Proficiency
Masterclass

Teacher's Book

Roger House

Kathy Gude

Michael Duckworth

OXFORD

UNIVERSITY PRESS

OXFORD
UNIVERSITY PRESS

Great Clarendon Street, Oxford OX2 6DP

Oxford University Press is a department of the University of Oxford. It furthers the University's objective of excellence in research, scholarship, and education by publishing worldwide in

Oxford New York

Auckland Bangkok Buenos Aires Cape Town Chennai
Dar es Salaam Delhi Hong Kong Istanbul Karachi Kolkata
Kuala Lumpur Madrid Melbourne Mexico City Mumbai Nairobi
São Paulo Shanghai Taipei Tokyo Toronto

Oxford and Oxford English are registered trade marks of Oxford University Press in the UK and in certain other countries

ISBN 0 19 432913 5

Printed and bound by Grafiasa S.A. in Portugal

Acknowledgements

The authors and publisher are grateful to those who have given permission to reproduce the following extracts and adaptations of copyright material. Special thanks to the staff and students of Access school, Thessaloniki and in particular Anna Parisi, Kiki Hatzi and Makkie Malyari for their help and support.

p20 'Skydoc', taken from *Reader's Digest* October 1996. Reproduced by permission of Los Angeles Times Syndicate International.

p21 'Is your house making you sick?' by Catherine Farror © *Reader's Digest* August 2000. Reproduced by permission of Reader's Digest.

pp25–26 Extracts from *The Hitchhiker's Guide to the Galaxy* by Douglas Adams. Reproduced by permission of Macmillan Publishers Ltd.

pp30–31 'The life of Mary Shelley' from www.4iq.com. Reproduced by permission of InteliQuest.

pp45–46 'August's winter on the ice cap' by Simon Courtauld, *The Spectator* 4 May 1991. Reproduced by permission of The Spectator.

pp57–58 'Walking on eggshells' © Sanjida O'Connell, *The Guardian* 10 May 2001. Reproduced by permission of Guardian Newspapers Ltd.

p71 'Whatever happened to Baby Doe?' Extracted from an article by Patrick Brogan first published in *The Independent Magazine* 5 October 1991. Reproduced by permission of Independent Newspapers (UK)Ltd.

p94 'Flash feet' by Lucy Muir, *GNER Livewire* June/July 2001. Reproduced by permission of The Illustrated London News.

pp94–95 'Mega-bookseller on the Web' by Cécile Margain, *Eurostar Magazine* November 2001. Published by permission of Textuel.

pp103–104 'Hidden clues to crime' by Judy Williams © *The Guardian* 4 February 1992. Reproduced by permission of Guardian Newspapers Ltd.

p113 'Some like it hot' by Pat Chapman, *GNER Livewire* December/January 2001. Reproduced by permission of The Illustrated London News.

pp121–122 Extract from *Make the Most of Your Mind* by Tony Buzan. Reproduced with enthusiastic permission of the Buzan Organisation, www.buzancentres.com

p140 Extract from *Visions* by Michio Kaku. Reproduced by permission of 'Blake Friedmann Literary Agency Limited on behalf of Michio Kaku.'

p165 Adapted extracts from 'You might catch malaria' by Jennifer Frankel, 'You might lose your spleen' by Desmond Balmer, 'You might draw in the wrong language,' 'You might drive off a cliff' by Lisa O'Kelly, 'You might need a drip' by Kim Bunce, *The Tiddler, No. 27 - The Don't Travel Issue* © The Observer. Reproduced by permission of Guardian Newspapers Limited.

The publisher is grateful to the University of Cambridge Local Examinations Syndicate for permission to reproduce material from the revised CPE handbook.

Although every effort has been made to trace and contact copyright holders before publication, this has not been possible in some cases. We apologize for any apparent infringement of copyright, and if notified, the publisher will be pleased to rectify any errors or omissions at the earliest opportunity.

Contents

Listening Paper 4 V =vocabulary	Speaking Paper 5	Writing Paper 2	Overview
Part 1 Multiple-choice questions	Part 2 Themed discussion Health campaign	Part 1 Proposal Making recommendations	Lexical cloze, cloze, word formation
Part 2 Sentence completion V Book expressions	Part 3 Extended speaking Technological advances	Part 2 Set book composition Preparing for the tasks	Lexical cloze, cloze, word formation
Part 3 Multiple-choice questions	Part 3 Extended speaking Risks and dangers	Part 1 Letter Expressing opinions	Lexical cloze, cloze, gapped sentences
Part 4 Three-way matching	Part 2 Themed discussion Travel – its future role in our society	Part 2 Article Descriptive language	Lexical cloze, word formation, key word transformations
Part 2 Sentence completion V Animal expressions	Part 2 Themed discussion Local environment campaign	Part 1 Essay Organisation and cohesion	Lexical cloze, cloze, gapped sentences
Part 3 Multiple-choice questions	Part 3 Extended speaking English as an international language	Part 2 Report Complex sentences	Lexical cloze, word formation, key word transformations
Part 1 Multiple-choice questions V Expressions with *help*	Part 2 Themed discussion Influences on our lives	Part 1 Article Illustrating with examples	Lexical cloze, cloze, gapped sentences
Part 4 Three-way matching V Expressions connected with communication	Part 3 Extended speaking Families	Part 1 Letter Responding	Lexical cloze, word formation, key word transformations
Part 1 Multiple-choice questions V Homonyms, Business expressions	Part 2 Themed discussion Advertising campaign	Part 2 Proposal Describing benefits	Lexical cloze, cloze, gapped sentences
Part 3 Multiple-choice questions V Expressions connected with the law	Part 2 Themed discussion Civil liberties report	Part 1 Essay Organising paragraphs	Lexical cloze, word formation, key word transformations
Part 2 Sentence completion V Expressions connected with food, drink and eating, Spelling	Part 3 Extended speaking Television	Part 2 Review Creating interest	Lexical cloze, cloze, gapped sentences
Part 4 Three-way matching V Expressions with *ears*	Parts 1, 2 and 3 Exam simulation, school, careers and work	Part 2 Report Giving explanations	Lexical cloze, word formation, key word transformations

Introduction

This new edition of *Proficiency Masterclass* has been updated to reflect the changes in the revised Certificate of Proficiency in English examination. In addition to offering students extensive guidance and exam training, it also contains interesting, lively and challenging materials for the classroom.

The revised CPE examination consists of five papers: Reading, Writing, Use of English, Listening and Speaking. Each paper has equal weighting and accounts for 40 out of a possible 200 total marks in the examination. The level of the examination remains the same (Level 5 in the ALTE Framework, corresponding to Mastery C2 in the Council of Europe Framework). A comprehensive guide to the examination appears in the introduction to the Student's Book.

The syllabus of the course now reflects the test focus of the revised CPE examination. Each exam task is covered several times within the course. Guidance on how to approach these tasks is given through *Exam tips* and exercises which explore different elements of the questions. The tasks are clearly labelled so that students can build up familiarity with the formats and gain a sense of progress in their exam preparation.

The following components accompany the Student's Book:
- Class Cassettes or Class Audio CDs
- Teacher's Book
- Exam Practice Workbook & Cassette Pack (available in with and without key versions)

There is also a Michigan ECPE Workbook & Cassette Pack, and a Michigan ECPE Teacher's Booklet.

The Student's Book

The Student's Book consists of 12 theme-related units divided into seven sections. Each section focuses on one particular skill to give greater clarity to the coverage of the exam tasks. However, additional skills are integrated into each section, making the material more varied. The final section in each unit is an overview of what has been covered in the unit.

Reading

Texts come from a wide variety of authentic sources. They have been selected to reflect the complexity of language and ideas students will come across in the exam, as well as for their interesting subject matter. A different examination task type is covered in each unit, with help in the form of *Exam tips*. Each task is given equal prominence, and exam format is replicated throughout. In addition, the vocabulary in the texts is exploited and extended, and students are encouraged to react to the texts they read.

Language in use

This section contains a review of Proficiency level structures and systematic practice in the first four parts of the Use of English paper. *Exam tips* and hints help students to understand what the tasks are testing and how they can draw on their grammatical and lexical knowledge to complete them successfully.

Comprehension and summary

This section focuses on Part 5 of the Use of English paper, which contains tasks in which students have often had little previous practice. This section increases students' awareness of how language is used in the texts (explored in the comprehension questions), and develops their summary writing skills by helping them to select relevant information and express ideas concisely and appropriately. Practice is given in referencing, paraphrasing, proof-reading and eliminating irrelevance.

Listening

Each listening section focuses on one examination task type from Paper 4. Throughout the course, students listen to a wide range of texts and learn to identify the function and purpose of the text, recognise feelings, attitudes and opinions, and infer meaning from what speakers say. Again, texts come from a wide variety of authentic sources and have been selected for their subject matter as well as their appropriacy for examination texts. There is also vocabulary work based on the content of the listening texts, and students are offered an opportunity to react to what they have heard.

Speaking

This separate speaking section offers structured practice in the tasks students perform in Paper 5. In

Proficiency Masterclass, Paper 5 Part 2 (the collaborative task) is referred to as 'Themed discussion', and Part 3 (the long turn) is referred to as 'Extended speaking'. Students practise the relevant functional language in contextualised exam-type tasks, and build up their ability to respond quickly and fluently to the extended speaking required in the long turn. Timings for the different stages of the extended speaking are not suggested in every unit as it is important for students to practise functional language and feel comfortable when performing this collaborative task.

Exam tips help students to think about the purpose and function of the tasks and perform to the best of their ability.

Writing

Each task type is introduced through a sample task and a sample answer. Students analyse how effectively the answer meets the requirements of the task. Students learn how to interpret the task and identify the target reader, write in the appropriate register and format, and use a wide range of structures and vocabulary.

A skills development section focuses on a particular point relevant to the task. The five-stage approach (Read, Think, Plan, Write and Check) guides students through all steps in the writing of their compositions.

Overview

The two-page Overview gives students the opportunity to practise some of the Paper 1 and Paper 3 tasks they have come across in the unit. The theme of the unit is continued, thus providing further exposure to related vocabulary.

The Exam Practice Workbook

This provides comprehensive revision of the material in the Student's Book, and practice for the revised examination. There are 12 units in total, each of which contains three or four full examination tasks which recycle, as far as possible, the themes, vocabulary, structures and task types in the Student's Book. Each set of four units combines to provide a complete set of Papers 1–4.

The material can be used in two ways: students can either work through the tasks unit by unit after completing the material in the Student's Book, or they can wait until they have completed four units, then tackle Papers 1–4, under examination conditions, if they wish, following the order of the tasks as they appear in the exam.

Exam guidance appears throughout tests 1 and 2. This consists of a step-by-step *Answering strategy*, which introduces each part of the examination. In addition, *Question hints* also appear alongside the texts. Test 3 is unguided and contains advice for filling in examination answer sheets so that students become more familiar with examination procedures.

At the end of the book, there is a separate section on Paper 5. This section contains recorded extracts from a sample speaking test, an analysis of candidate performance, and additional practice for students. Students work out their scores for each part of the test, building up a profile of their overall results. They can then compare their results over all three tests. There are photocopiable answer sheets at the back of the book.

The Teacher's Book

The Teacher's Book aims to give teachers support in teaching the course effectively, and offers a range of supplementary material and tests. Clear teacher's notes are given on how to set up and work through all activities and exercises in the Student's Book. A full answer key for each exercise is given, including sample answers to summary tasks. An explanation of the answers is offered where relevant to help clarify why particular answers are correct. In addition to the procedural notes, the following supplementary materials are provided.

Alternative and Extra activities

Sometimes an Alternative activity is given to the procedure suggested for using the Student's Book material. Each unit also contains ideas for short, easy-to-set-up Extra activities, which reinforce and extend the work in the Student's Book.

Photocopiable activities

Some more substantial extra exercises and activities are provided in the form of photocopiable materials, which require minimal preparation time. The teaching notes, key and worksheets are on TB pages 150–175. References to these are given in the Teacher's Book units.

Extra vocabulary

At the end of the teacher's notes to some sections there is a list of Extra vocabulary, which is not directly studied in the Student's Book exercises. The suggested activities on TB page 176 can be used either to practise this vocabulary where it occurs in the Student's Book, or to revise vocabulary at the end of the unit. Each activity should take no more than ten minutes to do and requires little or no preparation. Teachers can select which vocabulary items they wish to focus on before they choose an activity.

Vocabulary Tests

There are 12 one-page photocopiable Vocabulary Tests on TB pages 126–137 which focus on vocabulary from each unit.

Progress Tests

There are three photocopiable Progress Tests on TB pages 138 – 143 which test the material from each block of four units using exam-format tasks. Each test should take approximately 1 hour 45 minutes. Since marks are allocated as in the exam, follow this procedure to convert students' marks into percentages: divide their totals by the maximum score possible, then multiply the result by 100 [(student's total ÷ maximum) x 100 = percentage total].

Guidance for marking

The following is intended as a guide to teachers awarding marks for examination tasks. The table indicates how marks are awarded for each task in the CPE examination. For information on Paper 2 and Paper 5, see *Marking Productive Tasks* below.

Paper/ Part	Task	Number of questions	Marks per question
Paper 1 Reading			
Part 1	Lexical cloze	18	1
Part 2	Four-option multiple choice	8	2
Part 3	Gapped text	7	2
Part 4	Four-option multiple choice	7	2
Paper 3 Use of English			
Part 1	Cloze	15	1
Part 2	Word formation	10	1
Part 3	Gapped sentences	6	2
Part 4	Key word transformations	8	2
Part 5	Comprehension questions	4	2
	Summary writing task	1	14 (4 for content, 10 for summary writing skills)
Paper 4 Listening			
Part 1	Three-option multiple choice	8	1
Part 2	Sentence completion	9	1
Part 3	Four-option multiple choice	5	1
Part 4	Three-way matching	6	1

Marking productive tasks

The marking criteria for the productive tasks are outlined below so that teachers can assess their students' work with an understanding of the mark schemes.

Paper 2 Writing

An impression mark is awarded to each composition using a **general mark scheme**. This is used in conjunction with a **task-specific mark scheme**, which focuses on criteria specific to each question. Each question in the paper carries equal marks.

The **general mark scheme** consists of marks between 0 and 5, with 5 being the highest. The detailed criteria for each band are given in the table below. Marks from band 3 upwards are pass grades. Within each band, one of three performance levels can be awarded, e.g. 5.1 is a slightly weaker performance within band 5, 5.2 is a typical performance within the band, and 5.3 represents the strongest performance within band 5. There are no such distinctions in band 0.

Writing General Mark Scheme

5

Outstanding realisation of the task set:
- Sophisticated use of an extensive range of vocabulary, collocation and expression, entirely appropriate to the task set
- Effective use of stylistic devices; register and format wholly appropriate
- Impressive use of a wide range of structures
- Skilfully organised and coherent
- Excellent development of topic
- Minimal error

Impresses the reader and has a very positive effect.

4

Good realisation of the task set:
- Fluent and natural use of a wide range of vocabulary, collocation and expression, successfully meeting the requirements of the task set
- Good use of stylistic devices; register and format wholly appropriate
- Competent use of a wide range of structures
- Well organised and coherent
- Good development of topic
- Minor and unobtrusive errors

Has a positive effect on the reader.

3

Satisfactory realisation of the task set
- Reasonably fluent and natural use of a range of vocabulary and expression, adequate to the task set
- Evidence of stylistic devices; register and format generally appropriate
- Adequate range of structures
- Clearly organised and generally coherent
- Adequate coverage of topic
- Some non-impeding errors

Achieves the desired effect on the reader.

2

Inadequate attempt at the task set:
- Limited and/or inaccurate range of vocabulary and expression
- Little evidence of stylistic devices; some attempt at register and format
- Inadequate range of structures
- Some attempt at organisation, but lacks coherence
- Inadequate development of topic
- A number of errors, which sometimes impede communication

Has a negative effect on the reader.

1

Poor attempt at the task set:
- Severely limited and inaccurate range of vocabulary and expression
- No evidence of stylistic devices; little or no attempt at register and format
- Lack of structural range
- Poorly organised, leading to incoherence
- Little relevance to topic, and/or too short
- Numerous errors, which distract and often impede communication

Has a negative effect on the reader.

0

- Totally incomprehensible due to serious error
- Totally irrelevant
- Insufficient language to assess (fewer than 20% of the required number of words)
- Totally illegible

Taken from the revised CPE handbook © UCLES 2001

The following are components of the **task-specific mark scheme**: Content; Range; Appropriacy of Register and Format; Organisation and Cohesion; Target Reader. Examples of sample compositions and assessment according to the task-specific mark scheme can be found in the Revised CPE Specifications published by University of Cambridge Local Examinations Syndicate (UCLES). The staged approach to writing in the Student's Book provides a summary of the content and planning issues that a student needs to bear in mind when answering an exam question and can be used as a checklist for marking.

The following points should also be considered when marking scripts:

- Underlength and overlength scripts will be penalised.
- Correct spelling is essential. American spelling is acceptable, but must be used consistently.
- Paragraphs must be used.

- Handwriting must be legible. If it interferes with communication, candidates will be penalised.

Paper 3 Use of English Part 5

Answers to the **comprehension questions** need not form complete sentences. A word or a short phrase is sufficient.

An impression mark is awarded to each **summary writing task** using a **general mark scheme**. This is used in conjunction with a **content mark scheme**. Four marks are awarded for content points in the summary. If a point is not included, marks are deducted.

The **general mark scheme** consists of marks between 0 and 5, 5 being the highest. Within each Band, two performance levels can be awarded, e.g. a student can score 4.1 or 4.2. The criteria for the **general mark scheme** are detailed in the table.

Summary Writing Task General Mark Scheme

5	Outstanding realisation of the task set: • Totally relevant • Concise and totally coherent • Skilfully organised, with effective use of linking devices • Skilfully reworded where appropriate • Minimal non-impeding errors, probably due to ambition Clearly informs and requires no effort on the part of the reader.
4	Good realisation of the task set: • Mostly relevant • Concise and generally coherent • Well organised, with good use of linking devices • Competently reworded, where appropriate • Minor non-impeding errors Informs and requires minimal or no effort on the part of the reader
3	Satisfactory realisation of the task set: • Generally relevant with occasional digression • Some attempt at concise writing and reasonably coherent • Adequately organised, with some appropriate use of linking devices • Adequately reworded, where appropriate • Occasional errors, mostly non-impeding Adequately informs, though may require some effort on the part of the reader.
2	Inadequate attempt at the task set: • Some irrelevance • Little attempt at concise writing, so likely to be over-length and incoherent OR too short • Some attempt at organisation, but only limited use of appropriate linking devices and may use inappropriate listing or note format • Inadequately reworded and/or inappropriate lifting • A number of errors, which sometimes impede communication Partially informs though requires considerable effort on the part of the reader.
1	Poor attempt at the task set: • Considerable irrelevance • No attempt at concise writing, so likely to seriously over-length and seriously incoherent OR far too short • Poorly organised, with little or no use of appropriate linking devices and/or relies on listing or note format • Poorly reworded and/or over-reliance on lifting • Numerous errors, which distract and impede communication Fails to inform, though requires considerable effort on the part of the reader.
0	Negligible or no attempt at the task set: • Does not demonstrate summary skills • Totally incomprehensible due to serious error • Totally irrelevant • Insufficient language to access (fewer than 15 words) • Totally illegible

Taken from the revised CPE handbook © UCLES 2001

Paper 5 Speaking

Candidates are assessed on their performance throughout Paper 5 by the Assessor and are awarded a mark of between 0 and 5 for five analytical scales. They can also be awarded 0.5 for each of the criterion Bands, e.g. 2.5 if they fall between bands 2 and 3. In addition, they are awarded a global achievement mark of between 0 and 5 by the Interlocutor. The mark 3 is regarded as an adequate performance mark for a Grade C.

Under the CPE analytical scales, the following criteria are used by the assessor in order to grade candidates:

Criteria	Candidates are expected to ...
Grammatical resource	use a wide range of structures accurately and appropriately.
Lexical resource	use a wide range of vocabulary accurately and appropriately.
Discourse management	produce relevant and coherent contributions of an appropriate length.
Pronunciation rhythm,	use appropriate stress, intonation and pronounce individual sounds in order to be understood.
Interactive communication	initiate and respond appropriately, without undue hesitation, and show sensitivity to turn-taking.

An impression mark for Global achievement is awarded by the Interlocutor based on overall performance.

Overall competence

Grades in the CPE Examination correspond approximately to the following percentage scores:

Pass:

A   80% and above
B   75–79%
C   60–74%

Fail:

D   55–59%
E   54% and below

For further information on any of the Cambridge EFL examinations, please contact

EFL information
University of Cambridge Local Examinations Syndicate
1 Hills Road
Cambridge
CB1 2EU
United Kingdom
Tel: +44 1223 553355
Fax: +44 1223 460278
www.cambridge-efl.org.uk

1 In sickness and in health

▶ *See unit summary on page 4.*

Exam training in this unit

Reading	Lexical cloze: collocations, idioms
Use of English	Cloze: identifying parts of speech
	Comprehension and summary: identifying question types, selecting relevant information
Listening	Multiple-choice questions on one text: prereading questions
Speaking	Themed discussion: techniques for describing
Writing	A proposal: making recommendations

Ask students where they might hear the phrase *in sickness and in health*. It is an extract from the vows that a couple take at an Anglican wedding ceremony. The overall theme of the unit is how to keep fit and healthy.

Reading SB pages 10–12

One man's meat is another man's poison

Draw students' attention to the title. Ask them how they interpret this expression and discuss answers as a class. The expression suggests that what is beneficial for one person may be harmful to another or that not everyone has the same tastes or preferences.

Introduce the activity by asking students as a class how effective they think giving up sugar would be as a way of keeping fit. Ask them to compare it with going swimming regularly, and to give reasons.

Students rank the suggestions and give justifications in their groups.

Invite one member of each group to present the group's views to the rest of the class for comparison.

Round off the activity by asking students if they think physical fitness is important in the modern world.

Lexical cloze Paper 1 Part 1

A Discuss each title in turn and put students' ideas on the board.

Ask students to read through the texts quickly, ignoring the gaps to find out what each one is about.

Discuss answers as a class and compare with earlier ideas.

> **Key**
>
> Text 1 is about people who are obsessed with exercise.
>
> Text 2 gives one person's view of the benefits of vitamin pills.
>
> Text 3 describes the advantages of physical work for the treatment of bad backs.

B Draw students' attention to the *Exam tip* before they begin B. Use the first gap in Text 1 as an example, emphasising the phrase *on the spot*.

Students read carefully through each text and circle their chosen option.

Check answers as a class.

> **Key**
>
> Text 1
>   1 C *on the spot* is a set phrase meaning in one fixed place
>   2 B *puts off* is an idiomatic phrasal verb meaning to postpone
>   3 C *coming to terms with* is a set phrase meaning to accept the way things are
>   4 D *the moment you do something* is a set expression equivalent to as soon as you do something
>   5 A *take heart* is a set phrase meaning to feel more positive about something
>   6 C *previous experience* is a collocation
>
> Text 2
>   7 D *emotionally and physically drained* is a collocation
>   8 B *pick myself up* is an idiomatic phrasal verb meaning to recover from some difficulty
>   9 C *pleaded to try*, because influenced and urged are followed by *me*, and recommended is followed by *that* or *-ing*
> 10 A *out loud* is a set phrase meaning in a voice that can be heard
> 11 C *a sparkle in my eyes* is a set phrase meaning a feeling of enthusiasm
> 12 B *cut down on* is an idiomatic phrasal verb meaning to reduce in amount
>
> Text 3
> 13 D *digging up* is a phrasal verb meant literally
> 14 C *handed over* is a phrasal verb meaning to pass responsibility for something

Comprehension

C Students answer the questions using their own words as far as possible.

Check answers as a class, and ask students to justify their answers by referring to relevant parts of the text.

Key

Text 1
1 People who take regular exercise see those who don't as being less important and they prefer not to waste time talking to them.
2 It can be negative because it can make you over-confident about your health. It is also time-consuming, expensive and you can't stop because you lose your fitness.
3 The path to true contentment lies in sitting at home on the sofa by the fire doing nothing.

Text 2
1 An advertisement through the post prompted the writer to try the pills for his/her depression.
2 The pills had a positive effect and made the writer glad to be alive.
3 The writer believes there is a link between feeling well physically and feeling well emotionally.

Text 3
1 Initially it made his back feel good.
2 A rub-down is a kind of massage to relieve pain in the muscles. Goldman thought rub-downs were unnecessary.
3 He concludes that hard physical work can be beneficial physically and mentally.

Vocabulary

Collocation

D Ask students to work in pairs. Remind them that they can check their answers by referring to the texts.

E Point out to students that they may be able to use more than one collocation in the same sentence, so they don't necessarily have to write five sentences.

Students read their sentences out to the class for comparison.

Key

1 d the correct, legal or best place for you, e.g. The chairman took his rightful place at the head of the table.
2 g a feeling of being healthy in both your mind and your body, e.g. A sense of emotional and physical well-being is important to our happiness.
3 h the instant of understanding, e.g. He saw what he had done wrong in a moment of realisation.
4 e to do some form of physical activity, e.g. You should take more exercise to lose weight.
5 b when someone gives the appearance of not paying attention, e.g. I could tell she wasn't listening to me from the far-off look in her eyes.
6 a to affect something either positively or negatively, e.g. Giving up cigarettes will have a wonderful effect on your health.
7 f the amount of medicine you have been advised to take, e.g. It's dangerous to take more than the recommended dose of these pills.
8 c a way of stressing that the price is too high, e.g. the restaurant we went to last night was ridiculously expensive.

Idioms

F Students look at the picture of a couch potato that accompanies the first text on SB page 10. Ask them what they think a couch potato is, based on the picture.

When students have given you a few suggestions, ask them to look through the explanations a–h and find which they think is the correct one.

Students match the remaining idioms with their explanations. The idiom *a stuffed shirt* is illustrated in the cartoon.

Check answers as a class.

Key

1 g 2 h 3 c 4 f 5 a 6 e 7 d 8 b

Note: Idioms 1 and 8 are based on the proverbs 'A new broom sweeps clean' and 'A rolling stone gathers no moss'.

⊞ Extra activity

Ask students whether any of the idioms could describe anyone they know.

Write this sentence on the board as an example. *My brother is a real stuffed shirt. He's forever giving his views about things using long, difficult words. He regards other people as less important than him.*

Students give similar descriptions of their own.

Expressions with *come*

G Ask students to read through the definitions before they complete the sentences. Remind them that they may need to change the form of the verb in some sentences.

Check answers as a class.

Key

1	come to terms with	6	came down with
2	comes down heavily on	7	came round
3	comes out with	8	come in for
4	come to the point	9	come round to
5	came up with		

Photocopiable activity 1.1   TB page 150

Extra vocabulary

See page 176 for ideas on how to exploit this vocabulary.

mortal (adjective) cannot live for ever, must die
primary (adjective) the most important or basic
sparkle (noun) a small flash of light from a shiny surface
devoid (adjective) completely lacking in something
soar (verb) to rise quickly and smoothly
delve into (verb) to try hard to find more information about something
exhortation (noun) a strong form of persuasion
deliberate (verb) to think carefully before taking action
to stand by someone (verb) to support someone in a difficult situation

Language in use SB pages 13–15

The sporting life

The sporting life is an expression used to describe a life of activity and outdoor pursuits. It is also the name of a British sports newspaper.

Divide the class into pairs or small groups for this activity. Students discuss the questions and note down their answers, then they share their answers with the other pairs or groups.

Discuss any items they are not sure about as a class. Some of the sporting activities are mentioned in the cloze exercise that follows.

Key

1 pins: bowling
running shoes: athletics
a football: football
a tennis racket / racquet: tennis
ice skates: ice skating
a paddle: canoeing
a golf club: golf
weights: weightlifting

2 bowling: bowling shoes
athletics: a stopwatch
football: boots, shin pads, goalposts
tennis: a net, balls
ice skating: protective clothing
canoeing: a safety helmet, a life jacket
golf: balls, tees, a glove
weightlifting: a belt

3 bowling: alley
athletics: track
football: pitch
tennis: court
ice skating: rink
canoeing: rapids
golf: course
weightlifting: gym

4 alley: skittles
track: motor-racing,
pitch: rugby, polo,
court: squash, badminton,
rink: ice-hockey
rapids: rafting
course: horse-racing
gym: gymnastics, aerobics

⊞ Extra activity

Round off the activity by asking students which of the sporting activities you either *do*, *play* or *go*.

Key
do   athletics, weight-training
go   bowling, ice-skating, canoeing
play football, tennis, golf

❏ Alternative activity

With a large class you could conduct a survey by inviting students to find out all the sports students either enjoy watching or playing. Students then report back to you using the phrases below.

the majority	about half
most of us	a few
quite a few	hardly anyone

Cloze Paper 3 Part 1

A   Allow students 2 minutes to skim read the text. Remind them not to fill in the gaps yet.

Discuss answers as a class.

Explain that it's important for students at this stage to get into the habit of reading through the whole text quickly to get a general idea of what it is about before they fill in the gaps. The missing word may depend on the context or overall meaning of the text.

> **Key**
>
> Doing exercise or sports training to music

❏ Alternative activity

Students read through the text quickly and underline the different sports mentioned. Ask them to find out what connects these sports according to the text.

> **Key**
>
> football, tennis, figure-skating, ice-dance, gymnastics, skiing, soccer, rugby, rowing, weightlifting, athletics
> They are all connected by training to music.

B   Tell students not to worry about the answers they are not sure about at this stage.

C   Draw students' attention to the *Exam tip* before they read through the text again.

Where they are still not sure, students note down the type of word that is missing by looking at the whole sentence.

Go through the text and check answers as a class. The key includes the type of word that is missing.

> **Key**
>
> 1   whether   (connector)
> 2   well / much   (adverb / part of a connector)
> 3   not (adverb) / nothing   (pronoun)
> 4   on   (preposition)
> 5   are   (verb)
> 6   forms / examples   (nouns)
> 7   to   (preposition)
> 8   both   (determiner)
> 9   greater   (adjective)
> 10   any   (determiner)
> 11   up   (preposition)
> 12   their   (pronoun)
> 13   take   (verb)
> 14   which   (pronoun)
> 15   makes   (verb)

Structure

Defining and non-defining relative clauses

D

> **Key**
>
> 'that are also pleasing to the eye'
> 'both of which demand high standards of balance, co-ordination and suppleness.'
> 'which seem to demand muscular strength more than any other physical requirement'
> 'who take part in weightlifting'
> 'which demands enormous physical strength'
>
> A relative pronoun introduces a relative clause, e.g. *that, which, who, whose, whom, where, when* and *why*.

E   Go through the questions one by one and discuss answers as a class.

> **Key**
>
> 1   The first sentence is a *defining* relative clause. The sentence tells us that of all the golfers it was the one who attended the dinner that had won two previous championships. The sentence tells us which golfer we are referring to.
> The second sentence is a *non-defining* relative clause. The sentence tells us that there is likely to be only one golfer in question. The fact that the golfer attended the annual dinner is additional information. Point out the use of commas in this sentence. It would still be a complete sentence if the additional information was taken out. Ask students to look back at the idioms on page 12 exercise F.

Ask them what type of relative clause is used in the explanations. They are all defining relative clauses.

2 The relative pronoun can be omitted in the second sentence. This is because it is the object of the verb in the relative clause. In this case the subject is *spectators*. The relative pronoun cannot be omitted in the first sentence because it is the *subject* of the verb in the relative clause. This rule only applies to defining relative clauses. In non-defining relative clauses the relative pronoun can never be omitted.

3 *That* cannot be used in the second sentence. This is because *that* is never used in a non-defining relative clause. In this case *which* should be used. The first sentence is a defining relative clause.

4 *That* cannot be used after a preposition in a relative clause. In this case *which* should be used. *Whom* is used after a preposition when referring to people. Also it is a non-defining relative clause.

5 The relative pronoun is *whose* and it refers to the boxer. It is a possessive relative pronoun meaning *belonging to*.

6 The relative pronoun *which* refers back to the whole of the previous clause 'he resigned as manager of the club.'

F Remind students that all types of relative clause mentioned in E 1–6 are practised in this exercise. Reference is made to this in the key.

Check answers as a class.

Key

1 The American journalist who / that interviewed the tennis champion reminded me of my brother.
See E 1.

2 The liver, which is about 30 centimetres long, helps in the digestion of food.
See E 1 and E 3.

3 We decided to engage the two young dancers who / that / whom we had seen perform on television.
See E 2.

4 The new concert hall, which holds two thousand people, was opened yesterday.
See E 1 and E 3.

5 The band ICE, whose manager has just resigned, is/are currently touring the USA.
See E 5.

6 He had never had any formal education, which amazed me.
See E 6.

7 Skiing and snowboarding, both of which are exciting sports, can now be practised all year round on dry-ski slopes.
See E 4.

8 The new stadium won't be finished for another two years, by which time it will be out of date.
See E 4.

G

Key

The relative pronoun can only be omitted in sentence 3.

Note: A common mistake students make with this type of sentence is to use object pronouns in the relative clause as if it was a separate sentence, e.g. 'We decided to engage the two young dancers (who) we had seen *them* perform on television.'

Point out that the relative clause defines 'the two young dancers'. The relative pronoun *who* can be used in the relative clause. However, an object pronoun like *them* cannot be used in English to refer again to 'the two young dancers' within the relative clause.

Reduced clauses

The three exercises that follow focus on different types of reduced relative clauses. These are sometimes referred to as non-finite or participle clauses.

H Ask students to compare the two sentences in the example. Point out that the verb in the relative clause is passive so the past participle or *-ed* form is used in the reduced clause. If the verb is active the *-ing* form is used in the reduced clause.

Remind students to consider whether the verb in the relative clause is active or passive when rewriting the sentences.

Check answers as a class.

Key

1 Athletes using these techniques show a marked improvement in performance. The verb is active.

2 Competitors selected when they are young stand a greater chance of being successful. The verb is passive.

3 Trainers working with up-and-coming athletes say that more money needs to be spent on facilities. The verb is active.

> 4 The stadium being built for the event is already an architectural talking point. The verb is passive but refers to something not completed yet.

I Ask students to read the introduction and example. Point out how the position of the subject *the striker* changes in each sentence.

Remind students again to consider whether the verb is active or passive before they rewrite the sentences.

Check answers as a class.

Key

1 The losing team, who were humiliated by their defeat, trudged towards the dressing room.
The verb is passive.
2 The champion, who was beaming with joy, received her gold medal.
The verb is active.
3 The English FA cup, which was founded in 1871, is the oldest football cup competition.
The verb is passive.

J Ask students to look at the example and the three original sentences in I. Point out that this type of sentence is only possible when the subject is the same in both clauses.

Now ask students to look at the two example sentences and compare them with the sentences in I. Ask them if it is clear who is 'driven to desperation by hunger'. Is it the frog or someone else? The potential misunderstanding is illustrated in the cartoon.

Students look at the next three sentences and consider how the subject can be made the same before they rewrite them.

Check answers as a class.

Key

1 Thinking of how their lives would be together, the couple were pronounced man and wife (by the vicar).
2 Looking through the binoculars, I saw that the distant eagle seemed to be preparing to swoop on its prey.
3 I began to realise she was no longer my baby girl when I saw her dressed in her new school uniform.

Photocopiable activity 1.2 TB page 150

Comprehension and summary

SB pages 16–17

Under the weather

Ask students what they imagine when they visualise the phrase *under the weather*. Explain that it can be a metaphor for health and ask students what they think it implies. The phrase means that somebody is not feeling in good health.

1 Students work in pairs to rearrange the words and find the eight complaints.

Tennis elbow is illustrated in the cartoon.

Check answers as a class.

Key

writer's cramp, a sprained ankle, tennis elbow, a torn ligament, eye strain, a splitting headache, an ear infection, a slipped disc

2 Students discuss these questions in pairs or as a class.

Comprehension Paper 3 Part 5

A Before the students read the two texts, draw their attention to the photograph and ask them to predict what the two texts might be about.

Students read the two texts quickly to get an impression of who wrote them. Discuss answers as a class.

Key

Both texts were written by doctors.
The first text was written by a doctor who has also been a patient.

❏ Alternative activity

Write these four titles on the board:
A doctor's view of patients' expectations
What do patients really think of their doctors?
A hospital doctor's routine
The doctor/patient relationship seen from both sides

Ask students to read both texts quickly and choose one title for each text. Ask them to justify their choice.

Discuss answers as a class.

Key

Text 1
The doctor / patient relationship seen from both sides.
The writer mentions his / her experience as a junior surgeon and compares it with his / her experience as a patient.
Text 2
A doctor's view of patients' expectations
The writer mentions what patients want and don't want from him / her.
'A hospital doctor's routine' is too general for either text.
'What do patients really think of their doctors?' doesn't fit either text because both of them focus on the doctors' view, not the patients'.

B Ask students to underline a key word or phrase in each question to help them decide which type it is.

Check answers as a class.

Key

a question 4 'What impression does the writer give …'
b question 2
c questions 1 and 6 'Which word is used … ?', 'Which two words … contrast with …?'
d questions 3 and 5 ' Explain why the writer has chosen to use the phrase / expression …'

C Draw students' attention to the *Exam tip* before they begin the exercise.

Note: In the revised CPE Paper 3 Part 5 there are only four comprehension questions.

Use the key for examples of how their answers can be written.

Check answers as a class.

Key

Text 1
1 shuttling (line 14)
The writer mentions shuttling between clinics, the operating theatre, the wards, etc. in lines 15–18
2 a war
'You begin to think of the patients as *the enemy* and the nurses as *your first line of defence* against them.' (line 22)

3 to imply that doctors on their rounds are distant and uninterested
An *armada* is a large fleet or group of ships which would be impossible to stop.

Text 2
4 that by making things complicated they seem to be in control
'Illusory' is something that seems real but is not and it applies to the 'sense of control' so the doctors create a false sense of reality.
5 to show that a patient's problems are fairly ordinary compared to the difficulty of dealing with their expectations of the doctor.
A *pedestrian* is a person walking in the street, but as an adjective it can suggest that something is common or ordinary. In this context, it refers to the patient's angina which suggests that the doctor regards this illness as something uninteresting or unimportant.
6 friendly and charming
Patients want 'real doctors' who appear efficient because they think they are being treated better rather than a doctor who appears friendly and charming.

Summary writing Paper 3 Part 5

Identifying information

D Point out to students that it is important to accurately identify what they need to summarise as they won't be asked to summarise the whole texts.

Key

how doctors and patients generally feel about each other

E Students read through all the summary phrases and choose the relevant ones before they check with the text. They can do this in F.

Key

1   2   4   5   7
Sentences 3, 6, and 8 are not relevant to the task as they don't refer to the attitudes held by doctors and patients towards each other.

F Draw students' attention to the *Exam tip* first. Remind students to use this exercise to check their choices in E.

Check answers as a class.

G Point out that their summaries should not just be a list of points. Their sentences should be fluently linked. Before they begin the task, elicit some possible linking phrases they could use, e.g. firstly, furthermore, and, but, besides this, in addition, finally.

Sample summary

Firstly, both texts mention that doctors and patients have difficulty communicating with each other. Also doctors sometimes regard patients as an intrusion into hospital efficiency, while patients feel that doctors won't listen to what they say and often seem to be avoiding them. Besides this, doctors feel that patients expect them to give an impression of control which may be false. (61 words)

✚ Extra activity

Write these words on the board:

kept   prepared   written   matched   mannered
attended   conceived   timed   informed   worn

Divide the class into pairs or small groups. Ask them to add *ill* or *well* to the words and find a noun that matches them. Use this example: *a well-written essay*

Students make as many similar phrases as they can. Point out that both *ill* and *well* can be used with some words.

Each pair read out their phrases. This can be done competitively with the pair or group with the most correct phrases winning.

Possible answers:
a well-kept secret / garden / room or an ill-kept secret
an ill-prepared or well-prepared speech / presentation

well-prepared or ill-prepared for the exam / match / race / competition
a well-written essay / book/ composition / story etc.
a well-matched couple or two well- or ill-matched teams
a well-mannered or ill-mannered person
a well-attended concert / meeting / match / party / conference etc.
an ill-conceived or well-conceived plan / scheme/ proposal
a well-timed or ill-timed comment / action
a well-informed or ill-informed person / article / account
you can be well- or ill- informed about something
well-worn shoes / trainers / clothes / tyres

Extra vocabulary

See page 176 for ideas on how to exploit this vocabulary

perceptive (adjective) having the ability to understand things quickly
perspective (noun) an attitude or way of seeing things
bolster (verb) to make something stronger or improve it
demented (adjective) behaving in a crazy way due to an upset
belligerent (adjective) unfriendly or hostile
intrusion (noun) something unwelcome that comes into people's lives

Listening SB page 18

Alternative medicine

Write the words *conventional* and *alternative* on the board and ask students how the words might apply to medicine and /or education.

Students work in pairs to match the names to the pictures. Discuss what the treatments involve.

Discuss answers as a class.

UNIT 1   19

Discuss what conditions these methods might be used to treat.

❏ Alternative activity

Refer students to the list of complaints in *Under the weather* on page 16 and ask which of the alternative methods might best be used to treat these complaints.

Multiple-choice questions Paper 4 Part 1

Identifying the context

A 🎧 Remind students to listen for key words and phrases that will give them clues about the context.

Play the recording.

Check answers as a class.

> **Key**
>
> Extract 1: Two friends comparing an experience of hypnosis.
> Extract 2: An advertisement for a hypnosis technique.
> Extract 3: A journalist speaking on a radio programme
> Extract 4: A woman describing a disastrous holiday.

Listening for specific information

B 🎧 Draw students' attention to the *Exam tip* before they begin the listening exercise. In the exam, students will hear each extract separately. They will hear each extract twice.

Ask students to read through the questions and options for Extract 1.

Deal with any vocabulary questions. Ask them to make guesses about possible answers based on what they remember from the short extracts in A.

Play Extract 1 and pause recording while students think about their answers. Continue to play the recording.

Repeat the procedure for each extract in turn.

At the end of all four extracts allow students a minute to compare answers in pairs. Check answers as a class.

> **Key**
>
> 1 C   2 B   3 C   4 C   5 B   6 C   7 B   8 B

Note: Sections of the tapescript in italics highlight parts of the text relevant to the key.

Tapescript

Extract 1

WOMAN Well, I was having trouble sleeping. I'd done a great deal of research into hypnosis, and, um, although there's no doubt that it can be incredibly effective *I was very apprehensive*, I can tell you. I'd been prescribed …, well, given some mild sleeping pills and I … went to a hypnotherapist because I honestly felt that I was becoming addicted to them. Although I never felt that I went under, the insomnia sort of cleared up. And after the session, I had the best night's sleep I'd had for years. So, perhaps I well, learned something subconsciously.

MAN That's interesting. I actually had hypnosis for about two years. After the session, *my mind seemed razor sharp and I had this feeling of great power*. It only took a minute or so to put me to sleep. Then, when I woke up, I felt that I could fight King Kong! But it also helped me to concentrate on my game and block out the crowd. I have to say that I'm fascinated by the fact that apparently we only use ten per cent of our brains. I've read that the creative possibilities of our sub-conscious are enormous!

Extract 2

MAN Ever tried to give up smoking? The first time – yes – it does work - up until lunchtime! The second time - you don't feel like having a cigarette for 24 hours, but the urge slowly comes back. And *you know you are going to fail*. You feel cynical about it – tell your friends the timing just wasn't right. Why not try our new hypnosis treatment? We give you a word – freedom – and you think of it every time you have a craving. But, by the time you think of the word – you have no desire to light up! All you have to do is want to give up enough. And it's not only smoking that it works for! Do you ever suffer from stage fright? With the help of hypnosis, *you will find all your first night fears are dissolved!* All you then need to do is look forward to playing the character, and, while on stage, you should simply be that character! Try a session under hypnosis and see. You will be able to talk yourself into a semi-hypnotic state any time you're under stress, for instance, when you're flying. *You won't be scared any more – it will just help you to relax!*

Extract 3

MALE PRESENTER *It's everyone's biggest nightmare: suddenly falling ill on a long journey*, particularly when medical emergencies occur on aeroplanes. A first-aid kit may not be enough and it's a very long way to the nearest hospital. One major airline now boasts about a next-generation improvement: *a doctor who can monitor a patient's condition from the ground via satellite transmission*. The 'telemedicine' link shows vital signs such as blood pressure, temperature and oxygen in the blood. To check on a passenger, flight attendants – who have undergone basic medical training – first attach sensors. A monitoring unit then plugs into the plane's satellite-communication system which allows continuous two-way communication between the plane and the airport. The doctor on the ground receives the signals through a computer and decides whether the patient could safely be treated by the crew, or if an emergency landing is necessary.

Extract 4

WOMAN It all started during a party in the cellar of a friend's house in London. I could feel my chest tightening and began to find it hard to breathe. Every time I tried to inhale, my lungs became irritated – and within minutes I was coughing uncontrollably. I was afraid I was going to pass out so I ran outside, gulped in some fresh air, and eventually I regained control but I wasn't able to go back to the party. Then, about two months later, I suffered identical symptoms while on holiday with my husband in Cornwall. We'd rented a cottage and the only way I was able to breathe comfortably indoors was by inhaling through a damp tissue with the windows open and an electric fire to dry the air. We had to cut our holiday short in the end. We were bitterly disappointed. When I got back home, I decided to have some tests done. *It turned out that I'm strongly allergic to 'Aspergillus', a strain of ordinary household mould.*

Your views

B In pairs, students discuss the questions, then each pair compares its answers with another pair or compares answers with the class.

Extra vocabulary

See page 176 for ideas on how to exploit this vocabulary.

craving (noun) a very strong desire for something
retain (verb) to keep or to continue to have something
prudent (adjective) sensible and careful in making decisions or judgements
undergo (verb) to experience something, often unpleasant
monitor (verb) to watch and check something for changes

Speaking SB page 19

Themed discussion Paper 5 Part 2
Divide the class into pairs for all the activities.

A Allow students 2–3 minutes to compile their lists.

Compare lists as a class.

Possible answers

relaxing, public health, soothing, protection, therapeutic / therapy, prevention, treatment, diseases, sense of well-being, injection, contentment, hypodermic needles, beneficial, innoculation, good for your skin, apprehensive / scared / fearful, alternative medicine, health scheme / policy, health club, conventional medicine

Speculating

B Students discuss the pictures in pairs. Encourage the use of language for giving impressions and speculating.

Ask students to compare ideas with another pair.

> Speculating
> … could / may / might be …
> I would assume …
> … appear / seem to be …
> I get the impression …
> … look as though / if …

C 🎧 Play the recording twice if necessary. Discuss as a class what was different or similar to their descriptions.

Tapescript

INTERLOCUTOR Now I'd like you to look at pictures A and B and talk together about what you think the people are doing and why they might be doing these things.
FEMALE CANDIDATE Yes. So, I think the picture number one, this consumer is choosing … vitamin tablets. I assume that he needs some maybe some energy because he's feeling a bit stressed or he needs some vitamin tablets because he's going to take an exam, for example, or something.
MALE CANDIDATE Well … I wouldn't say that. It seems to me that, maybe he's … working in a shop like *Boots* … some … you know, some kind of …
FEMALE Oh no, I don't agree with you.
MALE … and he's in charge of providing the medicines to the customers, you know …
FEMALE No I think he could be – I think to me – From my point of view I think he's a customer. He doesn't seem to work for – for *Boots* at all.
MALE Don't think he's in a drugs rail – drugs stall.
FEMALE Yes he is. But not working for the company
MALE Well, on to the second photo. The little girl looks ill. She looks ill. (Yes) I think
maybe she's treated for a disease. The – the – the other woman seems to be a nurse.

FEMALE It may have been. Yes, maybe you are right, you are right, she could be a nurse – nurse. Yes.
INTERLOCUTOR Thank you.

Evaluating

D Ask students what health campaigns currently exist in their countries, what health issues the campaigns are about, and how they are presented.

Draw students' attention to the *Exam tip* and use one of the pictures as an example. Ask what message they think it is intended to convey. Then ask them whether they think it is successful and give reasons.

> **Possible answer:**
>
> I think the idea the first picture attempts to convey is that there is a variety of ways in which we can take care of our health and ensure fitness. However, I don't think it gets its message across very well because it shows a rather expensive form of treatment or therapy that most people may not be able to afford.

Students discuss the other pictures in the same way. They report their views to the rest of the class.

Suggesting alternatives

E Refer to the *Exam tip* and encourage students to make and invite suggestions from each other, and, if they disagree, to do so politely.

> **Suggesting and disagreeing**
> *One possibility could be …*
> *Another option for this would be …*
> *I see what you mean, but don't you think …*
> *I don't entirely agree with you there …*
> *I take your point but perhaps … might be a better idea.*

F Students report their decisions to the class. Take a vote on the two best suggestions.

Writing SB pages 20–21

A proposal Paper 2 Part 1

Understanding the task

A The questions are designed to check that students have understood what is required in this type of writing task.

Check answers as a class.

> **Key**
>
> 1 The proposal is for the senior manager. The style should be formal, professional and impersonal.
> 2 The reader will expect to find suggestions / recommendations for ways in which the health and fitness of staff at the company could be improved.
> 3 Using the results of the questionnaire as the basis for the suggestions / recommendations would give the proposal a sense of authenticity.
> 4 There will be a balance of both. The investigation of existing facilities will be with reference to the results of the questionnaire. The new ideas will be the suggested plan of action or recommendations based on these results.

Analysing the sample

B Refer to the answers in A and ask students to use them as a checklist as they read through the sample. When they have read the sample, ask students if the proposal has done what it is supposed to do.

Point out that the three questions are designed to focus students' attention on the style and layout of the sample proposal.

Discuss answers as a class.

> **Key**
>
> 1 The style is formal and impersonal
> 2 The proposal is divided into sections. Each section has a short heading.
> 3 This type of layout makes the proposal easier to read. The required information is clearly presented.

Writing skills

Making recommendations

C Draw students' attention to the *Exam tip* and write this sentence on the board: *I would strongly recommend making notes before you start writing as this will enable you to organise your ideas and write more fluently.*

Ask students which part of the sentence gives a positive proposal and which part gives a clarification.

Students look through the sample proposal again and find other examples of these functions and make lists in the categories provided.

Key

Positive proposals
I suggest that we investigate ways
Consideration should be given to …
I would strongly recommend providing
The restaurant menu could be revised

Clarifications
… as this would result in …
… since this would result in …
… on the grounds that …
… this would have the additional advantage of …
… as this would help …

Negative proposals
It would be inadvisable to provide …

D Students look at the cues in 1–6 and choose an appropriate structure for making a positive or negative proposal before they write their sentences. Remind them to write complete sentences bearing in mind that the form of some verbs may need to be changed and other words added.

Check answers as a class focusing on accuracy of form and sentence structure.

Possible answers

1 It would be a good idea to go cycling regularly, and this would have the additional advantage of helping you to get fit.
2 I am opposed to the idea of allowing cigarette advertising on TV, since this will result in more young people smoking
3 Consideration should be given to having a more balanced diet, as this would enable us to feel healthier and lose weight.
4 It would be inadvisable to open a wine bar at school, on the grounds that it would inevitably lead to students developing bad habits.
5 I would strongly recommend playing sports regularly because this would allow people to feel more energetic.
6 I suggest we stop watching TV so much because this might encourage us to get more exercise.

Writing your proposal

E Go through the stages in turn and discuss questions and brainstorm ideas as a class.

Unit 1 Overview key

SB pages 22–23

Lexical cloze Paper 1 Part 1

A

1 C	2 C	3 B	4 A	5 C	6 C
7 C	8 C	9 D	10 C	11 B	12 D

Cloze Paper 3 Part 1

B

1	whether		9	under
2	up		10	such
3	make		11	both
4	by		12	of
5	with		13	well
6	much / far / considerably		14	this
7	reason		15	time
8	taking			

Word formation Paper 3 Part 2

C

1	beneficial		6	subconsciously
2	circulation		7	enables
3	significance		8	intrusion
4	incredibly		9	incurable
5	uncontrollable		10	muscular

Vocabulary Test Unit 1 TB page 126

2 Written in the stars

▶ *See unit summary on page 4.*

Exam training in this unit

Reading	Multiple-choice questions on one text: dealing with distractors
Use of English	Word formation: affixation Comprehension and summary: referencing devices, meaning of idiomatic phrases
Listening	Sentence completion: looking at context before listening
Speaking	Extended speaking practice: responding to the long turn
Writing	A review: vocabulary range for creating interest

Ask students if they can understand the meaning of the title of the unit. *It's written in the stars* is a phrase used to imply that the outcome of something is dependent on fate or luck. The overall theme of the unit is scientific fact and fiction.

Reading SB pages 24–26

Masters of the universe

Introduce the activity by asking students to name a famous scientist from their own country and explain what their contribution to science was.

Students discuss the questions in pairs or small groups.

Check answers as a class.

> **Key**
>
> a pendulum Galileo Galilei (1564–1642) discovered that the swing of a simple pendulum depends only on its length.
> an apple Sir Isaac Newton (1642-1727). It is said that an apple falling on his head lead to his formulation of the idea of gravity.
> a light bulb Michael Faraday (1791–1867) was the first scientist to produce an electric current from a magnetic field.
> radioactive warning sign Marie Curie (1867–1934) was a Nobel Prize-winning physicist who discovered the radioactive element radium. Radioactivity itself was discovered by Henri Becquerel.

> solar system Nicolaus Copernicus (1473-1543) Polish astronomer who proposed that the Earth and other planets orbit the Sun.

Multiple-choice questions Paper 1 Part 4

Background notes Albert Einstein was the man responsible for the Theory of Relativity and our understanding of space and time.
Max Planck (1856–1947) was a physicist and originator of the quantum theory of sub-atomic physics.
Werner Karl Heisenberg (1901–1976) was a physicist and philosopher who helped establish the science of quantum mechanics.
Gonville and Caius college is one of the Cambridge University colleges.

A Draw students' attention to the picture of Stephen Hawking and ask if they know anything about him. Students read through the text quickly and find out how Stephen Hawking communicates. Point out that it is important to read through the whole text to get an overall idea of the gist before attempting the multiple choice questions.

Check answers as a class.

> **Key**
>
> He uses a computer attached to his wheelchair which has speakers that transmit an artificial voice from the words he types on the keyboard. His important ideas have been communicated through the books he has written, *Black Holes*, *Baby Universes* and *A Brief History of Time*.

B Draw students' attention to the *Exam tip*.

> **Key**
>
> 1 D   2 C   3 B   4 C   5 C   6 C

Vocabulary

C Deducing the meaning of unknown words from context is an essential skill at this level. Use the word *chimera* as an example.

Ask students to look at the first paragraph and find the word *chimera*. It occurs twice. Then ask the following questions: What does it refer to? (The Great Unified Theory); What type of word is it e.g. noun, verb, adjective, adverb, etc.? (noun); What other words does it connect with? (chasing, no chimera, but a real beast) Students can use the questions as a general checklist for deducing meaning from context in future.

Remind students to look at each of the words as they are used in the text before they match them to a definition.

Check answers as a class.

Expressions with *time*

D Ask students to explain to you any expressions with *time* they have in their own languages.

Ask students which expression they think is illustrated in the cartoon (*killing time*).

Remind students to replace the whole phrase with one of the expressions.

Check answers as a class.

Round off the activity by asking students whether they were *on time* or *in time* for the lesson. (*on time* is at the correct time; *in time* is early, with time to spare)

✚ Extra activity

Ask students to recount something that happened to them recently using as many of the expressions with time as possible.

E ⌾ The recording is an example of how explaining the universe has become part of popular science. Students read the question before they listen.

Play the recording.

Check answers as a class.

F Spend a few minutes discussing students' reactions to the extract.

Tapescript

NARRATOR Inside the building, the room was much as Slartibartfast had described it. In seven and a half million years it had been well looked after and cleaned regularly every century or so. The ultramahogany desk was worn at the edges, the carpet a little faded now, but the large computer terminal sat in sparkling glory on the desk's leather top, as bright as if it had been constructed yesterday. Two severely-dressed men sat respectfully before the terminal and waited.

LOONQUAWL The time is nearly upon us, Phouchg.

PHOUCHG Seventy thousand generations ago, our ancestors set this program in motion, and in all that time we will be the first to hear the computer speak.

LOONQUAWL An awesome prospect, Phouchg.

PHOUCHG We, Loonquawl, are the ones who will hear *the answer to the great question of Life* …!

LOONQUAWL *The Universe* …!

PHOUCHG *And Everything* …!

LOONQUAWL Ssh, I think Deep Thought is preparing to speak!

NARRATOR There was a moment's expectant pause whilst panels slowly came to life on the front of the console. Lights flashed on and off experimentally and settled down into a business-like pattern. A soft low hum came from the communication channel.

DEEP THOUGHT Good morning.

LOONQUAWL Er … Good morning, O Deep Thought, do you have … er, that is …

DEEP THOUGHT An answer for you? Yes, I have.

NARRATOR The two men shivered with expectancy. Their waiting had not been in vain.

PHOUCHG There really is one?

DEEP THOUGHT There really is one.

LOONQUAWL To Everything? To the Great Question of Life, the Universe and Everything?

DEEP THOUGHT Yes.

NARRATOR Both of the men had been trained for this moment, their lives had been a preparation for it, they had been selected at birth as those who would witness the answer, but even so they found themselves gasping and squirming like excited children.

PHOUCHG And you're ready to give it to us?

DEEP THOUGHT I am.

LOONQUAWL Now?

DEEP THOUGHT Now.

NARRATOR They both licked their dry lips.

DEEP THOUGHT Though I don't think you're going to like it.

PHOUCHG It doesn't matter! We must know it! Now!

DEEP THOUGHT Now?

LOONQUAWL Yes! Now …

DEEP THOUGHT Alright.

NARRATOR The two men fidgeted. The tension was unbearable.

DEEP THOUGHT You're really not going to like it.

PHOUCHG Tell us!

DEEP THOUGHT Alright. The answer to the Great Question …

LOONQUAWL Yes …!

DEEP THOUGHT Of Life, the Universe and Everything …

LOONQUAWL Yes …!

DEEP THOUGHT Is …

PHOUCHG Yes …!

DEEP THOUGHT Is …

PHOUCHG Yes …!!! …?

DEEP THOUGHT Forty-two.

NARRATOR It was a long time before anyone spoke. Out of the corner of his eye, Phouchg could see the sea of tense expectant faces down in the square outside.

PHOUCHG We're going to get lynched aren't we?

DEEP THOUGHT It was a tough assignment.

PHOUCHG Forty-two! Is that all you've got to show for seven and a half million years' work?

DEEP THOUGHT I checked it very thoroughly, and that quite definitely is the answer. I think the problem, to be quite honest with you, is that you've never actually known what the question is.

PHOUCHG Look, alright, alright, can you just please tell us the question?

DEEP THOUGHT The Ultimate Question?

PHOUCHG Yes!

DEEP THOUGHT Of Life, the Universe and Everything?

LOONQUAWL Yes!

NARRATOR Deep Thought pondered for a moment.

DEEP THOUGHT Tricky.

PHOUCHG Yeah, but can you do it?

NARRATOR Deep Thought pondered this for another long moment. Finally.

DEEP THOUGHT No.

Extra vocabulary

See page 176 for ideas on how to exploit this vocabulary.

emit (verb) to send out something such as sound, heat, light

specify (verb) to state something by giving exact requirements

disconcertingly (adverb) causing surprise, confusion or embarrassment

immense (adjective) extremely large

interjection (noun) a short sound or phrase to express sudden emotion

formulate (verb) to create or prepare something very carefully

mirage (noun) an illusion that cannot be real

detrimental (adjective) harmful or acting against something

capacity (noun) the amount that something can hold; the ability to understand or do something

deterioration (noun) process of something getting worse

Language in use SB pages 27–29

Word formation Paper 3 Part 2

A This part of the section focuses on affixation in English. Prefixes are added to the beginning of the root word and suffixes to the end.

Students work in pairs to discuss the changes to the words.

Discuss answers as a class.

> **Key**
>
> *strike* – meaning to hit someone or something; to stop working as a protest; to come into one's mind suddenly
> *striking* – adjective used to describe something or someone that is unusual or interesting enough to attract attention
> *strikingly* – adverb used with the same meaning as the adjective
> *able* – adjective which describes ability to do something
> *enable* – verb meaning making it possible for somebody to do something
> *enabled* – past participle of the verb
> *help* – verb and noun
> *helpful* – adjective used to describe something which or someone who helps in a situation
> *unhelpful* – negative adjective
> *unhelpfully* – negative adverb

B

> **Key**
>
> Real Madrid is the name of a football team. *Real* is Spanish for royal.
> *realign* comes from the root word *align*. It means to change the position or direction of something slightly.

C Brainstorm other words as a class.

> **Key**
>
> realising, realism, realisable, realisably

D Students prepare their diagrams in pairs and then compare them with another pair.

Check answers as a class.

Possible answers

Legal	illegal, legalise, legalisation, legalised, legalising, legally, illegally
Care	careful, carefully, careless, carelessly, carer, cared
Appear	disappear, disappearing, appearing, appearance, disappearance, appeared, disappeared, apparent, apparently

E Check answers as a class, asking students to give a definition of the words or to use them in a sentence.

Key

1	nonconformity	conformity, conform
2	disrespectfully	respectfully, respectful, respect, disrespect
3	disentangle	entangle, tangle
4	misrepresentation	misrepresent, represent, representation, presentation, present
5	proportionately	proportionate, proportion
6	uncoordinated	coordinated, coordinate
7	reconstructive	reconstruct, constructive, construct
8	differentiation	differentiate, different
9	informality	informal, formality, formal
10	interchangeable	interchange, changeable, change

F Draw students' attention to the *Exam tip* before they do the exercise. They will have a sense of the type of multiple changes possible from E.

Ask students to read through the text quickly to find out what in general it is about (the possibility of asteroids hitting Earth).

Discuss answers as a class.

Students read through the text carefully and decide on the right form of the words.

Check answers as a class.

Key

1	unavoidably	6	abundant
2	catastrophic	7	extraordinary
3	alarmingly	8	destruction
4	disappeared	9	realisation
5	insignificant	10	unfortunately

☐ Alternative activity

Ask students to cover the words with a piece of paper. In pairs they read through the text and decide what type of word e.g. noun, verb, adjective, adverb goes in the space by looking at the other words in the sentence.

Then ask them to uncover the words and put them in the right form.

✚ Extra activity

Write these words on the board.

strength   weak   hard   soft   circle   close   large   rich   danger   courage   force   sure

Ask students to work in pairs and make verbs from all the words on the board by adding *-en* either to the beginning or the end of the word.

Then they should make sentences using five of the verbs, using a dictionary if necessary.

Check answers as a class.

Key

strengthen, weaken, harden, soften, encircle, enclose, enlarge, enrich, endanger, encourage, enforce, ensure

Structure

Stative verbs

Introduce this activity by asking students if it is possible to use the continuous form of the verb in the example sentences (no).

Then ask them to work in pairs to make sentences using the verbs in the continuous form but with a different meaning.

Ask some pairs to read their sentences out and to explain the meaning of the verb.
Students then classify the verbs and compare their lists with a partner.

Check answers as a class.

Key

Verbs related to the senses   hear, smell, sound, taste
Verbs related to thinking   believe, doubt, guess,
   imagine, know, realise, regard, remember, suppose,
   understand
Verbs related to possession   belong to, have, own
Verbs related to emotional states   dislike, hate, like,
   love, mind, prefer, want
Verbs related to appearance   appear, seem
Others   contain, depend on, involve, mean

H

Key

1 a I think   think is used to express an opinion
   b I'm thinking   think expresses the possibility of
      a course of action
2 a is   be is used for a general state or condition
   b are being   be is used to talk about someone's
      behaviour or attitude at that particular moment
3 a I'm not imagining   imagine indicates the action
      of using one's imagination at that particular
      moment
   b I don't imagine   imagine expresses the
      speaker's opinion of what is likely to happen
4 a is appearing   appear means performing in a
      play, film or TV show for a limited period
   b appears   appear means seem

Continuous aspect
I

Key

1 a The simple past is used to indicate a repeated,
      regular action in the past which doesn't happen
      now.
   b The past continuous indicates a single activity
      that was interrupted by another action.
2 a The present continuous indicates a temporary
      situation.
   b The present simple is used to show it is a
      permanent situation.
3 a The present perfect simple indicates that the
      action is completed.
   b The present perfect continuous indicates that
      the action isn't completed yet.
4 a The past simple is used to show the action had
      finished when the teacher intervened.
   b The past continuous is used to show the action
      was still going on when the teacher intervened.

J

Key

| 1 c | 2 e | 3 c | 4 d | 5 e | 6 c | 7 a |
| 8 b | 9 b | 10 a | | | | |

Photocopiable activity 2   TB page 151

Extra vocabulary

See page 176 for ideas on how to exploit this vocabulary.

abundant (adjective) existing in large quantities
celestial (adjective) relating to the sky or universe
compromise (noun) an agreement reached by making
   concessions
deprivation (noun) the fact of not having something you need
intervene (verb) to become involved in a situation in order to
   help it

Comprehension and summary

SB pages 30–31

The theory of inequality

Students discuss the questions in small groups.

Suggest that they should come up with some examples
to support their views.

Ask one student from each group to summarise the
discussion for the rest of the class.

Round off the activity by asking students whether they
think women are better suited to certain jobs than men.

Comprehension   Paper 3 Part 5

Background notes
Thomas Vaughan (1622–1665) was a British alchemist
and philosopher of nature. His writings deal with
magic and mysticism.
Sir Isaac Newton (1642–1727) is famous for his
universal law of gravitation and laws of motion.
Robert Boyle (1627–1691) was a British philosopher
and scientist who carried out a series of experiments on
the properties of air.
Charles Babbage (1792–1871) was a British
mathematician and engineer who developed the
'difference engine' as a calculating machine, but it was
never completed in his lifetime.

The Royal Society was founded in 1645 as a national academy of sciences and election as a 'fellow' or member was considered a great honour.

Sir William Herschel (1738–1822) was a German-born British astronomer who discovered the planet Uranus. He was the father of Caroline Herschel who also became an astronomer.

Ada Lovelace (1815–1852) was a British mathematician. Her portrait appears on SB page 30. The Fawcett Society was established by Dame Millicent Fawcett, a well known feminist, to promote women in science.

A Students read through the article quickly and choose an option. Ask them to justify their choice.

Check answers as a class.

Key

Women failed to become scientists because of male prejudice.

B Ask students to read through the article carefully to choose a heading for each paragraph.

Check answers as a class.

Key

Paragraph 1	Fear of the unknown
Paragraph 2	Women's understanding
Paragraph 3	A male preserve
Paragraph 4	A one-off visit
Paragraph 5	Forgotten talents
Paragraph 6	Lacking in strength?

Referencing

C Draw students' attention to the *Exam tip* before they do the exercise.

Remind students to look back at the article and read the sentences around the extract to find the answer.

Check answers as a class.

Key

1 a rebel
2 modern science
3 science
4 women's knowledge
5 the time of Newton / 1667
6 the 19th century

D Remind students that they should keep their answers to the questions as brief and simple as possible. This was practised in Unit 1.

Ask students to compare their answers in pairs.

Check answers as a class.

Key

1 to suggest that science had made ideas of magic and witchcraft old fashioned
2 the Royal Society
3 to emphasise the exclusive nature of science as a men's club
4 scientific discovery as demonstrated by Boyle's air pump
5 the reasons for women's inadequacy in science
6 that he believed she was physically incapable of doing mathematics

E Remind students to see how the adverbs are used in the text before they match them to a meaning.

Check answers as a class.

Key

1 d   2 e   3 h   4 b   5 g   6 a   7 c   8 f

⊞ Extra activity
Write these prompts on the board.
1 the law / enforced
2 the greatest team / the world
3 what you said / ridiculous
4 offered / lend / car
5 exam results / bad
6 one point of view / valid / another
7 world / close / destruction

Ask students to work in pairs and make complete sentences from the cues using suitable adverbs from the list in E.

Each pair reads out their sentences for comparison as a class.

Possible answers
1 The law must be *rigorously* enforced.
2 They are *unarguably* the greatest team in the world.
3 What you said was *utterly* ridiculous.
4 He *kindly* offered to lend me his car.

5 Our exam results were *disastrously* / *staggeringly* / *catastrophically* bad.
6 One point of view is as *equally* valid as another.
7 The world is *alarmingly* / *disastrously* close to destruction.

F Again, remind students to check how the expressions are used in the text before they choose a meaning. Some of the expressions are metaphorical. Check answers as a class.

> **Key**
>
> 1 B   2 D   3 B   4 A

Summary writing   Paper 3 Part 5

G The key information in the question is *the reasons…why women have been unable to participate in science.*

> **Sample summary**
>
> Firstly, it was believed that women were associated with witchcraft and the devil, which was the enemy of science. Furthermore, it was thought that only men had minds that were suitable for understanding the mysteries of science and therefore women were excluded from scientific activity. Finally, in the 19th century, women's minds were considered too weak for science. (58 words)

Extra vocabulary

See page 176 for ideas on how to exploit this vocabulary.

inherent (adjective) basic part of something that cannot be removed
conviction (noun) a belief in something
codify (verb) to arrange things into a system
subside (verb) to become calmer or quieter
indictment (noun) an indication that something is bad or wrong
offshoot (noun) a thing that develops from something else

Listening   SB page 32

To boldly go

Introduce the activity by asking students if they have seen a science fiction film or read a science fiction novel recently. Ask them to explain what it was about. Discuss the questions as a class.

Note: *to boldly go where no man has gone before* is a phrase used in the television series *Star Trek* and which

has now become an accepted phrase to describe any new and exciting venture.

> **Key**
>
> 1 The two photographs show scenes from *Star Trek* and *The X-files*.

Brainstorm ideas for questions 2 and 3 (students' own answers).

Sentence completion   Paper 4 Part 2

Background notes

Percy Bysshe Shelley (1792–1822) and Lord Byron (1788–1824) were both poets associated with the Romantic Movement. Both had radical views on morality and society and led unconventional lifestyles. The Great Exhibition 1851 was a celebration of the Industrial Revolution held at the Crystal Palace as a showcase for the latest developments in science and technology.

A Ask students to look at the examples and guess what goes in the gap from the context and the prompts.

Then ask them to read through the sentences and make similar guesses. Point out that they may need more than one word in some gaps.

B ⌒ Play the recording. Remind students to use the second listening to check what they noted down in the first listening.

Check answers as a class.

> **Key**
>
> 1 feminist
> 2 grave
> 3 sixteen / 16
> 4 storm
> 5 ghost
> 6 (waking) nightmare / dream
> 7 student
> 8 female
> 9 The Great Exhibition

Tapescript
───────────────────

PRESENTER Although science fiction is often considered to be a fairly modern literary genre, it has a long tradition. By the end of the 19th century, novels involving science and fantasy had already become popular, but as Sally Renshaw explains, the genre goes back even further…

RENSHAW The first novel that is generally recognised as a work of science fiction is *Frankenstein*, written by Mary Shelley in 1817. Mary Shelley had an unconventional and often tragic life. She was the only child of Mary Wollstonecraft, the famous *feminist*, and William Godwin, a philosopher and novelist. She never knew her mother who died in childbirth, but her father had the very highest expectations of her. Her earliest years were imbued with a peculiar sort of Gothicism. On most days she would go for a walk with her father to the St. Pancras churchyard to visit her mother's *grave*, and Godwin taught her to read and spell her name by getting her to trace her mother's inscription on the gravestone. From an early age she was surrounded by famous philosophers, writers, and poets: Coleridge made his first visit when Mary was two years old. At the age of *sixteen* Mary ran away to live with the twenty-one year old poet, Percy Shelley, despite the fact that he was already married at the time. Although she was cast out of society, even by her father, this inspirational liaison produced her masterpiece, *Frankenstein*. She conceived of the novel when she was just 19, and was spending the summer with Shelley in Switzerland. On the night of June 16th, Mary and Percy Shelley could not return to their home, due to an incredible *storm*, and spent the night at the Villa Diodati with the poet Lord Byron. The group read aloud a collection of German ghost stories, and this inspired Byron to challenge them all to write a *ghost* story. Mary spent a week thinking of a suitable subject for her story, and it came to her when she had what she called a *'waking' nightmare*:

MARY I saw the pale student of unhallowed arts kneeling beside the thing he had put together. I saw the hideous phantasm of a man stretched out, then, on the working of some powerful engine, show signs of life … . His success would terrify the artist; he would rush away … hope that … this thing … would subside into dead matter … he opens his eyes; behold the horrid thing stands at his bedside, opening his curtains …

RENSHAW In her story, the monster is created by a young *student*, Victor Frankenstein, who assembles the creature from various body parts he collects from graveyards and slaughterhouses. The creature he creates escapes, and flees to the woods. At first, he is innocent and lonely, but he begins to change when he is rejected and attacked by humans because of his horrifying appearance. The creature realises that the only hope of escaping from total isolation is for Victor Frankenstein to create a *female* for him, which he initially agrees to do. However, Victor then changes his mind and this leads the monster to embark on a course of horrifying revenge. Mary completed the novel in May of 1817 and when it was published the following year, it became a huge success. The same, however, could not be said of her personal life, which was marred by further tragedies. Mary and Shelley married, but fierce public hostility toward the couple drove them to Italy. Initially, they were happy, but two of their children died

there, and Mary never fully recovered. When Mary was only twenty-four her husband drowned, leaving her alone with a two year old son. For her remaining twenty-nine years she lived in England which she despised because of the morality and social system. She was shunned by conventional circles and worked as a professional writer to support her father and her son. Mary became an invalid at the age of forty-eight. She died in 1851 of a brain tumour with poetic timing. *The Great Exhibition*, which was a showcase of technological progress, was opened. This was the same scientific technology that she had warned against in her most famous book, *Frankenstein*.

Your views

C Discuss the question as a class. Ask students whether they think Mary Shelley would be regarded as unconventional nowadays.

Vocabulary

Book expressions

D Ask students to read through all six sentences before they choose a suitable expression.
Remind them that they may need to change the wording of some of the expressions to fit in with the meaning of the sentence.

Check answers as a class.

> **Key**
>
> 1 throw the book at you (illustrated in the cartoon)
> 2 take a leaf out of her book
> 3 turn over a new leaf
> 4 speaks volumes about her
> 5 I'm in Mrs Lawson's good books
> 6 does everything by the book
>
> *Leaf* in sentences 2 and 3 means a page of a book.

Speaking SB page 33

The price of progress

1 Students discuss the pictures in pairs.

> **Key**
> Picture 1 Satellite technology
> Picture 2 Games consoles
> Picture 3 Genetic research
> Picture 4 Hand-held computers

2 Discuss answers as a class.

Extended speaking Paper 5 Part 3

A Allow a few minutes for the pairs to discuss their ideas with each other.

Students work on their own to make their notes.

B While students are speaking, go round and monitor. Check on their fluency in presenting their ideas and note any errors you would like to deal with.

Responding

C Remind students that they don't have to agree with what their partner has said but if they disagree they should do so politely. See Unit 1 Speaking, exercise D. When they have finished, do a quick feedback session on B and C.

Exploring the topic

D Introduce the activity by brainstorming as a class any recent controversial technological advances they know about e.g. cloning or genetic engineering.

Divide the class into small groups. Allow them 2–3 minutes to discuss the statement.

Invite one student from each group to report their discussion to the class.

Writing SB pages 34–35

A set book composition Paper 2 Part 2

Preparing for the tasks

A This checklist aims to help students prepare for writing on the set book by organising their study appropriately. In small groups, students discuss how they will approach the text that they have chosen. They should be prepare to give practical examples of how and when they will prepare.

Each group presents its plan to the class.

B Make a list on the board of any other study suggestions given by the students.

C This exercise practises some useful vocabulary for writing about the set book.

Check answers as a class.

Key

1 protagonist
2 opening
3 climax
4 denouement
5 pace
6 hero / heroine
7 style
8 events
9 theme
10 suspense

Writing your set book composition

D Students may be asked to write about the set text within any one of the five formats in the example exam questions in this section. Each of the formats has been practised in previous units. This activity aims to focus on how these formats can be applied to the set text writing task.

Deal with each exam question in turn and discuss answers to the questions as a class.

Key

1 a The balance should be fairly even as the review asks for an illustration of society through the characters.
   b The article is for readers of all ages in the local area. They will expect to gain information about attitudes in society at a particular time in history as represented in the book.
   c The style should be informal but also informative.
2 a The main focus is on the relationship between the two characters and their different personalities, although some mention must be made of the external influences on their relationship.
   b An introduction giving details of the beginning of the relationship.
   A paragraph explaining why the relationship could be considered doomed by referring to the characters' personalities and other factors that affected their relationship.
   A paragraph explaining why the relationship wasn't necessarily doomed by making reference to how the relationship might have worked in different circumstances.
   A conclusion giving the writer's own interpretation of the nature of the relationship.
   c A formal style appropriate to an essay for a tutor.

3 a The editor of the magazine. You wish your suggestion to be taken up.

  b Details of the personality of the female protagonist and how she resolves the problem. Reasons why this particular book and its protagonist would be of interest to the readers of the magazine.

  c Formal and persuasive.

4 a The younger readers of the magazine.

  b To explain how the characters, their relationships and the themes of the book would be relevant to younger readers of the review.

  c An informal, personalised style.

5 a The head of English at your college

  b The report should have a formal, impersonal style and be organised into clear sections, possibly with headings.

  c The main focus should be on how the content of the book has provided you with an insight into the place where events take place and into how you think a teacher could make the book more relevant to students, perhaps by using video and drama.

E Remind students of the importance of planning their composition before they write by referring to the five stages used in previous units. Use the notes in the key for part D as a guideline for you and your students.

The illustration on page 35 depicts scenes from novels by Jane Austen, E M Forster, D H Lawrence, George Orwell, John Steinbeck and F Scott Fitzgerald.

Unit 2 Overview key

SB pages 36–37

Lexical cloze Paper 1 Part 1

A

1 B	2 A	3 D	4 D	5 A	6 B
7 A	8 A	9 A	10 B	11 C	12 B

Cloze Paper 3 Part 1

B

1	such	9	least
2	with	10	rather
3	ahead	11	of
4	on	12	result / consequence
5	where	13	those
6	over	14	whose
7	longer	15	doing
8	without		

Word formation Paper 3 Part 2

C

1	passionately	6	intellectual
2	consuming	7	irrespective
3	remainder	8	unsuccessful
4	characteristics	9	declining
5	unfortunately	10	embittered

Vocabulary Test Unit 2 TB page 127

3 Safety and danger

▶ *See unit summary on page 4.*

Exam training in this unit

Reading	Gapped text: looking for clues in the surrounding paragraphs
Use of English	Gapped sentences: thinking about multiple meaning
	Comprehension and summary: shortening sentences, reducing the number of words in a summary
Listening	Multiple-choice questions on one text: preparing to answer the questions
Speaking	Extended speaking: giving views and opinions, responding
Writing	A letter: writing a response to an article, expressing opinions

The overall theme of this unit is dangers and risks and their effects on our lives.

Reading SB pages 38–40

War and peace

Introduce the activity by asking students whether military service in their country is compulsory or voluntary.

Students brainstorm answers to the questions in small groups.

Discuss answers as a class.

Note: *War and Peace* is also the title of the famous novel by Leo Tolstoy (1828–1910).

Gapped text Paper 1 Part 3

Background notes
The passage is from the story *Transfigured Night* by William Boyd, which was written in the form of a journal.
Nietzsche (1844–1900) was a German philosopher who rejected conventional moral values.
Charles Dana Gibson (1867–1944) was an American illustrator famous for his pictures of young women.
A *trabuco* is a type of cigar.
Galicia is a region of Poland.
Lapps are semi-nomadic people from the arctic regions of Europe.

A Students skim read the text and decide on the period.

Check answers as a class, asking students to justify their choices.

> **Key**
>
> First World War. Russia entered the war in August 1914. The mood and atmosphere created in the extract also serve to give a strong impression of the period.

B This is a simplified version of the task in the exam, using five gaps instead of eight. Draw students' attention to the *Exam tip*.

Check students have understood the task by asking them to explain to you what they have to do.

Check answers as a class, asking students to justify why they have chosen a particular place for each paragraph.

> **Key**
>
> 1 C 'In my elation' links with 'glad to enlist' in the next paragraph and describes his feelings about joining the army.
> 2 F 'By the time I reached the Café Museum' links with 'Inside the place was busy' in the next paragraph.
> 3 A 'he was already fairly drunk.' refers to the soldier in uniform mentioned in the previous paragraph and links with 'his voice sounding slightly slurred' in the next.
> 4 B 'He offered me a Trabuco' refers to the cigar in the previous paragraph. 'When the wine arrived' links with 'he filled our glasses' in the next paragraph.
> 5 E ' "God preserve me from sanity" ' links with 'I … asked God to preserve me from sanity as well' in the next paragraph.

Ask students to check paragraph D and explain why it doesn't fit. Ask: Is it true that the writer had never seen the man before? (no, line 25)

Note: In the revised CPE Paper 1 Part 3, there are seven paragraph gaps.

C Remind students they can find answers to the questions by underlining relevant parts of the text. Ask them to use their own words as far as possible in answering the questions.

Check answers as a class.

Key

1 He wasn't making any progress with his work so he wanted to do something different. 'divert me from my intellectual work', 'I had reached an impasse'

2 The uniformed soldier 'students … casually and unaffectedly dressed. So I was a little surprised to catch a glimpse in one corner of a uniform'

3 The way he was sitting and his expression were so stern and unfriendly that no one wanted to join him. 'His posture and the ferocious concentration of his gaze clearly put people off as the three other seats around his table remained unoccupied.'

4 that he wanted to isolate himself 'I want to be lonely', 'All I do is pollute my mind talking to people', 'One-man army'

D This activity focuses on how the writer creates an impression of the characters.

Check answers as a class.

Key

the writer
'in my elation, subject myself to the rigours of a harsh routine, divert me from my intellectual work, reached an impasse, morbid despair, pleased to see a fellow soldier'

Georg
'staring intently at the table top, ferocious concentration of his gaze, put people off, I detest this sun and this city, I want to be lonely, pollute my mind talking to people, preserve me from sanity'
Georg seems the more pessimistic.

➕ Extra activity
Write these adjectives on the board.

depressed enthusiastic frustrated outgoing sociable gloomy sullen solitary open straight-forward cynical unsociable pessimistic honest

Ask students to work in pairs to choose which adjectives apply to Georg, which to the writer, and which could be used to describe both of them.

Students should justify their choices by referring to the text.

Accept any answers that seem reasonable.

Vocabulary

The right meaning

E Remind students to read the whole sentence first before making their choice.

Check answers as a class and clarify why the other words do not fit.

Key

1 a *recovered* suggests getting back something which was lost
salvaged is only used with objects
saved suggests the victims were still alive

2 c *declared* means to state something with emphasis
confirmed is normally followed by a *that*-clause
decreed is used to make official statements which have the force of law

3 c *averse* means disliking or being opposed to something
reluctant expresses a lack of willingness to do something, and is followed by the infinitive with *to*
antagonistic describes a negative attitude to other people

4 a *divert* means to make someone or something change direction
deflect means changing direction as a result of hitting something
detract usually *detract from*, means to make something seem worse

5 c *aroma* suggests a pleasant and distinctive smell
odour is a neutral word used in science to describe a smell
reek suggests a nasty or unpleasant smell

6 c *smashed* suggests the noise of something breaking into pieces
clinked describes a ringing sound
crashed describes the sound of two things hitting each other

Ask students to read out their new sentences to the class.

F

Key

1 d	2 e	3 f	4 b	5 i	6 c	7 a
8 h	9 j	10 g				

⊞ Extra activity

Write these adverbs on the board

briefly   steadily   quickly   secretively
continuously   intently   hardly   knowingly
longingly   furtively

Ask students to work in pairs to make sentences
using each of the ten verbs in F with a suitable
adverb above.

When they have finished, ask them to read out their
sentences to the class. Check correct word order,
especially with *glimpse*, *glance* and *hardly*.

Alternatively, divide the class into teams to write
their sentences and award a point for each correct
sentence they produce.

Possible answers

I briefly glimpsed him leaving.
I gazed longingly out of the window.
I stared intently at the page.
I quickly glanced at the picture.
She peeped furtively around the corner.
He peered intently at the contract.
Despite the shock, he hardly blinked.
We could hardly make out the ships on the horizon.
They wept continuously for their departed loved
ones.
He winked knowingly at me.

Expressions with *do*

G   Ask students which expression with *do* is illustrated
(doing the donkey work).

Remind students that they need to be careful with the
form of the verb *do* and that they may need to change
the order of the words.

Check answers as a class.

> **Key**
>
> 1 I'm fed up with *doing the donkey work* in the
>   barracks.
> 2 We had to *do it up.*
> 3 *I can do it with my eyes closed.*
> 4 I think too much army-type discipline *does more
>   harm than good.*
> 5 Could you *do me a favour*?
> 6 Some people say that military service *does
>   wonders* for character building.
> 7 He *did time* for being a conscientious objector.
> 8 A life of hardship will *do you no good.*

Extra vocabulary

See page 176 for ideas on how to exploit this vocabulary.

abolish (verb) to officially end laws or systems
to subject someone to something (verb) to force someone to
   experience something unpleasant
harsh (adjective) very difficult, unkind or even cruel
morbid (adjective) expressing strong interest in sad or
   unpleasant things
elation (noun) feeling of great happiness or excitement
ferocious (adjective) very fierce or aggressive
candidly (adverb) openly and honestly
resentment (noun) feeling of anger about something
   considered unfair
preserve (verb) to protect or keep something in good condition

Language in use   SB pages 41–43

Dizzy heights

Introduce the activity by asking students how the title
Dizzy heights is related to the picture.

Ask them to think of other adjectives they could use to
describe how they might feel in this situation. (Possible
answers: daunted, exhilarated, nervous, excited, scared,
horrified, unsafe)

Students work in groups to discuss the questions.

Discuss answers as a class.

> **Possible answers**
>
> The picture shows a construction worker on a crane
> high above the ground.
> 1 physical strength and fitness, fearlessness, manual
>   dexterity, calmness
> 2 risk of falling, exposure to all weather conditions
> 3 students' own answers

Structure

Background notes

Sydney Harbour Bridge was opened in March 1932
after 6 years of construction. It is the world's largest
steel arch bridge and the top of the arch is 134 metres
above sea level. It is a well-known symbol of Australia.

A   Allow students a minute to read the text quickly.

Check answers as a class.

> **Key**
>
> a guided tour to the top of Sydney Harbour Bridge

Modal verbs

B   This exercise serves as a quick revision of the different functions of modal verbs.

Check answers as a class.

Key

1	necessity	must, need
2	obligation	must, should, ought to
3	possibility	may, might, can, can't, could, couldn't
4	ability	can, can't, could, couldn't
5	permission	may, can, can't
6	deductions	may, might, can't, could, must, should

C   This exercise focuses on the meanings of past modals in context.

Check answers as a class. The key includes hint questions to help clarify meaning.

Key

1. an unlikely comparison 'It might just as well have been a mill pond' Hint: Was it really a mill pond?
2. an obligation that was not fulfilled 'We ought to have found this out' Hint: What didn't they find out? Was this a problem for the writer?
3. an action which proved to be unnecessary 'We needn't have worried' Hint: Why were they worried? Why was it unnecessary?
4. a positive deduction 'It must have been at least 50 feet high' Hint: How sure is he about the height of the ladder?
5. a negative deduction the prospect couldn't have been more daunting' Hint: Was it possible for it to be more daunting?

Possibility and speculation

D

Key

1. might / may have been
2. could / might / may have been standing
3. could / might / may have taken
4. could / might / may have been repairing
5. could / might / may have been taken

E   This exercise focuses on how *could*, *might* and *may* can change meaning according to the context of the sentence.

Draw students' attention to the example and explanation.

Remind them to find two endings for each sentence stem.

Ask students to read out whole sentences. Check answers and clarify changes of meaning as a class.

Key

2 b This was possible, but they didn't write back. The use of the phrase here also indicates that the speaker is annoyed.
  d Perhaps they wrote back but the speaker doesn't know for sure.
3 a It was possible for him to catch the train but he didn't.
  e It wasn't possible for him to catch the train.
4 g It was possible for Ted to phone, but he didn't.
  h The speaker doesn't know if Ted phoned or not.

Making deductions

F   Check answers as a class. Ask students to read out the whole sentence when they give their answers. The second half of the sentence gives the evidence for the deduction in the first half.

Key

1	c	must have been	4	f	must have been
2	d	can't have been	5	b	can't have been
3	a	must have been	6	c	can't have been

G   This is a freer activity to focus on making deductions about the past.

Students read out their sentences for comparison. There is more than one possible answer for some situations.

Possible answers

1. It must have been an expensive restaurant. / There must have been a mistake with the bill.
2. It can't / couldn't have been Patrick.
3. It must have been raining.
4. You must have forgotten about it. / The TV programme must have been exciting. / You can't have been listening to me.
5. We must have drunk it all. / We can't have drunk it all!
6. You can't / couldn't have worked hard enough on it. / You must have misunderstood something in the lesson.

Necessity and obligation

H See C2 and 3 on SB page 41 if necessary.

Key

1 e 2 e 3 d 4 d 5 a 6 b 7 c

I

Key

2 needn't have booked
3 should have / ought to have booked
4 didn't need to have, get, buy
5 shouldn't have / oughtn't to have taken, borrowed, driven
6 needed to get
7 needn't have spent
8 shouldn't have been driving

⊞ Extra activity

Ask students to match the sentences in I with the meanings a–e in H.

Key

1 d 2 a 3 b 4 d 5 c 6 e 7 a 8 c

Photocopiable activity 3.1   TB page 151

Gapped sentences   Paper 3 Part 3

J   Go through the example with the class.
Point out the missing word will always be the same part of speech and in the same form if it is a verb, i.e. *-ing*, *-ed*, infinitive.

Draw students' attention to the *Exam tip* before they begin the exercise.

Check answers as a class.

Key

1 task 2 break 3 summit 4 drained 5 pool
6 driven

⊞ Extra activity

Write this sentence from the article on the board:
Our belts would be tethered to a cable to break a fall.

Students work in pairs or small groups to make up two more sentences using *fall* as a noun.

Encourage the use of dictionaries.

Compare sentences as a class.

Possible answers
I had a bad fall and broke my arm.
We had a heavy fall of snow last weekend.
There has been a *fall* in prices recently.

As a further challenge, ask students to change their two sentences using fall as a verb but not changing its form.

Possible answers
If you're not careful, you'll fall and break your arm.
We're expecting snow to fall this weekend.
Prices may fall in the near future.

Extra vocabulary

See page 176 for ideas on how to exploit this vocabulary.

dizzy (adjective) a feeling as if everything is spinning round
daunting (adjective) a lack of confidence or fear about something
to embark on something (verb) to begin something new or difficult
reckless (adjective) showing a lack of care about danger
exhilarating (adjective) very exciting and enjoyable
vast (adjective) extremely large in area

Comprehension and summary

SB pages 44–45

Mind over matter

Draw students' attention to the phrase *mind over matter*. Ask them what they think it means (the use of willpower to overcome physical problems).

Ask students in what circumstances it might be necessary to use *mind over matter*.

Students work in small groups to discuss the risks as a group and note down their decisions. Encourage them to give justifications.

Each group presents its decision. Compare them as a class.

Comprehension   Paper 3 Part 5

Background notes
Rehabilitation is special treatment or therapy to help someone return to a normal life.
Angina is a heart disease marked by a sharp pain in the chest.

cardiologist is a doctor who specialises in heart eases.

onnel is a synonym for *staff*, the people who work ewhere.

A Students read through the texts quickly.

Check answers as a class. Ask students to justify their answers.

> **Key**
>
> Both articles describe the negative effects of stress and anxiety and mention ways of dealing with them.

B Remind students to look closely at the text to find suitable or correct answers.

Discuss answers as a class.

> **Key**
>
> Text 1
> 1 *powerful*, *important* and *emotional* are wrong because they are not used in the article to describe the results of the research. The correct answer is: *incredible*, *dramatic*, *overwhelming*
> 2 The answer is unsuitable because *staggering* refers to the results not the management programme. The correct answer is: to reinforce the idea of how surprising the results were.
>
> Text 2
> 3 *negative* and *worst* are insufficiently dramatic. The correct answer is: *doom* and *disaster*
> 4 The answer misinterprets the final paragraph – confident people aren't prevented from feeling frightened. The correct answer is: that they are just as afraid as you below the surface.

Summary writing   Paper 3 Part 5

Shortening a summary

C Check students have understood the instructions by asking them to explain the techniques for shortening the sentences to you.

Remind them that they should also take out words which are unnecessary.

Ask them to compare their reworded sentences in pairs.

Check answers as a class.

> **Key**
>
> 1 We work better when we think creatively.
> 2 Not having the determination to succeed shouldn't stop you trying.
> 3 After completing the course, their health improved.
> 4 Ignore demoralising negative sentences.
> 5 Taking a few risks will help you to become more responsible.
> 6 People who are apparently confident often turn out to be just as nervous as you.

D Remind students of the importance of underlining parts of the text.

> **Key**
>
> Text 1
> 'learning to relax' (line 7); 'think positively' (line 8); 'extent to which they feel in control of their own emotions' (line 25)
>
> Text 2
> 'People need to understand that they really are better than they believe' (line 17); 'taking risks' (line 21); 'learn how to deal with it' [fearfulness] (line 25)

E Ask students to read through the whole summary first.

Discuss as a class why the phrases have been deleted.

Students go through the rest of the summary and delete similar unnecessary phrases.

Ask them to compare their deletions in pairs.

Check answers as a class.

> **Key**
>
> 1 The first sentence is unnecessary as there is no need to introduce the subject of the summary. It's obvious that if you are healthy you may avoid surgery so it's unnecessary to state this with the phrase and 'perhaps even of avoiding surgery'. There is no need to qualify calm with 'quite'.
> 2 The following words and phrases can be deleted: *generally, Nevertheless, in staying healthy, own, In order to improve performance, you should, seem to, Furthermore, in spite of the fact that you may lack confidence, you need to, emerging, ensure that you*

Ask students to look at what they have left in the summary.

Remind them to consider how they can use the techniques in exercise C to rewrite the remainder.

Ask them to write their final summary then compare summaries in pairs.

Sample summary

Staying calm and remaining positive gives you a better chance of being healthy. How well you succeed depends on taking control of your emotions. Try to convince yourself that you can achieve more than you expect, even though others may have little faith in you. Come to terms with your deepest fears and meet each challenge positively. Thus you can learn from your mistakes.
(63 words)

Photocopiable activity 3.2 TB page 152

Listening SB page 46

Stormy weather

1 Students work in small groups to discuss the pictures.

When they have finished, discuss ideas as a class.

Possible answers

1 heavy rain / snow, flooding
2 drought, hot weather
3 hurricanes, storms, a tidal wave
4 hurricanes, storms, tornadoes

2 In their groups, students brainstorm ideas based on the pictures and make a list.

Compare lists as a class.

Multiple choice questions Paper 4 Part 3

A 🎧 Draw students' attention to the *Exam tip*. Play the recording. Ask students to use the second listening to confirm or change their choices.

Check answers as a class.

Key

1 C   2 D   3 B   4 A   5 C

Tapescript

PRESENTER Hello, and welcome to our programme 'Young hero or heroine of the week'. The subject this week is Cindy Talbot, a final year college student, who was on the third day of her five-day solo-hiking trip through a forested wilderness when she was struck by lightning. Lightning kills nearly a hundred Americans each year, more than hurricanes or tornadoes, and to survive a direct hit is almost a miracle. Luckily, Cindy was rescued and we are fortunate to have her with us in the studio today.

CINDY Hi!

PRESENTER Tell me, Cindy, what were you actually doing when the lightning struck?

CINDY Well, I'd noticed the thunderclouds gathering and I was, well, resting on a rocky peak people call Eagle Peak , when I heard the thunder rumbling in the distance, and *I was rather unnerved*. Fortunately for me, Rod and Mark, the two guys who came to my rescue were driving back home in their pickup ... they'd been cruising around in the forest checking their traps, I think. I must admit I thought *the thunder sounded kinda ominous*. So I said to myself: 'Cindy, time to get a move on' ... you see *I didn't want to get caught* in a storm like that. But, I was too late, I guess. I remember when the downpour started ... and it must have lasted for about an hour, ... at least an hour ... I knew it wasn't going to stop just like that, so I sheltered under some trees.

PRESENTER *Not a very wise thing to do* considering it was an electric storm, or so I'm told!

CINDY I didn't have much option, to tell the truth. Everything happened so quickly and there didn't seem to be anywhere else around where I might find shelter. But eventually the sun came out and the rain started to move away, so I came out from under the trees to dry off a little bit. And then, well, I'd just put my backpack on – it has a metal frame, by the way! – when the whole world exploded, and I felt an electrical charge surging through my body. It was literally 'a bolt out of the blue'! I realised that by some miracle I was still alive and had to get help. But I couldn't move my legs, so I had to crawl. It sure was heavy going, but after about an hour I reached a wet, muddy kind of track in a clearing in the forest, and was found by Rod and Mark, the two guys with the fur business. When they found me, *I don't think they thought there was a grain of truth in my story at first!* Rod told me later that *he thought what I'd told him was a bit far-fetched*, to say the least! They said they'd seen this weird-looking object – seemed to be kind of sprawling across the road ... not moving, but it wasn't a fallen tree – it looked human. I thought: Gee, thanks! Anyway, they'd jumped out of the truck to get a closer look, and they found me. They managed to get me to the nearest hospital in record time, and, er, in a few days, I was on my feet again. Thanks to the guys. But I've still got the scars on my back, ... on my hips and foot, too. And I'm scared to death of lightning now.

PRESENTER I suppose lightning's not normally something to be terrified about. But you've just got to know what you're doing, haven't you! So do you feel the experience has had any long term effect on you?

CINDY Hmn, I think it's made me realise that I'm a lot more resilient than I thought. *I'm not really a quitter and I'm determined, really determined to go on hiking.*

PRESENTER But perhaps not in electric storms?

CINDY I can't promise that, I'm afraid!

PRESENTER Cindy, thanks for talking to us today.

Your views

B Students discuss the questions in small groups. Ask them to try and come to an agreement as a group.

Each group presents their decisions to the class for comparison.

Extra vocabulary

See page 176 for ideas on how to exploit this vocabulary.

relieved (adjective) feeling happy because something unpleasant stopped or didn't happen
initial (adjective) first, at the beginning
outcome (noun) the result of an action
vow (verb) to make a serious promise to do something
unnerved (adjective) a feeling of fear or loss of confidence
ominous (adjective) suggesting that something bad will happen
far-fetched (adjective) something very difficult to believe
out of the blue unexpectedly, without warning

Speaking SB page 47

Extended speaking Paper 5 Part 3

Understanding the task

A Students decide who is Student A and who is Student B.

> **Key**
>
> Student A risks, modern world
> Student B fewer dangers than previous generations

Planning

B This stage is to help students prepare for their presentation. Draw their attention to the example and how the topic could be explored from the three different viewpoints.

Now ask them to look at their own prompt card and consider how they can use the three viewpoints with their topics.

Students make notes. This is a practice activity not a test so you can allow them a little time to prepare in order for them to develop good habits. In the exam, students are expected to give fluent and coherently linked responses to the prompts.

Speaking and responding

C Draw students' attention to the *Exam tip*.

Check that they have understood what they have to do by asking one or two individual students to explain the instructions to you.

While they are speaking, go round and monitor. Note down any errors you would like to deal with or any ways they could improve their fluency.

When the students have finished the activity, write any errors on the board and discuss corrections as a whole class. Also discuss any points about the fluency of their presentations that you want to deal with.

Exploring the topic

D See TB page 22 *Suggesting and disagreeing* for the language of disagreeing politely.

Encourage students to discuss each of the questions.

Groups report their conclusions to the class.

Writing SB pages 48–49

A letter Paper 2 Part 1

Understanding the task

A

> **Key**
>
> 1 The writer thinks that our personal freedom is being taken away.
> 2 the newspaper's readers
> 3 The style is quite formal and appropriate to a newspaper article. The writer uses a non-finite clause in the second sentence, 'Not content to' and a rhetorical question in the final sentence 'How far'. The writer's opinions are expressed quite strongly.
> 4 The newspaper would be interested in hearing strong opinions, both for and against the points the writer of the article makes.

Analysing the sample

B   Before students answer the questions, ask them to read through the sample and find out whether the writer agrees or disagrees with the opinions expressed in the article.

Key

1   Paragraph 1   purpose of letter and brief summary of main opinion

   Paragraph 2   positive aspects of government control

   Paragraph 3   negative effects of government controls

   Paragraph 4   why some attempts at control don't work

   Paragraph 5   conclusion restating overall opinion and making a suggestion

2   It is likely to suit the readers of the newspaper because it clearly and strongly presents its opinions in support of the article, but it also refers to a different point of view in paragraph 2.

3   The language is quite formal and strongly expresses the writer's opinions. It is very similar to the language in the original article.

4   'I would definitely agree that'

   'it would be infinitely preferable'

   'Having said that, it is also true'

   'However the main problem is'

   'Of course it is vitally important'

   'which is a complete waste of time'

   'it serves no purpose whatsoever'

   'it will never be possible to'

   'To sum up, I think'

   'There is no evidence that'

   'What we do need is'

Writing skills

C   Before students begin the exercise, ask them to look at the phrases they noted down in B 4.

Check answers as a class, asking students to read out their sentences for comparison.

Key

1   It would be infinitely preferable to ban dangerous sports.

2   It is vitally important that we resist attempts to restrict individual freedom.

3   Trying to ban sports would be a complete waste of time.

4   It serves no purpose whatsoever to introduce yet more regulations.

5   There is no evidence that watching dangerous sports encourages young people to take risks. (illustrated)

6   What we need is the elimination of unnecessary risks.

Writing your letter

D   Go through each of the stages in turn and discuss questions and brainstorm ideas as a class.

Unit 3 Overview key

SB pages 50–51

Lexical cloze   Paper 1 Part 1

A

1 C	2 C	3 C	4 B	5 D	6 A
7 B	8 D	9 A	10 C	11 C	12 B

Cloze   Paper 3 Part 1

B

1	further	9	down
2	with	10	only / just
3	Too	11	instead / unfortunately
4	By	12	as
5	through/ over	13	ago
6	if / though	14	for
7	well / badly	15	earth
8	over		

Gapped sentences   Paper 3 Part 3

C

1   enlisted   2   fell   3   struck   4   abandoned

5   raised   6   preserve

Vocabulary Test Unit 3 TB page 128

4 Small world

▶ *See unit summary on page 4.*

Exam training in this unit

Reading	Multiple-choice questions on 4 texts: identifying style and purpose of texts
Use of English	Key word transformations: inserting extra words, idiomatic expressions, verb changes
	Comprehension and summary: using linking phrases
Listening	Matching statements to speakers
Speaking	Themed discussion: suggesting alternatives
Writing	An article: descriptive language

It's a small world is used as an expression of surprise when meeting someone you know in an unlikely or unexpected place. Ask students how it can also be applied to the idea of travel in today's world. It refers to the fact that, as tourism opens up more and more destinations, the world seems smaller. The overall theme of the unit is travel and tourism.

Reading SB pages 52–54

Wish you were here

Introduce the activity by asking students where they would come across the phrase *wish you were here* (it is a set phrase used on holiday postcards sent to friends and family).

1 Look at the example with the class first, stressing the sound link between *v'nice* and *Venice*.

Small groups work out the word plays in the slogans. Ask them to note down the real phrases.

Check answers as a class.

> **Key**
>
> Genoa = Do you know a (better way?)
> Pisa = piece of (cake)
> Cannes = can (do)
> Rome = roam (around Europe)
> Paris = Pa is (happy, so is Ma)

2 Ask students which of the slogans above they found most effective.

Discuss the question as a class. Brainstorm ideas as to why the slogans may be effective and possible reasons why they may be ineffective.

Round off the activity by asking students what holiday advertising is used in their countries.

> ⊞ **Extra activity**
> Ask students to write a holiday advertising slogan for their own country in English.

Multiple-choice questions Paper 1 Part 2

Background notes
A pith helmet is a lightweight hat worn in tropical countries for protection against the sun.
Paul Theroux is a travel writer famous for his books such as *The Old Patagonia Express.*
A sanatorium is a kind of hospital where people go to recover from long-term illnesses.
Force majeure is a legal term, originally from French, used in contracts to refer to unexpected circumstances such as war.
A *gîte* is a French word for a small cottage in the country which is rented out for holidays.

A These two activities aim to develop students' awareness of the purpose and tone of the texts as well as the writer's style and attitude. An understanding of these elements is important for students at this level.

Ask students to read through all four texts quickly to get an idea of where they are taken from.

Check answers as a class. Discuss the reasons given for their choices.

Then ask students to read the texts again and underline the words which the writers use to create the mood.

> **Key**
>
> 1 Text 1 a newspaper article   The writer is giving their opinions on the subject of travel and compares the past with the present.
> Text 2 an autobiography   It is written in the first person and describes the writer's personal experience of visiting a place.
> Text 3 an insurance document   The text mentions offering alternative holidays or a refund of money if there is a cancellation. It also mentions promises on the part of the company and reads like a contract.

Text 4 a holiday brochure   It gives details of the facilities available and presents them in an attractice way to the reader, as in a brochure. e.g. 'Many of our properties are superb', 'be pleasantly surprised'.

2   **Text 1** disparaging   The writer uses phrases such as 'look down on mere tourists', 'get a perverse joy from spending all day squatting over a sordid cesspit'.
Text 2 anecdotal   The writer gives a personal account with phrases such as 'I had spent the summer'.
Text 3 legalistic   The text contains a number of words and phrases found in legal documents. e.g. 'force majeure', 'hereinafter', 'materially alter', 'full refund of monies', 'undertake to'.
Text 4 explanatory   The text tells the reader what to expect with phrases such as 'Do not expect luxury', 'Remember, however, that these are holiday homes'.

B   Remind students to underline the part of the text that helped them make their choice.

Check answers as a class and discuss students' justifications for their choices.

Key
1 C   2 D   3 D   4 B   5 B   6 C   7 A   8 C

Vocabulary

C   Remind students to look at how the words are used in the texts if they are not sure which one to use to complete the sentences.

Encourage them to get a feeling for how the word is used rather than concentrating on its exact meaning.

Check answers as a class.

Key

1	musty	5	unattractive
2	perverse	6	infested
3	obsessed	7	weary
4	sordid	8	arid

✚ Extra activity
Ask students to find positive adjectives, adverbs or phrases in texts 2 and 4.

Then ask them to work in pairs and use as many of them as they can to describe an ideal holiday location.

Allow students 5 minutes for this, then ask them to read out their descriptions to the class.

Key
Text 2 'captivated instantly', 'looked tidy and beckoning', 'impossible green lushness'
Text 4 'pleasantly surprised', 'are superb', 'justly proud', 'sophisticated'

Expressions with *run, look* and *catch*

D

1   Ask students to look at how the verbs are used in the texts before they explain the meanings. *Run off with* and *look down on* are in text 1, *catch you unawares* is in text 4.

Check answers as a class.

Key

run off with means to steal something or take it away
look down on means to think you are better or superior to someone
catch you unawares means to be surprised or unprepared for something

2   Allow students a few minutes to match the verbs to the phrases.

Check answers as a class.

Key

run	a business, out of, short of, for it
look	on the bright side, down your nose at, like a drowned rat, a gift horse in the mouth
catch	somebody red-handed, someone's eye

3   Ask students to compare their answers in pairs.

Check answers as a class.

Key

a catch someone's eye
b run for it
c look on the bright side
d look a gift horse in the mouth (illustrated)
e run out of something
f catch someone red-handed
g look down your nose at
h run short of
i run a business
j look like a drowned rat

4 Remind students that they may be able use more than one expression in the same sentence.

Ask them to read out their sentences for comparison as a class.

Photocopiable activity 4.1   TB page 152

Extra vocabulary

See page 176 for ideas on how to exploit this vocabulary.

to be caught up in (verb) to be involved in something involuntarily
eternal (adjective) existing or continuing for ever
sultry (adjective) weather that is hot and humid
accumulated (adjective) increased in amount over a period of time
dispel (verb) to make something go away
commonplace (adjective) ordinary, not unusual
scapegoat (noun) someone blamed for something bad although it may not be their fault
liability (noun) the state of being legally responsible for something
outstanding (adjective) not yet paid or done
rustic (adjective) typical of the countryside, simple

Language in use SB pages 55–57

Into the unknown

1 Introduce the activity by asking students whether they would like to visit either of the two places in the pictures. Ask them to give reasons why or why not.

Divide the class into small groups and ask them to note down their ideas.

Ask each group to present their ideas and discuss them as a class.

Round off the activity by asking students if they can think of any more unusual places to visit or take a holiday.

2 🎧 This listening activity provides background for the key word transformation exercise that follows and the grammar exercises with *wish*.

Ask students to read through the questions before you play the recording. Play the recording once.
Check answers as a class.

Key

1 150 days
2 He would have had to walk back to the base on his own.
3 young, average age 25, recently at university, inexperienced

3 Check students know the meaning of all the adjectives before they listen.

Remind them that they can choose several adjectives according to the impression they get of Uncle August.

Check answers as a class.

Key

resigned	This is suggested at the beginning by mentioning his 150th day alone.
resourceful	He was smoking tea-leaves.
optimistic	He never said he wished he hadn't gone.
courageous	He never regarded it as an ordeal.
amateurish	Possible, but it is mentioned that this was deceptive.

Tapescript

NARRATOR On 5 May 1931, my uncle, August Courtauld, was spending his *150th day* alone on the ice cap. Since the last week of March, his tented igloo had been covered by snow; his food was now running out, there was no light, and he was smoking tea-leaves in his pipe. On that day, his paraffin primus stove gave its last gasp.
Suddenly there was an appalling noise like a bus going by, followed by a confused yelling. The voice of his expedition leader came down the ventilator pipe, and his five-month incarceration through an Arctic winter was over. If he hadn't been rescued, *he would almost certainly have had to walk back to his base alone*, with no equipment whatsoever – that is if he'd been able to dig himself out! But August never regarded it as an ordeal; never said he wished he hadn't gone. He had, after all, volunteered to stay alone at the ice cap station, and take recordings of the weather there, something which had never been done before.
Uncle August was a member of an expedition which had gone to Greenland in the summer of 1930 to map the coast and mountain ranges. It was also important in considering the setting up of a regular air route over Greenland to North America, to see what the weather was like on the ice cap, particularly in winter.
There was, however, more to the expedition than that. Its members had an *average age of 25, many of them had not long ago been at university*, and there was *a clubbable*

spirit of youthful adventure among them. But the *air of gentlemanly amateurishness* could be deceptive: most significantly, and in contrast to Scott's expedition to the South Pole, they learnt how to use dogs for sledging.

Structure

Wishes and regrets

A

> **Key**
>
> In general *if only* expresses a strong regret or wish and can be more emphatic, especially in exclamations e.g. *If only you wouldn't do that!* Often the two are interchangable.

B

> **Key**
>
> 1 c 2 b 3 a

C Before students begin the exercise, remind them to consider whether the regret or wish refers to a past situation, a present situation or a change in the situation as discussed in B above.

Check answers as a class.

> **Key**
>
> 1 could
> 2 had
> 3 hadn't left
> 4 wouldn't smoke
> 5 would tell
> 6 hadn't told

D Remind students that *if only* tends to be stronger than *wish*, so they should choose which is a more suitable interpretation of the prompt sentence.

Check answers as a class.

> **Key**
>
> 1 I wish I wasn't a chain smoker.
> 2 I wish you were teaching our class next year.
> 3 If only it would rain soon, everything's so dry.
> 4 I wish Pat wouldn't always phone me at work when I'm busy.
> 5 I wish / if only our neighbours had let us know they were moving house.
> 6 Dave and Sue wish they'd bought a new car.
> 7 I wish David wouldn't eat with his mouth open.
> 8 If only I had taken up his offer of a job.

Note: A common error made by students is the confusion between a wish or regret about a present situation and a wish for a change in the situation. Point out that the use of *wish / if only* with *would / wouldn't* refers to something or someone else not yourself, so the pronoun *I* can't be used with *would / wouldn't* to express a regret or wish, e.g. *I wish I wouldn't have to do so much homework* is incorrect, but *I wish I didn't have to do so much homework* is correct.

✚ Extra activity

Tell students they can have three wishes.

Wish 1 must be an ability you would like to have (e.g. *I wish I could play the piano well.*)

Wish 2 must be a current situation you would like to change. It must be something outside your control. (e.g. *I wish I didn't have to do so much homework.*)

Wish 3 must be something from your past you would like to change. (e.g. *I wish I hadn't bought these green trousers!*)

Ask them to write down their three wishes on a piece of paper; they shouldn't be too personal as the rest of the class will read them.

Collect in the pieces of paper and distribute them round the class, making sure students don't get their own piece of paper.

Each student reads out the three wishes and the rest of the class guess who wrote it.

Conditionals

E

> **Key**
>
> 1 e 2 d 3 a 4 b 5 c

F

> **Key**
>
> 1 c 2 b 3 a 4 d

G

This exercise focuses on variations to the basic conditional forms.

Discuss answers to each of the questions in turn as a class.

Key

- a sentences 1, 2 and 3
- b sentences 4, 5, 6 and 7
- c If it had not been for, But for, Were it not for
- d sentences 1, 4, 7, 8 and 9. This can sound more formal.
- e sentence 2 *Should you* see Fred, give him my regards.
  sentence 3 *Were I* to go missing, what would you do?
  sentence 5 *Had it not been* for the traffic, I wouldn't have been late.
- f provided
- g unless

H   Remind students that they will need to consider all the different types of conditional sentence they have looked at in exercises E, F and G when rewriting the sentences. Reference is made to this in the key.

Check answers as a class.

Key

1 If it hadn't been for the bad weather, we could have gone camping.
   See G 5.
2 Had you told me about the party on Saturday night, I could have gone.
   See G 4.
3 If only we had gone by air, we could have saved time.
4 Should you need any help, you can always call me.
   See G 1.
5 Provided (that) your interview is successful, you'll get the job.
   Unless your interview is successful, you won't get the job.
   See G 8 and 9.
6 If he was / were a policeman, I would have seen him wearing a uniform.
   See G 2.

Round off by asking students if they can rewrite sentence 1 in two other ways (Had it not been for the bad weather … , But for the bad weather …).

Photocopiable activity 4.2   TB page 152

Key word transformations   Paper 3 Part 4

I   Go through the example with the class and draw students' attention to the *Exam tip*.

Remind students to think about the meaning and structure of the whole sentence rather than just what goes in the gap.

Check that students have understood what to do in the exercise by asking one or two students to explain the instructions to you.

Check answers as a class by asking students to read out the whole sentence.

Key

1 almost run out of
2 was more to the expedition than
3 would have been subjected
4 couldn't wait to be with
5 wedding took place
6 how he had been affected by
7 gave its last gasp
8 never regarded his incarceration as

Extra vocabulary

See page 176 for ideas on how to exploit this vocabulary.

intrepid (adjective) adventurous, not afraid of danger
appalling (adjective) shocking, extremely bad
incarceration (noun) imprisonment
dejected (adjective) unhappy and disappointed
resourceful (adjective) good at finding solutions to problems
perishable (adjective) likely to decay or go bad quickly
fraught with (adjective) a situation filled with something undesirable

Comprehension and summary

SB pages 58–59

A mixed blessing?

Students work in small groups to make a list of the arguments for and against tourism based on the newspaper headlines and adding their own ideas.

They compare lists as a class.

Ask students how the headlines connect with the title *a mixed blessing?* (a *mixed blessing* is something that can have both positive and negative effects).

Comprehension Paper 3 Part 5

Background notes Snowdonia is a national park in
North Wales famous for its picturesque mountain
landscape and the highest mountain in Wales, Mount
Snowdon.

A Ask students to read both texts first and find out
what each is about (the first text discusses both the
positive and negative aspects of tourism and mentions
one particular place, the second text gives advice about
having a positive impact as a tourist).

Remind students to keep their answers to the questions
as brief as possible.

Check answers as a class.

Key

1 to give an impression of the large number of
   connected footpaths
2 the negative effects of tourism
3 aware, sensitive
4 the potentially damaging impact of tourists in
   particular areas

B

Key

American	British
traveler	traveller
behavior	behaviour
trash	rubbish
minimize	minimise
maximize	maximise

Summary writing Paper 3 Part 5

Linking

C

Key

the positive effects that tourism can have on an area

D Remind students that it is important for them to get
into the habit of underlining the relevant parts of the
texts as the first step in the summary writing process.

Ask them to compare what they have underlined in
pairs and then check their work using the two sample
summaries in E.

Key

Text 1
'30 per cent of jobs can be directly attributed to tourism'
(line 3)
'Many village shops would have to close if they were not
supported by income from tourists and the money spent
on local souvenirs can prevent local industries from
going out of business.' (line 10)
'In some locations tourist operators have set up their
own trusts and put money back into the community by
making donations to local conservation projects.'
(line 33)

Text 2
'Local people will welcome you not only as a means of
increasing their income but also as an added interest in
their daily lives.' (line 12)
'Tourism can bring financial rewards and employment'
(line 16)
'Support local businesses during your ecotravels to
maximise the benefits of tourism on the local
community and, with your tourist dollars, help in the
conservation of the area.' (line 27)

E Draw students' attention to the *Exam tip*.
Then ask them to put the linking phrases into the gaps.

Check answers as a class.

Key

1	both	5	while
2	Furthermore	6	Moreover
3	Besides	7	as well as
4	also		

F

Key

1 The first summary presents the two economic
   benefits first, followed by conservation and finally
   the positive effect on local people's lives.
   The second summary begins with the positive
   effect on the local community and links it with
   conservation. The two economic benefits are
   mentioned last.
2 Yes. The information has been organised into three
   areas: economic benefits, investment in
   conservation, positive effect on local people.
3 Furthermore, Besides, Moreover

G Ask students to describe to you the procedures they have followed for this and previous summaries. See G on SB page 31.

> **Sample summary**
> Tourists can cause traffic congestion in narrow roads and make it difficult for local people to do their work. What is more, tourists can also cause harm to the environment not only by wearing down footpaths but by wandering from trails and disturbing the wildlife. Finally, many tourists leave their rubbish behind, which makes areas of natural beauty look ugly. (60 words)

Listening SB page 60

Time traveller

1 Students discuss their ideas in small groups and then present their ideas for comparison as a class.

> **Key**
>
> Picture 1 Ancient Egypt
> Picture 2 The European discovery of the Americas
> Picture 3 The USA in the gangster era
> Picture 4 Ancient Greece and Rome

2 Ask students to discuss the question in their groups.

Invite one student from each group to give a summary of the discussion.

Three-way matching Paper 4 Part 4

A 🎧 Draw students' attention to the *Exam tip*. Ask them to read the six statements before they listen.

Play the recording twice.

Check answers as a class.

> **Key**
>
> 1 B 2 D 3 B 4 D 5 M 6 M

Tapescript

AMERICAN Hi! Did you both have a good day?
DIANE It was great. Really interesting! We travelled through history – I suppose you could say that we went in a *rather different kind of time machine*.

MIKE *That's a good way of putting it*, actually. Basically, we went into the centre of Oxford and visited a permanent exhibition called the Oxford Story – and it sort of brings to life the history of the city.
DIANE That's right. In fact in the guide book I bought the other day, it says that the exhibition actually spans over 800 years. But the really unusual thing about it is that you can experience the sights, the sounds, and even the smells of the past. Mind you, *we could have done without some of the more gruesome smells*!
MIKE Oh, come on! They certainly had the desired effect – made the whole thing seem more realistic.
DIANE But, if you're thinking of going yourself, well, it's not a place you can linger for any length of time. You can probably spend about just over an hour or so – depending on how long you want to spend in the gift shop, of course. You see, you travel at a fairly slow speed sitting at a sort of electrically powered scholar's desk – and it goes through three different levels.
MIKE *Wish I'd had one of those when I was at school!*
DIANE Come to think of it, *it would certainly have livened up some of the lessons I used to have.* Anyway, you travel into this world of academics, eccentrics …
MIKE … and scientists and great writers from the university's history. It's certainly very informative and educational, if that's the kind of thing you're looking for as a tourist, that is! But it also offers a glimpse of what student life must have been like in those days. It really is a fascinating insight into how education's changed since then.
DIANE Or perhaps just the opposite, as the case may be! *I must say that I was astonished to see that so many things were not as different as I'd imagined.*
MIKE And we both enjoyed the short audio-visual presentation of what student life is like today. In fact, I'd certainly recommend the visit. *But perhaps not if you're the physical type who likes to travel under his own steam!* Still, it's one of the city's main tourist attractions – and it certainly gives you a feel for the days gone by. In any case, as the whole trip only lasts for about an hour, you can always go punting on the river afterwards.
DIANE Yes, we did that, too. Mike insisted that if we were going to spend some time in Oxford, then we would never forgive ourselves if we didn't go punting. But to tell the truth, it's not an experience I'd like to repeat. I can't say it was the most relaxing thing I've ever done.
MIKE Still, you have to admit, it was great fun, especially when we lost the pole! But honestly, it wasn't my fault. *It looks so easy when you see someone else do it – but try it yourself and it's a completely different story, I can tell you!* Anyway, fortunately some people in another punt stopped to help us out, otherwise we'd be there now.
AMERICAN Well, thanks for the tips, but I guess I'll give the punting a miss!

Your views

B   Use the three questions as the basis for a class discussion. Allow students a short time to consider their responses to the questions.

Invite one student to begin the discussion by presenting their views. Elicit responses from other students and open up the discussion to the whole class.

If you have a large class, divide them into groups for the discussion.

Extra vocabulary

See page 176 for ideas on how to exploit this vocabulary.

brawl (noun) a noisy and violent fight
dreaded (adjective) causing fear
unsightly (adjective) not pleasant to look at
detrimental (adjective) harmful to something
designated (adjective) given a particular role or job

Speaking   SB page 61

Themed discussion   Paper 5 Part 2

Speculating

A   Encourage students to think of as many effects of the development of railways and air travel as possible, and to try to agree on which has had the greatest effect.

B   Ask the groups to report back to the class.

Evaluating

C   Students should evaluate each picture in turn, concentrating on how well they think the picture relates to the topic of the magazine article. Useful phrases for this task can be found on TB pages 21 and 22.

> ### ➕ Extra activity
> To give students further practice in evaluating pictures, bring into class a number of pictures from magazines connected with travel that you have selected yourself.
>
> Divide the class into small groups and give them 2 or 3 pictures each.
>
> Ask each group to discuss the suitability of their pictures for the article and to select four images for the article in total, choosing from those in the Student's Book and the ones you brought in.

Suggesting alternatives

D   Draw students' attention to the *Exam tip* and remind them that they don't have to confine themselves to selecting means of transport – other images of travel can be used, e.g. people waiting at a railway station, an airport departure lounge, a petrol station in the middle of nowhere.

Writing   SB pages 62–63

An article   Paper 2 Part 2

Understanding the task

A

> **Key**
> 1 People who are interested in travel and read travel magazines.
> 2 An unusual or adventurous journey, perhaps in a train or car, with descriptions or events that make it memorable.
> 3 An ordinary or conventional journey where nothing in particular happened.
> 4 That it was spoiled by a travelling companion.
> 5 Possible answer: introduction to the location of the journey and the reason why you made it; what made it memorable and how it was spoiled by your travelling companion.

Analysing the sample

B

> **Key**
> 1 Only the final paragraph mentions how the journey was spoiled by a travelling companion. It doesn't connect with the rest of the description and seems to have been added on as an afterthought.
> 2 By describing how irritating Emma's voice was and making it part of the description of the journey itself.
> 3 It uses a range of descriptive language to make the journey more vivid and interesting to the reader and includes the writer's feelings and reactions. It is also well-organised with a clear beginning and end.
> 4 'The train started on the long twelve-hour haul to', 'City buildings drifted past the window', 'The train soon reached' , 'The train began to move slowly uphill', 'The train clanked on up to', 'the train finally came to a halt'

✚ Extra activity

Ask students to go back to the sample and to add sentences and phrases to describe how irritating Emma's voice was.

Possible answers

At the end of paragraph 2, replace the final sentence with: No sooner had we found an empty seat and settled in than Emma began chatting.

In paragraph 4: The train clanked on up to an empty plateau … but my enjoyment of the view was spoiled by Emma's persistent questions.

In paragraph 6: I hired one of the horse-drawn carriages at the station, and breathed in the sweet smell of fresh rain. At last I was free of Emma's voice as she had gone to …

Writing skills

Descriptive language

C   Ask students to consider what they have discussed about the sample article as they read through the passage.

Check answers as a class.

> ### Key
>
> The verb *went* is repeated too many times which makes the description less vivid and interesting to read.

D   Ask students to rewrite the passage in pairs.

Ask them to compare their work with another pair. Use the key to check their work.

> ### Key
>
> We *drove* down the rough track towards the jungle until we reached the river that *cut* across the road. We parked in the shade of some rubber trees and got out. We *waded* across the river, which fortunately was not too deep, and then, as we were in no hurry, *walked* through the rice fields on the other side towards the forest. The path that *led* through the trees was entirely overgrown, so we *hacked our way* through it with considerable difficulty. It was nearly mid-afternoon when we finally *emerged* from the thick undergrowth and *reached* the bottom of the mountain. Although we were all by now feeling exhausted, we *clambered* up the steep slope and *arrived* at the rendezvous point just as the sun was going down.

Writing your article

E   Go through each of the stages in turn and discuss points and brainstorm ideas as a class.

Extra vocabulary

See page 176 for ideas on how to exploit this vocabulary.

haul (noun) a distance to be covered
desolate (adjective) empty and without people
plateau (noun) an area of flat land that is high up
savour (verb) to enjoy the full taste of something
undergrowth (noun) a mass of bushes and plants under trees in forests

Unit 4 Overview key

SB pages 64–65

> ### Lexical cloze Paper 1 Part 1
>
> **A**
>
> | 1 C | 2 D | 3 B | 4 A | 5 B | 6 D |
> |-----|-----|-----|------|------|------|
> | 7 B | 8 D | 9 C | 10 D | 11 D | 12 B |
>
> ### Word formation Paper 3 Part 2
>
> **B**
>
> | 1 monumental | 6 disillusioned |
> |--------------|-----------------|
> | 2 enabling | 7 non-payment |
> | 3 maximise | 8 amateurish |
> | 4 unforeseen | 9 hoteliers |
> | 5 uninspiring | 10 disastrous |
>
> ### Key word transformations Paper 3 Part 4
>
> **C**
>
> 1 is beyond our control
> 2 were none the worse
> 3 tendancy to look down on
> 4 someone/somebody had run off with
> 5 looked on the bright side
> 6 was caught red-handed
> 7 never look a gift horse in
> 8 makes it difficult for local traders to go

Vocabulary Test Unit 4 TB page 129

Progress Test Units 1–4 TB pages 138–139

5 Back to nature

▶ See unit summary on page 4.

Exam training in this unit

Reading	Lexical cloze: collocation
Use of English	Cloze
	Comprehension and summary: editing
Listening	Sentence completion: identifying exact words
Speaking	Themed discussion: evaluating and suggesting images
Writing	An essay: organisation and cohesion

Ask students what they understand by the phrase *back to nature*. The phrase means leading a more natural life without the aid of modern technology. The overall theme of the unit is the environment.

Reading   SB pages 66–68

In safe hands?

Introduce the activity by asking students what is implied by the phrase *in safe hands*. It means that somebody has been taken care of well.

1

Key

Picture 1   endangered, nature reserves, poaching
endangered refers to species which are under threat of extinction.
nature reserves are places where the natural environment is placed under special protection by law.
poaching is the illegal killing of animals, most of which are protected.

Picture 2   biodiversity, deforestation, medicine
biodiversity refers to the range and variety of different species or types. Some species are disappearing thus reducing the range and variety.
deforestation refers to the cutting down of large areas of forests which causes a reduction in the amount of oxygen produced and other problems such as flooding.
medicines are often based on rare plants that are found to have health-giving properties.

Picture 3   disposable, landfill sites, recyclable
disposable is often used to describe everyday objects which can be thrown away once they have been used.
landfill sites are areas where ordinary domestic rubbish is deposited.
recyclable refers to types of waste that can be re-used e.g paper

2   In pairs or groups, students discuss issues related to the pictures before comparing their ideas as a class.

Lexical cloze   Paper 1 Part 1

A   The questions aim to encourage students to read the whole text to get a general idea of the content before they attempt the Lexical cloze.

Students discuss their ideas in pairs before comparing them as a class.

Key and possible answers

Text 1
1   The purpose is to provide general information about terrapins.
2   What you need to know about terrapins

Text 2
1   The purpose is to point out the negative effects of light pollution and give the writer's opinion on the issue.
2   Light pollution – a modern menace

Text 3
1   The purpose is to give a warning about the potential dangers of global warming.
2   The threat of global warming

B   Remind students that the correct answer may depend on collocation, set phrases or complementation, and they should read around the gap before making their choice.

Key

Text 1					
1 A	2 B	3 A	4 D	5 C	6 A

Text 2					
7 A	8 D	9 A	10 A	11 C	12 D

Text 3					
13 B	14 A	15 C	16 B	17 B	18 C

Vocabulary

Collocation

C

> **Key**
>
> reach the size   verb + noun
> stage a protest   verb + noun
> raise the alarm   verb + noun
> controlled environment   adjective + noun
> vast amounts   adjective + noun
> grave danger   adjective + noun

D

> **Key**
>
> 1 hold   4 tremendous
> 2 call   5 harsh
> 3 drastic   6 run

E In pairs, students match the adverbs and the adjective groups.

Check answers as a class.

> **Key**
>
> 1 bitterly   5 deeply
> 2 greatly   6 highly
> 3 seriously   7 most
> 4 perfectly   8 fully

F Remind students to use each of the eight adverbs once only to complete the sentences.

Check answers as a class.

> **Key**
>
> 1 seriously wounded   5 most kind / generous
> 2 perfectly simple   6 fully conscious
> 3 greatly mistaken   7 deeply moved
> 4 bitterly cold   8 highly qualified

➕ Extra activity

Students work in pairs and choose four more adverb + adjective combinations from the list and make sentences of their own.

Ask each pair to read out their sentences to the class.

Expressions with *light* and *dark*

G Ask students to make guesses if they are not sure of the meaning of some expressions.

Check answers as a class.

> **Key**
>
> 1 g   2 f   3 d   4 c   5 e   6 i   7 a
> 8 h   9 b

H Check answers as a class.

> **Key**
>
> 1 a dark horse
> 2 came to light
> 3 makes light of
> 4 went out like a light
> 5 a leap in the dark (illustrated)
> 6 kept them in the dark
> 7 the light at the end of the tunnel
> 8 to see the light
> 9 the bright lights

I In their pairs, students invent their sentences, then read their ideas out to the class for comparison.

Photocopiable activity 5   TB page 153

Extra vocabulary

See page 176 for ideas on how to exploit this vocabulary.

indignant (adjective) showing anger because of unfair treatment
mellow (adjective) soft, rich and pleasant
nook and cranny small inaccessible places
glaring (adjective) extremely bright or obvious
penetrate (verb) to get into or through something
accelerate (verb) to gather speed, to go faster
swell (verb) to grow in size or become rounder
plight (noun) a difficult or sad situation
sombre (adjective) sad and serious in mood

Language in use SB pages 69–70

Tomorrow's world

Students work in small groups to discuss questions 1–3.

Compare answers as a class.

❏ Alternative activity

This activity aims to encourage students to read through the whole text to get a general idea of what it is about before they attempt to fill in the gaps.

Students speculate about the purpose of the building. Put their ideas on the board.

Direct students to read the text quickly and find out if their answers were close to the real purpose and location of the building. The picture shows the experimental building *Biosphere 2* that the text describes.

Cloze   Paper 3 Part 1

Background notes
hectares are units of measurement of land.
ecosystems are the complete systems of relationships between plants, animals and humans living in the same environment.

A   Remind students that the word which goes into the space may depend on the context. Ask them to check that the word they have chosen fits in with the meaning of the whole sentence and possibly the other sentences around it.

Check answers as a class.

Key			
1	in	9	until / unless
2	inside	10	not
3	due	11	other
4	within / in	12	forward
5	far	13	such
6	fact	14	Unlike
7	by	15	nowhere
8	much		

Structure

Future time

B   This exercise is a quick revision of the basic future forms.

Check answers as a class.

Key			
1	opens	4	am playing
2	will continue	5	am going
3	is going to rain	6	'll take

C   This exercise focuses attention on the grammatical explanations for the answers in B.

Check the answers as a class.

Key			
1	sentence 1	3b	sentence 3
2	sentence 4	4a	sentence 2
3a	sentence 5	4b	sentence 6

D   This exercise focuses on both the form, meaning and use of more complex ways of referring to future time.

Ask students to read through the five sentences and match one of the forms from the list to each sentence first.

Discuss each sentence in turn as a class, analysing the use of each form.

Key

1   future continuous
    This is used to refer to an action in progress at a particular point in the future, or to imply that something is part of the normal course of events.
2   past continuous
    This is used to refer to a plan or intention that was made previously but has changed due to the circumstances.
3   *be* + infinitive
    This is used as a formal declaration to refer to an event that is scheduled to happen.
4   future perfect
    This is used to refer to a state or an action before or leading up to a given time in the future.
5   future perfect continuous
    This is used to refer to a state or an action before or leading up to a given time in the future, and implies either repetition or incompleteness.

E   Ask students to underline the different future forms used in the paragraph and match them to a function from C and D. *Future perfect, future continuous* and *will* as an auxiliary are all used.

Ask students whether the views expressed in the paragraph are optimistic or pessimistic.

F   Divide the class into small groups. Ask them to write a similar paragraph using the same future forms.

Provide them with the following prompts if necessary: environmental problems, pollution, crime and violence, travel to other planets, global warming, virtual reality and the internet, artificial intelligence, new types of buildings, deforestation.

Each group reads out their paragraph for comparison as a class.

Tenses in future time clauses

G Ask students to read through the three examples.

Discuss questions 1 and 2 as a class.

> **Key**
> 1 The present simple is used in a future time clause to refer to the time of an event in the future.
> 2 The present perfect is used in a future time clause to emphasise that the event has been completed before the event in the main cause takes place.
> 3 The present continuous is used in a future time clause to emphasise that the event is an ongoing or incomplete situation.

H Remind students to consider the meaning of the whole sentence before they decide on the appropriate verb form.

Check answers as a class.

> **Key**
> 1 am   4 have read
> 2 is leaving   5 want
> 3 have been swimming 6 are waiting

Future phrases

I Discuss the questions as a class.

> **Key**
> 1 is about to, is due to, is expected to
> 2 is about to

J

> **Key**
> will happen – certain to, bound to, sure to, set to
> may happen – likely to
> probably won't happen – unlikely to

K In pairs, students write their paragraphs. Remind them to use as many phrases from parts I and J as they can.

Students read out their paragraphs for comparison as a class.

> ❏ **Alternative activity**
> Ask students to make predictions about their own lives using two of the phrases.

Comprehension and summary
SB pages 72–73

Born to be wild
Students works in groups to discuss questions 1–4.

Discuss answers as a class.

> **Key**
> 1
> Picture 1 a fox, which can be found both in urban and rural environments in most regions of the world
> Picture 2 a giant panda, which originates in mountainous forests in Asia but is also found in many zoos
> Picture 3 a pair of male caribou, a species of deer found in the arctic regions of North America
> Picture 4 a herd of wildebeest migrating across the plains of Africa

Comprehension Paper 3 Part 5

A Discuss answers to the questions as a class, focusing on relevant parts of the texts.

> **Key**
>
> 1 Both authors think that zoos play an important role in conservation and education. The second text also mentions relaxation as a benefit of zoos.
>
> Text 1
> 'Modern zoos are not grim prisons.' (line 16)
> '[Zoos] are as essential to our future as Victorian free education.' (line 29)
>
> Text 2
> 'Zoos, at their best, provide an example of how to [conserve species] right on our doorsteps.' (line 6)
> '…they also have the opportunity to educate us.' (line 21)

2 The author of the first text dismisses opponents by implying that they have a false, unthinking impression of what life is like in the wild.
'A moment's reflection shows that this attitude is a ludicrous perversion.' (line 13)
The author of the second text refers to zoos facing 'an onslaught of criticism from some quarters' (line 9) but emphasises the benefits of zoos rather than attacking the criticism.

3 The author of the first text uses forceful language.
'sheer anthropological romanticism and we all know it' (line 3)
' …this attitude is a ludicrous perversion.' (line 13)
The author of the second text writes in a more moderate tone, emphasising the need to protect zoos. The style is more like a warning.
'If we want the human race to survive too,…' (line 4)
' …zoos are an endangered species.' (line 8)
' …they would do well to emphasise their other benefits.' (line 14)

B Remind students that they should keep their answers to the questions as brief as possible. A short phrase or sometimes even one word is enough.

Check answers as a class.

Key

Text 1
1 to suggest that the view that 'man is born free' is a fantasy
2 that they are based on misinformation and not the reality of the wild
3 grim

Text 2
1 a fragile web with species dependent on each other
2 to show how close and accessible zoos are
3 the difficulties that zoos face: criticism, costly conservation programmes, lower visitor numbers

Summary writing Paper 3 Part 5

C This and the next exercise provide a guided approach to selecting relevant information for the summary.

Students compare their answers in pairs.

Check answers as a class.

Key

a statements 2, 5, 7, and 8
b statements 1 and 3
c statements 4 and 6

D Ask students to underline the key words in the exam question first (*reasons given … for why zoos should be maintained*).

Remind them that they could approach the task by eliminating the irrelevant statements to leave the relevant ones.

Check answers as a class.

Key

Statements 3, 4, 6, 7 and 8

Editing

E This exercise aims to focus students' attention on the need for their summaries to be accurately as well as fluently written.

Students compare their corrections with a partner.

Check corrections as a class.

Key

1 provide – providing
   acted – act
2 in addition to – in addition
   the better scientific understanding – better scientific understanding
3 aspect – role
   jeopardised – endangered
   like – as
4 oportunities – opportunities
   were – where.
5 zoo's – zoos
   There should be a full stop at the end of the paragraph.

F Ask students to describe to you the procedures they have followed for previous summaries.

Draw their attention to the *Exam tip*.

Extra vocabulary

See page 176 for ideas on how to exploit this vocabulary.

insulated (adjective) protected from heat, sound or electricity passing through
stimulated (adjective) situation of being more active or interested
ludicrous (adjective) ridiculous and unreasonable
broadscale (adjective) wide ranging in its effects
restore (verb) to return something to its original state
unravel (verb) the act of woven threads becoming separated
onslaught (noun) a strong or violent attack

Listening SB page 74

Walking on eggshells

Ask students what they imagine when they picture the expression *walking on eggshells*. Elicit suggestions about what it might mean metaphorically. If they find this difficult, ask them if they have ever been in a situation requiring special sensitivity. (*Walking on eggshells* is an expression meaning that you have to behave carefully to avoid upsetting or angering somebody.)

Discuss the questions as a class. Elicit what they know about these animals and encourage them to speculate about what they are not sure of.

Sentence completion Paper 4 Part 2

Background notes

Megafauna in this context refers to large extinct animals. A number of these animals are referred to in the listening text. Reassure students that they don't need to know what these animals are in order to do the task.

A 🎧 Remind students that it is important to read through the sentences before they listen. Ask them if they can find out from any of the sentences why these animals became extinct.

Draw attention to the *Exam tip*, pointing out that the sentences are summaries of what the speaker says but that the missing words are the same as they will hear on the tape.

After playing the recording the first time, allow students some time to think about their answers.

Continue to play the recording a second time.

Ask students to compare answers with a partner and then check answers as a class.

Tapescript

PROFESSOR Thousands of years ago, Australia was inhabited by huge animals such as the marsupial lion, the three-metre long diprotodon, the quinkana, a seven-metre crocodile, and the kangaroo of the Pleistocene which weighed in at 200kg. At some point in Australia's history, 85% of this so-called megafauna became extinct. For more than a century, the timing of this extinction has been controversial. However, new discoveries have been made that may pinpoint this demise more precisely. The controversy has remained mainly because studies of bones become less accurate the further back you go. However, a new discovery has started to shed more light on the question. Preserved eggshells from flightless birds are surprisingly common, and this breakthrough came when specimens from two species of birds were found in the same place. These were the emu and the two-metre tall Genyornis Newtoni. Finding them together suggested these species co-existed and nested close to one another. That is until 50,000 years ago, give or take five thousand years. From that point on, there's an abrupt lack of genyornis egg shells, though the emu ones remain. This has provided the best evidence yet of an extinction date for this giant animal and the other megafauna. There is a suggestion that it may have been due to changes in climate which the emus, for whatever reason, were able to survive, but which the genyornis couldn't. But the most complete information for this period comes from New South Wales, and suggests a landscape characterised by lush vegetation, an environment in which genyornis would have survived. Could humans have killed off the megafauna? It's true that humans are known to have had quite a severe impact on flightless birds in particular. The dodo is the classic example, and, in New Zealand, the eradication of the moa has been well documented. In that case, it was due to people hunting the birds and starting fires. Whether humans could have killed off the megafauna by hunting them for food depends on the date modern humans first arrived in Australia. We do have evidence to suggest that their arrival coincides exactly with the demise of the genyornis. However, there is not a great deal of evidence to suggest that these early peoples hunted the birds to extinction. That isn't to say they had no impact, but it may have been by changing the landscape, largely as a result of fires which destroyed the birds' food, rather than through hunting. It's possible to examine the egg shells of genyornis and the emu, and, by checking the types of carbon in them, we've been able to reconstruct the diet of these animals. One conclusion from this is that genyornis had a more limited range of food. A further clue has been found in a physiological study of the genyornis. The shape of the beak shows that it was highly dependent on plants, and, of course, the fires would have resulted in a dramatic decrease in trees and shrubs, which put an enormous stress on the genyornis. This stress, together with possible climate changes, led to their extinction and also to that of other species of megafauna. Twenty-two out of thirty-eight species of megafauna died out. The majority of those relied on plant matter for food. As that went, predators were also unable to survive. In addition, genyornis bones are found with other megafauna bones, such as the giant kangaroo and the marsupial lion, often crammed into the same sites, so it is likely that these creatures died out at the same time. There must have been extraordinary demands on the ecology of this

environment for the extinctions of the megafauna to have happened at the same time. Fortunately, scientists now have a new insight into the reasons behind this event.

Your views

B Refer students back to the listening task to make comparisons.

Invite one or two students from each group to summarise their discussion for comparison with the class.

Vocabulary

Animal expressions

C Introduce the exercise by asking students to explain any animal expressions they have in their own languages.

Remind them to have a guess if they're not sure about some of the expressions by thinking about the meaning of the whole sentence.

Check answers by asking students to read out the whole sentence. The expression *in the dog-house* is illustrated.

Key			
1	dog	5	frog
2	whale	6	fish
3	crocodile	7	horse
4	wolf	8	snail

Speaking SB page 75

Note: Monitor all the activities and give feedback at the end focusing on any points of fluency or accuracy that you want to deal with.

1 Students complete the questionnaire by ticking the appropriate boxes.

2 In their groups, each student in turn presents their opinions based on the questionnaire.

Compare opinions as a class.

✚ Extra activity

Read out the following text and ask students to note down phrases which are used to link the different aspects. These are in italic in the text.

Read the text twice if necessary.

As far as litter *is concerned*, my area is good *as* the streets are cleaned regularly and the rubbish is collected everyday. *However, this is not true for* the noise levels and air quality which are both poor *due to the fact* that it is in the centre of the city and there is a great deal of traffic at all times. *In terms of* road safety and public transport, mine is a good area to live in *on account of the fact* that the council has invested money on improving the system. *Unfortunately though*, there are not enough green spaces owing to it being a built up area. *On the other hand* the street lighting is good *because of* this.

Themed discussion   Paper 5 Part 2

Speculating
A

> **Possible answers**
>
> 1 pollution, litter, community responsibility, voluntary work
> 2 green spaces, community gardens, education

Evaluating

B   Students remain in their pairs to discuss all four pictures. Encourage them to justify why they think the solutions are either effective or not, in relation to the purpose.

Invite one student from each pair to present their ideas to the class for comparison.

> **Possible answers**
>
> 1 See A above
> 2 See A above
> 3 traffic fumes and congestion, pedestrianisation
> 4 parks, dogs fouling parks, play areas for children

Suggesting alternatives

C   Each pair decides on two more images. Encourage the use of language for making suggestions and agreeing / disagreeing.

Ask each group to present their ideas to the rest of the class for comparison.

Writing   SB pages 76–77

An essay   Paper 2 Part 1

Understanding the task
A

> **Key**
>
> 1 The essay is for a college, school or university tutor and the reason for writing it is that it could be part of your studies or a course requirement.
> 2 The essay should be more academic in tone and contain reasoned arguments in support of a particular point of view.

Analysing the sample
B

> **Key**
>
> 1 The first paragraph gives a general introduction to the subject and briefly presents the writer's point of view by referring to the idea in the original statement. The final paragraph refers back to the extract and gives a brief overview of the writer's argument.
> 2 The writer's ideas are indicated by the use of the following phrases:
> '… is a highly dubious proposition'
> 'It is clear that …'
> 'It is therefore quite wrong …'
> 3 The writer introduces the view that industrialised countries have done a lot to reduce pollution. The writer attributes this view to other people, 'It is often suggested …'
> 4 The writer says that this view is '… an oversimplification.'
> 5 The writer gives the opinion that the west contributes a great deal more to the pollution of the environment in comparison to developing countries.
> 6 The structure is the same as paragraph 2. The writer introduces an opposing view, discredits the view by giving reasons why it is wrong, then finally the writer's own point of view is presented.

Writing skills

Organisation and cohesion

C Students work individually, then compare their lists with a partner.

Check answers as a class.

Key

Introducing an opposing view
It could be argued that …
It is often suggested …
Some people would argue …

Discrediting the opposing view
This is partly true but …
To a certain limited extent, there is some truth in this but …
… is an over-simplification.
This argument has a certain superficial logic to it, but, on closer examination …

Proposing your own view
It is clear that …
It is therefore quite wrong …
The real situation …
Ultimately, …

D Students look at the four ideas in D and consider how they could structure a paragraph according to the suggested outline.

Students write a short paragraph based on each idea. Remind them to add their own views and structure their paragraphs using phrases from C.

Sample paragraph

It is often suggested that taking up cycling instead of using a car is too dangerous. *To a certain limited extent, there is some truth in this but* if everyone were to continue using cars instead of cycling, then the pollution levels would only get higher and life in cities would become unbearable. *It is clear that* we must impose restrictions on the use of cars in the cities and encourage people to cycle by introducing car-free zones. Only this way can we make our cities safer and less polluted for everyone.

Writing your essay

Go through each of the stages in turn, discuss points and brainstorm ideas as a class. Draw students' attention to the *Exam tip*.

Unit 5 Overview Key

SB page 78–79

Lexical cloze Paper 1 Part 1

A

1 A	2 A	3 B	4 A	5 C	6 D
7 C	8 D	9 D	10 C	11 A	12 A

Cloze Paper 3 Part 1

B

1	be	9	to
2	not	10	above
3	contrary	11	if
4	in	12	would
5	since	13	led
6	growth	14	by
7	that	15	most
8	some		

Gapped sentences Paper 3 Part 3

C

1	tasteless	4	put
2	lights	5	due
3	threat	6	raise

Vocabulary Test Unit 5 TB page 130

---

6 Culture vultures

▶ *See unit summary on page 4.*

Exam training in this unit

Reading	Multiple-choice questions on four texts: identifying style, attitude and purpose
Use of English	Word formation: negative affixes Comprehension and summary: connotation
Listening	Multiple-choice questions on one text
Speaking	Extended speaking: fluency, exploring the topic
Writing	A report: complex sentences

Ask students what kind of animal a vulture is and how they normally eat. Ask if they can imagine what a *culture vulture* is. A *culture vulture* is a colloquial phrase meaning a person who is eager to acquire culture. The overall theme of the unit is language and culture.

Reading SB pages 80–82

Speaking the same language?

Explain that the phrase *speak the same language* can also mean to be able to communicate easily with another person since you share a similar outlook on life.

1 🎧 Pause the recording after each passage and ask students to choose the period from the list they think it is from. Encourage them to speculate.

Discuss answers as a class. Ask students if there are any words or phrases they recognised in the passages from early English.

Key

Extract A   1611, taken from the Authorised or King James Bible.
Extract B   8th century, taken from the Old English text *Beowulf* by an unknown author.
Extract C   1726, taken from *Gulliver's Travels* by Jonathan Swift.
Extract D   1999, taken from *Lock, Stock and Barrel*.
Extract E   14th century, taken from *The Prologue* to *The Canterbury Tales* by Geoffrey Chaucer.

---

2   Students discuss the questions in groups.

One student from each group presents a summary of the group's discussion to the class.

Round off the activity by asking students whether they think English will remain as an international language or whether another language will take over in the future.

Multiple-choice questions Paper 1 Part 2

Background
The *Transcaucasus* is a region associated with the Caucasus mountains. It includes parts of modern-day Russia, Georgia, Armenia and Azerbaijan.
The *Tower of Babel* comes from a biblical story in which the people of Babel attempted to build a tower to reach heaven. Displeased with this act, God made them all speak in different languages so as to be unable to communicate with each other and thus fail in their plan to build the tower.
A *neologism* is a new word or expression which has been made up to suit the circumstances. Recent examples are *walkman, internet, cybercafé, website* etc.
Carolingian refers to the period and territories of the dynasty descended from Charlemagne.

A   Remind students that some answers to the multiple-choice questions may seem correct in themselves but may not fit with the stem of the question. Students work individually.

Key

1 D   2 B   3 D   4 B   5 A   6 B   7 C   8 C

❏ Alternative activity
Ask students to underline key words in the question stems before they look at the choices.

Possible answers
1 the origins of
2 as an example of
3 the author's main intention is
4 What does the writer imply about
5 the stories that the minstrels related
6 Scholars … disagree principally on
7 with a sense of exaggeration
8 the writer's implied attitude towards

Check answers as a class. Encourage students to give reasons for their choices.

Identifying style

The following two activities aim to develop students' awareness of aspects of language used in the texts.

Draw students' attention to the *Exam Tip*.

B Deal with each text in turn and discuss answers as a class.

> **Key**
>
> Text 1
> 1 To give an explanation of the origin and development of different languages from a common source.
> 2 A university teacher, an expert in linguistics or a journalist from a specialist periodical.
> 3 People interested in the history of languages or students of linguistics.
> 4 In a book on the history of languages or in a specialist journal or magazine.
> 5 Formal / neutral.
>
> Text 2
> 1 To give a description of the uses and effects of the Babel fish, which is imaginary.
> 2 A novelist or short story writer.
> 3 People who like reading fiction, particularly science fiction.
> 4 In a science fiction novel or short story.
> 5 Neutral / informal.

> Text 3
> 1 To give examples of a recent trend to create new words.
> 2 A journalist or linguist.
> 3 People interested in language and words.
> 4 In a general interest magazine or book about language.
> 5 Neutral / informal.
>
> Text 4
> 1 To give information about aspects of French literature before 1200.
> 2 A university teacher or research student of literature.
> 3 Students or people interested in literature.
> 4 A book on medieval literature or a specialist journal or magazine.
> 5 Formal.

Background notes
Text 1 comes from a specialist journal (Scientific American).
Text 2 comes from *The Hitchhiker's Guide to the Galaxy* by Douglas Adams, a humorous science fiction novel.

Text 3 comes from *The Cambridge Encyclopedia of the English Language* by David Crystal.
Text 4 comes from an encyclopedia text on early medieval literature.

C Ask students what they think the difference is between these two texts and the other two texts. These two texts are less serious or academic in tone than the other two. There is an element of humour or irony in both these two texts.

Discuss answers as a class

> **Key**
>
> Text 2
> 1 'leech–like'
> 'the oddest thing in the Universe'
> 'upshot of all this'
> 'if you stick a Babel fish in your ear'
> 'the poor Babel fish'
> 2 'brainwave energy'
> 'unconscious mental frequencies'
> 'a telepathic matrix'
> 'conscious thought frequencies
> 'nerve signals'
> 'speech patterns'
> 'decode'
> 'brainwave matrix'
> 3 'The practical upshot of all this is'

> Text 3
> 1 ingenious
> 2 *juvenile* would suggest that the writer found it silly and immature

Vocabulary

D This activity focuses on connotation; the positive or negative associations of words with similar meanings.

Students read the sentences and find any words they think might have negative associations. Ask them to think about possible differences in meaning between the other words.

Discuss each sentence in turn as a class.

➕ Extra activity

Read out or write on the board the following local news item: 'A large number of students entered the college buildings today in protest. They are asking for better library facilities.'

Write these words on the board:
unreasonable invaded angry demonstration
mob riot occupied legitimate violent
crowd demands requests

Divide the class into pairs. Ask students to write a brief report of the local news item using six of the words on the board. Student A writes a report supporting the college authorities. Student B writes a report supporting the students.

When they have finished, ask students to read out their reports for comparison as a class.

Possible answers
Students' report
A crowd of angry students occupied college buildings today in a demonstration, making legitimate requests for better library facilities.
College authorities' report
A mob of violent students invaded college buildings today in a riot, making unreasonable demands for better library facilities.

Expressions connected with reading and speaking

E

Ask students which expression they think the cartoon illustrates (mince words).

F   Remind students they may need to change the form of the verb in some expressions.

Check answers as a class by asking students to read out the whole sentence.

➕ Extra activity

Ask students to tell each other about an occasion in their lives or something they have done which can be best described using one or two of the expressions.

Language in use

SB pages 83–85

Word formation Paper 3 Part 2

A

> **Key**
>
> 1 a 2 d 3 b 4 h 5 f 6 j 7 g 8 c
> 9 e 10 i

B Students answer the questions individually.

Discuss answers as a class.

> **Key**
>
> 1 *il-* comes before a word beginning with *l*.
>   *ir-* comes before a word beginning with *r*.
> 2 *im-* comes before words beginning with *m* or *p*.
> **Note** Point out that *un-* can be used before words
> starting with any letter.
> 3 inauspicious, misunderstood, immodest,
>   dishonest, unenthusiastic, disproportionate,
>   unbiased, unconnected / disconnected,
>   non-alcoholic, illiterate, careless, unworthy

C Check answers as a class.

> **Key**
>
> | | | | |
> |---|---|---|---|
> | 1 | relentless | 6 | illiterate |
> | 2 | unconnected | 7 | non-alcoholic |
> | 3 | disproportionate | 8 | incoherent |
> | 4 | ungrateful | 9 | careless |
> | 5 | inauspicious | 10 | implausible |

D Remind students that they will need to consider the
type of word, e.g. noun, verb, adjective, adverb, that fits
in the space as well as the negative prefix.

Check answers as a class.

> **Key**
>
> | | | | |
> |---|---|---|---|
> | 1 | disproved | 6 | dispossesed |
> | 2 | disappear | 7 | injustice |
> | 3 | undeniably | 8 | incapable |
> | 4 | innumerable | 9 | invariably |
> | 5 | unauthorised | 10 | unlike |

⊞ Extra activity

Ask students to work in pairs and find as many
words as they can with the negative prefixes *dis-*,
non- and *mis-*. Encourage them to use dictionaries
to do this but remind them to choose words which
they think will be useful, not obscure words.

Compare answers as a class.

Alternatively, this could be set as a homework task.

Structure

Emphasis

E Encourage students to say the sentences out loud.

Check answers as a class.

> **Key**
>
> 1 <u>I</u> have read most of Dickens's novels.
> 2 I <u>have</u> read most of Dickens's novels.
> 3 I have read <u>most</u> of Dickens's novels.
> 4 I have read most of <u>Dickens's</u> novels.
> 5 I have read most of Dickens's <u>novels</u>.

Cleft sentences with *it*

F Students work in pairs to discuss the differences and then discuss their answers as a class.

> **Key**
>
> 1b It was <u>Dickens</u> who captured the imagination of Victorian England.
> This sentence emphasises that Dickens, rather than any other novelist, captured the imagination of Victorian England.
> 2b It was <u>because his personal life was unhappy</u> that Dickens devoted so much time to writing.
> This sentence emphasises that because his personal life was unhappy, rather than any other reason, Dickens devoted his time to writing.
> 3b It was <u>in 1836</u> that Dickens published Pickwick Papers.
> This sentence emphasises the date of publication.
> In each sentence the emphasised information is preceded by *it + verb to be* and followed by a relative pronoun, *who* or *that*.

Cleft sentences with *what*

G Students analyse the example sentences and then discuss answers as a class.

> **Key**
>
> Sentences 1b and 2b focus on the information in italics more strongly than 1a and 2a.
> 1 *all* means *the only thing that*.
> 2 Great expectations was all I bought.

H This activity focuses on changes in the structure of cleft sentences when an action is emphasised.

Students analyse the example sentences and then discuss answers as a class.

> **Key**
>
> 1 The verb *to do* is used.
> 2 The infinitive form with or without *to*
> 3 ever

I This exercise practises all the cleft sentences. Before students begin the exercise, encourage them to look back at the activities and make a note of the different types of cleft sentences.

Remind them that sentences 1–8 can be rewritten in more than one way.

Check answers as a class, paying attention to accuracy of form and word order in their sentences.

> **Key**
>
> 1 What really irritates me is his arrogance.
> It is his arrogance that really irritates me.
> 2 The doctor said that all I needed was a good holiday.
> The doctor said that what I needed was a good holiday.
> 3 It was the busy main road that put us off buying the house.
> What put us off buying the house was the busy main road.
> 4 She hardly ever sees her husband because all he ever does is work all the time.
> It is because he works all the time that she hardly ever sees her husband.
> 5 He knew he would never be able to afford a Mercedes, so what he did was steal one.
> 6 I've no idea why she's crying, all I did was smile at her.
> 7 What I can't understand is why you didn't come and see me earlier.
> It is why you didn't come and see me earlier that I can't understand.
> 8 She says it was your lies that upset her.
> She says that what upset her was your lies.

Photocopiable activity 6.1   TB page 153

Comprehension and summary

SB pages 86–87

Reading between the lines

Test the students on what the phrase in the title means. It was introduced on SB page 82 of the Student's Book.

Monitor each pair or group by asking questions or making suggestions.

Discuss answers as a class.

❏ Alternative activity

Introduce the activity by eliciting from students what different types of books there are.

Possible answers
fiction / non fiction
coursebooks / textbooks
thrillers / detective stories / crime fiction
romance
social drama
humour
science fiction
war / action stories / adventure stories
biography / autobiography
historical novels
travel books

Comprehension Paper 3 Part 5

A This activity aims to encourage students to read through the texts in order to identify the main points before they attempt the comprehension questions and summary task which follow.

Check answers as a class.

> **Key**
>
> Text 1
> Sentences 2, 3 and 5
> Text 2
> Sentences 1, 4 and 6

B Remind students to keep their answers as brief as possible.

Discuss answers as a class.

> **Key**
>
> Text 1
>   1 reading for entertainment
>   2 it is intellectually challenging
>
> Text 2
>   1 higher level skills or schemata that the reader brings
>   2 the reader cannot understand the text

Connotation

C Remind students that the writer's choice of words reflects his or her attitude and an understanding of this is sometimes tested in the comprehension questions.

Discuss answers to the question as a class.

> **Key**
>
> b is the best answer to the question.
> It is correct because it explains how the use of the word *dubious* shows the writer's opinion, not what it means or what it refers to.
> For this reason, the phrase 'to give the impression…' is useful for answering this type of question.

D This activity focuses students' attention on how the writer's choice of words relates to the point he or she is trying to make.

Remind students to consider the context in which the words or expressions are used.

Discuss answers as a class.

> **Key**
>
> Text 1
>   1 It is used ironically to show that the past was not so wonderful as some people think.
>   2 to show that these research studies contain important information about the problems of reading.
>   3 to give the impression that, in the writer's opinion, much of what has been written about reading problems is exaggerated for effect.
>
> Text 2
>   4 to highlight in more technical language the point that the reader makes a contribution to the text as well as the writer.
>   5 to suggest a gradual process of loss of understanding
>   6 to suggest the process of reading can be compared to a technical process.

Summary writing Paper 3 Part 5

E Students underline the key words in the exam question first 'why students find reading difficult'.

Ask students to underline the parts of the texts which are relevant to the summary task. Then ask them to compare what they have underlined with a partner.

Check answers as a class.

Key

Text 1

'it was shown that the more lead, aluminium or zinc … the lower the reading scores'

'It is because we stop developing reading skills except in the teaching of literature.'

Text 2

'if the reader's schemata are inadequate … , then comprehension breaks down.'

'and some of these differences [in the way readers process text] may account for the fact that there are good and bad readers.'

F

Sample summary

Firstly, a high level of metals in the body can negatively affect reading skills. Furthermore, too much attention is paid to teaching reading through literature rather than for learning in the early stages. Also, the lack of higher level skills or schemata can cause a failure to understand texts properly, and differences in how readers process texts must be taken into account. (62 words)

Listening SB page 88

Getting the picture

Students discuss the questions in groups and note down their answers.

Discuss students' opinions as a class.

Multiple-choice questions Paper 4 Part 3

A 🎧 Students read through the multiple-choice questions before they listen and make guesses about any of the answers based on the notes they made in their discussions in the introduction above.
After playing the recording the first time, allow students some time to think about their answers.

Continue to play the recording a second time.

Check answers as a class and discuss why the other options are not correct by referring to the tapescript.

Key

1 D   2 B   3 C   4 B   5 C

Tapescript

TEACHER Now, let's move along to the next gallery … whose turn is it to tell us about the next painting? Amanda, is it you?

AMANDA Yes, this is the one I've prepared.

TEACHER Good … now I've got one or two questions for Amanda to guide us through this painting, so if you could all pay attention, we can get started … Brian … thank you. Now, as you can see it's a pre-Raphaelite painting, so we're talking 1880, 1890 … and what can you tell us about this – and other pre-Raphaelite paintings for that matter – compared to what came before?

AMANDA Well, there was very definitely a reaction against some of the earlier concerns – for example the pre-Raphaelites didn't believe in the idea that it was important to be true to nature or realistic … This is a good example – it's by the painter Burne Jones, completed in 1884, and it shows a lot about his philosophy of painting …

TEACHER OK. And what was it exactly?

AMANDA Well in his own words, … is it OK if I use my notes?

TEACHER Yes of course.

AMANDA He said that a painting should be '*a beautiful romantic dream of something that never was, never will be, in a land that no-one can define or remember, only desire.*'

TEACHER So in other words *the very opposite of realism* – no practical lessons for modern industrial societies or whatever.

AMANDA Yes, exactly, and this painting is in many ways very typical of Burne Jones – in fact his wife later said it was his most distinctive work, the one that really summed up what he thought.

TEACHER OK, tell us about the story it tells.

AMANDA It's called King Cophetua and the Beggar Maid, and it's based on an old legend from early medieval times about a king who falls in love with a beggar girl, and finds that his love for her is greater than all his wealth and power.

TEACHER Was it a well known story?

AMANDA Yes – *most people knew it well, but only through reading Tennyson's poetry*, in which he wrote about it, rather than from the original story.

TEACHER So it's another example of what we were talking about earlier – the link between the romantic movement in literature and the movements in art … do go on.

AMANDA In the painting, the artist imagines the King sitting at the girl's feet, gazing at her in adoration. Burne Jones said he was determined that the King should look like a king and the beggar should look like a Queen, and *he had certain details such as the crown and the maid's dress specially made for him* so that he could capture the detail. The setting has echoes of 15th century Italian art, particularly Mantegna and Crivelli, and it's all elaborately decorated with highly wrought textures and jewel-like colours. If you look at the clothing you can see what I mean. The two characters in the background have got these rich flowing clothes, and there's the same richness in the King's flowing cloak.

TEACHER So what is he trying to tell us about here ... what about these anemones ... do they have any particular significance do you think?

AMANDA Yes, the maid is holding a bunch of anemones, and if you look closely you can see that some of them have fallen on the steps by the King. The flowers are a symbol of unrequited love, and there's a lot of personal feeling in this painting, as there is in much of his work. At the time he was doing this, Burne Jones had met and fallen in love with a girl called Frances Graham, but she then married someone else. So it's likely that the King represents Burne Jones and the Queen represents Frances Graham, and *the painting shows his feelings about losing the woman he loved*.

TEACHER Are there any other themes that the audience in 1884 would have recognised apart from on this personal level?

AMANDA Yes, to the general public it would have had a completely different meaning, which *they would have recognised quite easily* – they would interpret the painting as being about the rejection of worldly wealth and the elevation of love above everything else.

TEACHER Yes, absolutely ... and that was a message that was very close to Burne Jones's heart and was very relevant for late Victorian Britain ... Well thank you Amanda, and now we'll move on to the next artist ...

Your views

B   Students discuss the questions in groups.

Round off the activity by comparing opinions as a class.

Speaking SB page 89

Mind your language

Draw students' attention to the title. Ask them when someone might use the phrase *mind your language*. The phrase is normally spoken as a warning when someone has used foul or abusive language. The word *mind* here has the meaning 'be careful with'.

Students discuss the questions in groups.

Ask them to check their answers to question 2 with the key on Student's Book page 180.

Discuss the other answers as a class. For question 3 ask students to consider differences in pronunciation of

English words in their language. Ask them also to consider 'false friends' – English words that are used in their own languages but with different meanings.

A   Students discuss the questions in groups and then as a class.

> **Key**
>
> The first writer is discussing the advantages of having a global language.
> The second writer is discussing the bad effects that can happen when a language dies out.
>
> The first writer considers a single language for international communication to be a good thing, whereas the second writer thinks the consequences would be negative.

B

> **Key**
>
> 1   opportunities for business, access to information, improvements in international relations
> 2   loss of cultural identity, loss of history, people's influence on the world

C   Draw students' attention to the *Exam tip*.

Remind students that they can present their responses to the questions more fluently by linking their ideas together rather than just reciting a list.

Monitor and give feedback at the end on any aspects of fluency or accuracy you want to deal with.

Exploring the topic

D   Students discuss the questions in groups and then as a class.

Writing SB pages 90–91

A report   Paper 2 Part 2

Understanding the task

A   Students read through the exam task and underline the parts that relate to the four questions.

Discuss answers to the questions as a class.

Key

1 The report is for the school principal.
2 The reader will find out details about the trip and the festival and the writer's opinions.
3 A description of the festival itself and some of the events, including the writer's impressions of them.
4 An assessment of the personal benefits of the trip.

Analysing the sample

B

Key

1 It is divided into sections with suitable headings.
2 The language is formal but not impersonal.
3 Narrative tenses, mostly past simple, are used to describe the festival, the events and the benefits the writer gained. Present simple and *will* are used in the introduction.
4 The report is mainly based on opinions. Some factual details of the festival are given.
5 The report includes all the details and opinions requested and is written in an appropriate style.

Writing skills

Complex sentences

C Students compare the notes with the sentence and underline words and phrases that have been added.

Discuss the answers as a class.

Key

Despite and *although* have been added to show contrast. A relative clause with *which* has been used to combine information.

D Students work in pairs to arrange the sentences into the three areas.

Check answers as a class before they write their sentences.

Key

a 1, 5, 8   b 2, 4, 9   c 3, 6, 7

Students work in pairs to write their sentences and then compare what they have written with another pair.

Use the sample to check their sentences.

Possible answer

Blenheim Palace and its grounds were a gift from Queen Anne to the Duke of Marlborough, who was the commander of the British army when it defeated the French at Blenheim in 1704. The gardens, which are a particular feature of the palace and comprise such features as lakes, woods and sweeping vistas, were designed by Capability Brown. The main building, which took nearly 20 years to complete, is a neo-classical structure designed by John Vanburgh.

Writing your report

Go through each of the stages in turn, discuss points and brainstorm ideas as a class. Draw students' attention to the *Exam tip* and ask students to look back at the sample report and comment on which details they think are likely to be made up.

Photocopiable activity 6.2   TB page 154

Unit 6 Overview key

SB pages 92–93

Lexical cloze Paper 1 Part 1

A

1 B	2 A	3 C	4 C	5 A	6 A
7 B	8 A	9 B	10 A	11 D	12 B

Word formation Paper 3 Part 2

B

1	singularly	6	psychological
2	supposedly	7	comparatively
3	considerable	8	preference
4	simplicity	9	addition
5	complexity	10	appealing

Key word transformations Paper 3 Part 4

C

1 do not have a good command of
2 some striking similarities between
3 what fascinates him most
4 all you ever do is
5 gives you an insight into
6 was no shortage of
7 incapable of completing
8 take it as read

Unit 6 Vocabulary test TB page 131

7 Only flesh and blood

▶ *See unit summary on page 4.*

Exam training in this unit

Reading	Multiple-choice questions on one text: using question stems to find information in the text
Use of English	Gapped sentences: parts of speech, multiple meanings
	Comprehension and summary: paraphrasing skills, prompted summary
Listening	Multiple-choice questions on four short extracts
Speaking	Themed discussion: thinking laterally to find alternative ideas for images
Writing	An article: presenting opinions in an informal style

Ask students to suggest a meaning for the expression *only flesh and blood*. The expression is used to explain that somebody is only human and that humans are vulnerable. The overall theme of the unit is human interaction and communities.

Reading SB pages 94–96

From rags to riches – and back!

Introduce the activity by asking students if they personally know of any 'rags to riches' stories (ones that involve people moving from poverty to extreme wealth).

1 Encourage students to give more fluent descriptions by linking the phrases together and adding any other suitable words of their own.

Discuss answers as a class.

Possible answers

The man
He has straight, greying hair with a receding hairline. His bushy moustache and staring eyes give him a rather worried expression. He is not at all shabbily dressed as he is wearing a formal suit and tie.
The woman
She has fair, curly hair but dark eyebrows. She has an attractive smile and is very elegantly dressed in expensive-looking clothes.

2 Elicit some suitable adjectives for describing personality and character and encourage students to express their personal impressions, e.g. *I would say* the man is a rather stern and serious person whereas the woman *gives me the impression of being* outgoing and lively.

3 Draw students' attention to the heading, *from rags to riches – and back!* and ask how it might apply to the two pictures of the woman.

Discuss ideas as a class.

Multiple-choice questions Paper 1 Part 4

Background notes

The text is taken from a magazine article which recounts the true story of Horace Tabor and Baby Doe. Lily Langtry (1853–1929) was a well-known British actress, greatly admired by Edward VIII.
Sarah Bernhardt (1845–1923) was the stage name of French actress Rosine Bernard who achieved great fame as a classical actress.
Oscar Wilde (1854–1900) was an Irish writer best known for his plays including *The Importance of Being Earnest* and his novel *The Portrait of Dorian Gray*.
Benvenuto Cellini (1500–1571) was an Italian sculptor and artist famous for his autobiography.
Nouveaux riches is a French term for people who have recently acquired wealth as opposed to those who inherited it from old families.

A Allow students a few minutes to read through the text. Remind them not to worry about unknown vocabulary at this stage.

Check answers as a class.

Key

The events took place in Leadville, Colorado, USA in the 1880s and 1890s.

B This activity is designed to encourage students to answer the multiple-choice question stems from their reading of the text before they read the options. Remind them to express the ideas they get from the text in their own words. This will encourage them to try and paraphrase any new vocabulary by using the context.

Check answers as a class.

Key

1 It was a town of contrasts between obviously rich and very poor. *'vulgar opulence and Western austerity'* (line 10)
2 Oscar Wilde thought that this was the most logical approach to art criticism he had seen. *'rational method of art criticism'* (line 26)
3 It remains famous for the story of Horace Tabor and Baby Doe. *'the town's celebrity comes from'* (line 37)
4 The writer implies that she was able to manipulate and exploit the men she met for her own purposes. *'acquired and disposed of'* (line 54), *'she met and captivated'* (line 56), *'she induced him'* (line 60)
5 He wasn't actually elected as senator and was only given the 30 days left of the previous senator's term to keep him happy. *'but as a consolation prize'* (line 65)
6 The writer implies that they disapproved of her, probably because of her past. *'a girl of doubtful antecedents'* (line 51)
7 They became bankrupt due to a change in the law which resulted in silver no longer being valuable. *'which had made silver legal tender … was repealed'* (line 81)

C Ask students to look at the four options for each question and compare them with their answers to the questions in B before they make their choice.

Check answers as a class.

Key

1 C 2 D 3 A 4 D 5 C 6 C 7 B

D 🎧 Play the recording and ask students to note down what they think the main events are. They don't need to write down the exact words they hear.

Ask students to compare notes with a partner, then discuss answers as a class.

Possible answers

Horace became a day labourer, then postmaster of Denver. When he died he asked Baby Doe not to give up the mine.
She devoted the rest of her life trying, unsuccessfully, to reopen the Matchless mine. She even moved with her daughters to a shack at the minehead. The children both left her, and she died a recluse at the age of 80.

Tapescript

NARRATOR 'Whatever happened to Baby Doe?' is a question often asked by visitors to Leadville and the answer, I'm afraid, is not a happy one! The Tabors were reduced to destitution. Horace worked as a day labourer to save his wife and two daughters from starving. In 1899, an old friend got him appointed postmaster of Denver and his fortunes briefly revived. But he died a year later. His last words to Baby Doe were, 'Don't give up the mine.' This is where the story becomes a tragedy. The former courtesan, who had spent 17,000 dollars on her daughter's christening robe and had given her 100 peacocks as pets, moved back to Leadville and devoted the rest of her life to working the Matchless. She became a wild eccentric, a bag lady who sailed forth every few months to try to raise money from the bankers in Leadville and Denver to reopen the mine. Eventually, she moved with her daughters to a shack at the minehead – a small squalid building exposed to the elements, whose walls she pasted with pictures of her days of glory, cut out from magazines. The oldest daughter ran away. The younger, Silver Dollar, who had inherited her mother's youthful morals but none of her later obduracy, died an alcoholic in Chicago in 1925. Still Baby Doe tried to work the mine, descending into the depths itself, well into her seventies, trying in vain to find the new silver lode which would restore her fortunes. She finally died an old, mad recluse, frozen to death aged 80, in a blizzard, in 1935.

Vocabulary

E This exercise deals with vocabulary items from the reading text and related words. Encourage the use of dictionaries.

Students work in pairs to do the exercise. Remind them to refer back to the text to check how the words labelled A are used.

Check answers as a class and discuss the meaning of the unused words. Definitions of these words are included in the key.

Key

1 C *destitute* means without food, money and other necessities of life
   dejected means unhappy and disappointed
   desolate describes an empty place without people, or a feeling of loneliness and unhappiness

2 A *discerning* means able to show good judgement about the quality of something
   observant means to be quick at noticing things
   distinguishing means seeing the difference between things that are similar, or being different from other similar things

3 A *austerity* is having no money due to bad economic conditions
   sobriety is the state of not being drunk, or the fact of being sensible and serious
   gravity means the extreme importance of a situation

4 B an *objection* is the reason why you are opposed to something
   criticism is the expression of disapproval
   censure is an act of very strong criticism or disapproval

5 C a *bequest* is the action of leaving possessions to a person by the means of a will
   heritage is the history, values and traditions of a country that are passed down through generations
   an *inheritance* can be possessions or money left to you after the death of someone

6 A *lucrative* means producing large amounts of money
   acquisitive means wanting to get many possessions
   affluent means wealthy, well-off

7 B *deposed* means to be forcibly removed from a powerful position
   disposed means to be got rid of or be willing or prepared to do something
   dispersed means to be moved apart, separated and sent somewhere else

8 A *captivated* means being kept extremely interested in or attracted by something
   captured means to take into one's possession by control or force
   enslaved means to make someone a slave, or to cause someone to lose their freedom of choice or action

9 B *exaggerated* means made to seem larger (better or worse) than it really is
   extravagant means spending a great deal of money, more than necessary
   exceptional means unusually good

10 A *dilapidation* is the state or process of falling into decay, or being in disrepair
   disintegration is the process of coming to pieces
   devastation is the state or process of being destroyed or ruined

11 A consolation is given to someone to make them feel better when they are disappointed
   compensation is money given to someone because of damage, injury or loss
   conciliation is the act of bringing two opposing sides together in agreement

✚ Extra activity

Write the following two columns of words on the board:

exceptional	place
desolate	ancient treasures
gravity	crowd
heritage	feature
dispersed	society
distinguishing	situation
affluent	talent

Ask students to work in pairs and match the words in the left hand column, which have been taken from E, with those on the right.

Allow students a few minutes to write as many sentences as they can using the words they matched.

When they have finished, ask students to read out their sentences for comparison as a class.

Possible answers

He had an *exceptional talent* for music.
The small village in the mountains was a very *desolate place*.
I don't think they realised the *gravity* of the *situation*.
Ancient treasures are the *heritage* of every nation.
The police *dispersed* the *crowd* following the demonstration.
The large dome is the building's main *distinguishing feature*.
Nowadays we live in a much more *affluent society* than we used to.

Expressions with *gold* and *silver*

Ask students to explain to you or the class any expressions with gold or silver they have in their own languages.

Check answers as a class.

Extra vocabulary

See page 176 for ideas on how to exploit this vocabulary.

down-at-heel (adjective) no longer in a good condition

discerning (adjective) able to show good judgement about the quality of something

heyday (noun) a time of greatest popularity or success

fragile (adjective) easily broken

debris (noun) pieces of material left over after something is destroyed

antecedents (noun) people or events that come before

dispose of (verb) to get rid of something unwanted

prominent (adjective) important or well-known in a particular field

induce (verb) to cause something to happen or persuade someone to do something

paupers (noun) poor people

shun (verb) to avoid someone

oust (verb) to force someone out of a job or position of power

Language in use

SB pages 97–99

Rome wasn't built in a day

This expression can be used to give encouragement to someone who is getting overwhelmed by the size of a task.

1 Elicit names of other empires and discuss as a class what these empires contributed to our civilisation now.

Ask students whether they think it was only military power that created these great empires or were there other factors, e.g. culture, language, trade or science.

Discuss whether such empires could exist nowadays.

2 Elicit from students a possible list of reasons for the downfall of the Roman Empire. Ask them to say either what they know from history lessons or to speculate.

Structure

Passive verb forms

A

Key

1 He discovered malaria in the bones of a child who died around 450AD.
2 It suggests that malaria might have been instrumental in weakening the Roman Empire.
3 They will have to reconsider the reasons for the downfall of the Roman Empire.

B

Key

1 'Ancient Rome *may have been destroyed* by the mosquito' (line 00)
   'Rome's downfall *had been caused by* a combination of' (line 00)
2 'The Roman's ability to fight off the barbarians *would have been weakened*' (line 00) In this sentence the agent (malaria) is not necessary as it has already been mentioned and is therefore obvious.
   'he *would have been better advised* to' (line 00)
   The agent in this case would be whoever had given the advice, and since this is not known or is hypothetical, then it can't be used.

C This activity aims to raise students' awareness of the change of focus or register between active and passive sentences.

Ask students to read through the pairs of sentences and discuss the questions with a partner.

Discuss answers as a class using the key for reference.

Key

There is no difference in meaning between the two sentences in each pair, only a change of context and, therefore, register.

1 a an informal conversation
   b a more formal context such as a news report or newspaper article
2 a an informal conversation
   b a more formal context such as a news report or statement
3 a an informal announcement of the event
   b a more formal notice of the event
      The agent is necessary here because it is important that we know the speaker will be an expert.
4 a a student's notebook or a spoken description of an experiment
   b an impersonal description of the experiment in a textbook

D This exercise focuses on the appropriate choice of active or passive according to the context.

Remind students to consider the tense of the verb as well as whether it should be active or passive. They should pay attention to accuracy with verb forms especially the auxiliary *have* in the present and past perfect tenses and word order with the adverbs *never*, *also*, *wrongly*.

Check answers as a class.

Key

1 was
2 was used
3 had been affected
4 was given
5 was wrongly thought
6 have now shown
7 was found
8 arrived
9 have also found
10 has never been proved

E This exercise focuses on the use of the passive in everyday speech. Remind students to consider what seems a natural response to the prompts as well as the correct tense.

Check answers as a class by asking students to read out both the prompt and the response.

Key

1 is being done / prepared
2 was sent
3 have been bitten
4 are being followed
5 hasn't been seen

F This exercise focuses on common noun + verb collocations used with the passive.

Ask students to compare their answers with a partner, and then check answers as a class.

Key

1 decision has been made
2 warning has been issued / given
3 agreement has been reached on a site
4 offer of £4,000 has been made
5 advice was given

⊞ Extra activity

Write the following verbs and noun phrases on the board:

verb	*noun phrases*
enforce	our requirements
make	the law
stage	an official statement
voice	an effort
raise	a protest
hold	strong opinions
issue	an objection
meet	an important meeting

Ask students to work in pairs and match each of the verbs with one suitable noun phrase.

Allow students a few minutes to make as many sentences as they can using the matched verbs and noun phrases. Encourage them to use the passive in their sentences.

When they have finished, ask students to read out their sentences for comparison as a class. This can be done competitively if you wish, with the pair who has the most correct sentences winning.

Possible answers

The law should be properly *enforced*.

An *effort* to rescue victims of the disaster *was made* yesterday.

A *protest* over the building of a new motorway *was staged* in the village centre.

Strong opinions about this *have been voiced* by the local community.

An objection was raised at the meeting.

An important meeting will be held to discuss this issue.

An official statement was issued by the government this morning.
Our requirements were not met by the hotel management.

G

Key

1	don't often get invited	5	got stung
2	didn't get promoted	6	get damaged
3	got hurt	7	got stolen
4	got run over	8	got stopped

Note There is further practice in the use of *get* with the causative *have* forms in Unit 11 on SB pages 153–154.

Photocopiable activity 7 TB page 154

Gapped sentences Paper 3 Part 3

H Draw students' attention to the *Exam tip* before they begin the exercise.

Ask them to compare answers with a partner, and then check answers as a class.

Key

1 rich	2 stings	3 bred	4 fell	5 hold	6 spread

Comprehension and summary

SB pages 100–101

A sense of community

Ask students what they understand by *a sense of community*. Ask them to describe what types of community they feel part of.

Discuss the different types of community represented in the pictures as a class and ask if students have had similar experiences.

Comprehension Paper 3 Part 5

A Allow students 5–6 minutes to read through both texts before they answer the questions.

Check answers as a class.

Key

1 to emphasise the present climate of change
2 they are less close than they used to be
3 limited, bounded
4 common experience

Summary writing Paper 3 Part 5

Paraphrasing

B Draw students' attention to the *Exam tip*. Point out that it may not be possible to paraphrase some words and that they should consider the meaning of the whole phrase.

Check answers as a class.

Key

1 d 2 e 3 f 4 c 5 a 6 b

C Remind students to refer to the two texts and find alternative wording for the phrases in these contexts. Encourage the use of dictionaries.

Discuss answers as a class.

Possible answers

bounded by	restricted or limited by
in a particular location	in a certain place
founded on	based on
recently expanded	increased / made larger
taken into account	considered
constrained	restricted / limited
it was costly	it was expensive
interacted	met and spoke to / mixed with

D Ask students to tick relevant points in the list. Remind them to refer back to the texts to confirm their choices.

Students compare their answers with a partner.

Check answers as a class.

Key

2, 5, 6, 7, 9

E Remind students to use appropriate linking phrases to create a well-expressed and fluent summary.

> **Sample summary**
>
> Firstly, a change in our working lives has led to people being more likely to move on to a different job in another area. So they frequently live away from family and relatives who could provide support. In addition, the change in shared experience due to improved communications technologies has resulted in less personal contact with friends and neighbours. (59 words)

Listening SB page 102

Every little helps

Introduce the section by asking what ideas the pictures and headline suggest.

Divide the class into pairs or small groups to discuss the three questions. Ask them to prepare a list of suggestions and ideas for questions 2 and 3.

Allow a few minutes for the discussion and then ask each pair or group to present their ideas to the rest of the class.

Multiple-choice questions Paper 4 Part 1

A 🎧 Ask students to read through the questions and options for extract 1. Play extract 1 and pause the recording. Allow students 5–10 seconds to think about their answers.

Continue to play the recording for students to confirm their answers.

Repeat the procedure for each extract in turn. At the end of all four extracts, allow students a minute to compare answers in pairs.

Check answers as a class.

> **Key**
>
> 1 C   2 B   3 B   4 C   5 A   6 B   7 C   8 B

Tapescript

Extract 1

ANNE So, how did the trip go?

JIM Honestly, it was the most amazing experience. I wouldn't have missed it for the world.

ANNE I just can't believe that *you actually succeeded in raising enough money.*

JIM Well, we really did push the boat out trying to drum up support in our spare time.

ANNE Even so, it's amazing that you managed to fill two lorries with toys and clothing, isn't it?

JIM Oh yes, and blankets, too – all sorts of things. But remember that we had to drive them ourselves – one thousand five hundred miles! The 'Save the Children' charity gave us a lot of practical help, too, though.

ANNE You must have been really proud of yourselves when you got there.

JIM Pride really didn't come into it. *Just seeing the faces of those children when we gave them some of the toys – the compassion you feel* – you really want to load up the lorry with all the kids and bring them back here! But at least they were being cared for at that stage. So we left feeling that we'd done a really worthwhile job and that we could always retrace our steps – once we'd refinanced another venture, of course.

ANNE Hmmn … I might even come with you next time …

JIM Now, there's a thought!

Extract 2

MUSICIAN Good evening, and welcome. Tonight, I'm appealing to everyone out there – not just those of you who have come to hear us perform! This live Helpline Round-the-clock Special is in aid of the famine-stricken province we've been hearing so much about recently – and seeing on our TV screens night after night. And, believe me, however little you pledge – we will make sure that it reaches its destination. Last year (in between giving concerts to raise money), I myself went out to supervise the deliveries of aid to stricken areas, and I know from my own first-hand experience that whatever we do is a mere drop in the ocean – we can never, never send enough to help these people. *But what we do send will be greatly appreciated*, so it all depends on you. Pick up the phone. The number will be appearing on your TV screens shortly, and will be announced on radio programmes throughout the evening. You can ring and quote your credit card number or, if you can't get through, just send us a cheque, and *you can sleep easily in your bed knowing that you've done your bit for Helpline!* Thank you …

Extract 3

FEMALE REPORTER In-depth Special Report this afternoon looks at the World Bank's role in lending to the nations of the world. More than a third of the World Bank projects completed last year were judged unsuccessful by its own staff, according to a *leaked internal World Bank report* *obtained* last week. The report lends considerable weight to long-running charges by critics that bank loans have contributed to environmental and social destruction in some countries.

The World Bank lent billions of dollars last year to countries in need of financial aid, and the largest sums were spent on development projects like dams, roads and timber management.

Critics have long said that projects such as the Bank's forestry management plans *have done nothing but result in the destruction of environments* such as the rainforests. They also claim that irrigation projects *have destroyed areas of land because faulty designs have allowed the intrusion of sea water*, and they allege that plans for major dam projects *threaten to displace hundreds of thousands of people*. So on today's programme we examine the issues surrounding the controversy and ask you, the listeners, for your views.

Extract 4

INTERVIEWER So, I understand you and your wife sponsor six-year-old Ana from Africa. Why did you decide to take on a sponsorship like this?

MAN Basically, we had wanted to do something to help people in the poorer regions of the world for some time. When we saw an advertisement in a magazine we made up our minds to do something positive. Opportunity International seemed like a good scheme, not least because our donation is sent straight to Ana, her family, and the village where she lives – not too many middle-men, as it were.

INTERVIEWER So you know where your donation ends up and who's getting the benefits?

MAN Absolutely. *But what I found most extraordinary about Opportunity International was the way in which they work with the locals*: you see, the people themselves decide how the money can best be spent in the community where the children live.

INTERVIEWER And how much do you know about Ana?

MAN Quite a bit, actually. They've sent regular reports on the community's progress since we started paying, and we've found out quite a lot about the charity's activities elsewhere too. We donate monthly, and it's not such a lot to find, in all honesty. *It's not as if we can't manage without it, or anything like that, but it's great to see that so much good can be done with the little that we give!*

Your views

B Discuss the question as a class and encourage students to evaluate and justify their answers.

Vocabulary

Expressions with *help*

C Ask students to read through all five sentences first and then choose an appropriate expression for each one. Remind them to consider the meaning and structure of the whole sentence as they may need to add words or change the form of the verb.

Check answers as a class by asking students to read out the whole sentence.

> **Key**
>
> 1 *lend a helping hand* to, assist someone willingly
> 2 *she can't help herself,* can't help doing something
> 3 *help yourself, to* take what you want
> 4 *it can't be helped,* that no one can change the situation
> 5 *helped me out,* assist someone in a difficult situation

Speaking SB page 103

Themed discussion Paper 5 Part 2

Speculating

A Divide the class into pairs and ask them to consider what factors the images in the poster represent.

Allow 2–3 minutes for students to talk in their pairs.

Discuss their ideas as a class.

> **Possible answers**
>
> religion / beliefs / traditions / culture
> wealth and poverty / difference between rich and poor / economic and social factors
> health and sickness / medicine / well-being

Evaluating

B Ask students to think about what the poster lacks in their view. What, in their opinion, are the most significant factors which influence our lives?

Allow students 2–3 minutes for the discussion.

Discuss their ideas as a class.

Suggesting alternatives

C Draw students' attention to the example first. Ask them to explore other factors they feel are important and to make notes about them similar to the example. They can use their ideas from the discussion in B above. Remind them to think of images which represent the alternative themes.

Draw students' attention to the *Exam tip* and ask them to consider how they can present their ideas more fluently by linking points in their notes together and extending the range of vocabulary and structures. Allow about 2 minutes for this and then ask each pair to present their ideas to the class for comparison.

Give feedback on any points of fluency or range that you want to deal with.

Writing SB pages 104–105

An article Paper 2 Part 1

Understanding the task

A Ask students whether the views expressed in the extract are optimistic or pessimistic about the future of the countryside.

Discuss answers to the three questions as a class.

> **Key**
>
> 1 the *Features and Opinions* page
> 2 that the articles will contain contributors' personal opinions on topical issues and may be expressed strongly
> 3 an informal style and a personal tone

Analysing the sample

B Ask students to read through the sample first and find out whether the views expressed are optimistic or pessimistic about the future of the countryside.

Students work through the questions on their own or in pairs.

Check answers as a class, asking for specific examples in the text.

> **Key**
>
> 1 The writer uses less formal or neutral language and includes personal experience – 'the village that I live in', 'explains Mary Foxwood, one of the oldest residents'.
> 2 The writer's opinions are clear. The article is balanced in that both sides of the issue are presented, but the writer's own more optimistic view is presented more strongly in the final paragraph.
> 3 The writer suggests that the media has exaggerated the situation. The writer's own experience shows that village life is thriving. Finally, the writer mentions that rural life has changed and adapted to the modern world and has improved when compared to life in the city.
> 4 'flavour of the month', 'but the thing is', 'doom and gloom'.

Writing skills

Illustrating with examples

C Students work in pairs to discuss which text is more appropriate.

> **Key**
>
> 2 is more appropriate since it gives examples without assuming that the reader knows the area.

D Students write short paragraphs using ideas from their own experience. Remind them to use paragraph 2 in C as a model.

Writing your article

E Essentially, this task requires a discursive piece of writing giving the students' own opinions on the topic of life in the city nowadays. Compare this task with the more formal discursive writing tasks in Unit 3 (a letter to a newspaper) and Unit 5 (an essay for a college tutor). Also compare this type of article with the descriptive / narrative type in Unit 4 (a nostalgic journey).

Remind students that it is important to read the exam task carefully as the purpose of the article and the intended readership are important in determining the appropriate style and register that students should use.

Go through each of the stages in turn and discuss questions and brainstorm ideas as a class.

Unit 7 Overview key

SB pages 106–107

Lexical cloze Paper 1 Part 1

A

1 B	2 D	3 A	4 D	5 C	6 B
7 D	8 B	9 C	10 A	11 C	12 B

Cloze Paper 3 Part 1

B

1	whole	9	which
2	no	10	down
3	why	11	so
4	their	12	were
5	Over / Throughout	13	else
6	on / along	14	even / far / more
7	some	15	without
8	as		

Gapped sentences Paper 3 Part 3

C

1 vacant   2 wipe   3 mass   4 access   5 steps
6 aid

Vocabulary Test Unit 7 TB page 132

8 The ties that bind

▶ *See unit summary on page 4.*

Exam training in this unit

Reading	Gapped text: referencing pronouns
Use of English	Key word transformations
	Comprehension and summary: error correction, proof-reading a summary
Listening	Three-way matching
Speaking	Extended speaking: responding to your partner's views
Writing	A letter to a newspaper: responding to opinions

Ask students if they know the meaning of the expression *the ties that bind*. The expression refers to the responsibilities that prevent us from always doing exactly what we want. Ask students what ties they have and in what way they are bound by them. The overall theme of the unit is family relationships and friendship.

Reading SB pages 108–110

The urban jungle

Ask students as a class how they can explain the contrast between the words *urban* and *jungle* in the title. **Possible answer:** Although cities offer a supposedly more sophisticated way of life with better facilities, life there can be a struggle for survival (like it is in the jungle), especially if you are poor.

Students discuss the situation in pairs and note down their ideas.

Ask each pair to present their ideas for discussion as a class.

Gapped text Paper 1 Part 3

Background notes
Crack is a highly addictive form of cocaine.
A ghetto is a part of the city inhabited almost exclusively by socially-disadvantaged groups.
The sixth grade is the sixth year in the American education system normally reached at the age of eleven or twelve.
The Bronx and Queens are districts of New York City.

A Introduce the activity by drawing students' attention to the title and subtitle of the article. Ask them why parents might be 'at the end of their tether' and how they might 'win sympathy'. What do they think 'mean streets' might be?

This activity aims to encourage students to read through the main text first before looking at the removed paragraphs in order to get a general idea of the overall content.

The three questions can be answered without referring to the removed paragraphs. Allow 2–3 minutes.

Check answers as a class, asking students to refer to parts of the text to support their answers.

> **Key**
>
> 1 They chained their daughter to a radiator.
> 2 She seems to be uncontrollable.
> 3 The writer is sympathetic to the parents and regards their 'crime' as justifiable.

B Draw students' attention to the *Exam tip* and ask them to list all the people who have been mentioned in the article so far.

Ask them to read through paragraphs A–H and add to the list if appropriate.

Then they should underline any pronouns or phrases that refer to people or things and work out who or what the pronoun or phrase refers to (whether or not the latter are mentioned in the paragraph itself). This will also help the process of choosing the correct paragraph.

Check answers as a class.

> **Key**
>
> 1 B 2 H 3 F 4 C 5 G 6 D 7 A

Note: Paragraph E is not needed: it refers to 'her statement to the police', but there is no mention of a statement made by Linda to the police in the article.

C

Key

1 They were trying to protect her from drugs and the dangers she encountered on the streets.
2 Because they were actually trying to protect their child rather than being cruel.
3 She ran away from the foster home and returned to her former circle of friends in the world of drugs.
4 Encourage students to speculate on the outcome based upon what they have read in the text.

Vocabulary

D

Key

1	tipped off	6	tracked her down
2	wound up	7	bail was set
3	accused of	8	fall through the cracks
4	dropped out	9	be hard pressed
5	be mixed up in	10	walk away from

British and American spelling

E Ask students to note down the American spelling as used in the text.

Check answers as a class.

Key

1 meager (line 49) center (line 56) meter (paragraph H)
2 leveled (paragraph F)
3 neighbors (line 28)
4 specializes (paragraph D)

Expressions with *fall*

F Ask students to read the sentences first and then choose an appropriate expression for each one. Remind them that they may need to change the form of the verb to fit in with the sentence.

Check answers as a class, by asking students to read out the whole sentence.

Key

1	have fallen in with	6	fell short of
2	fell apart	7	fallen into place
3	fell on	8	fell for (illustrated)
4	fall behind	9	fell through
5	fall back on	10	have fallen victim to

Extra vocabulary

See page 176 for ideas on how to exploit this vocabulary.

intimidation (noun) act of threatening someone into doing what you want

norm (noun) situation or behaviour that is accepted or standard

petition (verb) to make a formal request to an authority

meager/meagre (adjective) small in quantity

notion (noun) idea or understanding of something

beguiling (adjective) very attractive in a mysterious or dangerous way

exile (noun) state of being sent to live in another country as punishment

outbreak (noun) sudden start of something unpleasant

Language in use

SB pages 111–113

Seen and not heard?

The expression *Children should be seen and not heard* is an old saying which suggested that children were supposed to keep quiet when in adult company.

1 Ask students to think about what life was like for children in the nineteenth century and what aspects they think have changed most.

2 Students work in pairs or small groups.

Discuss answers as a class.

3 The ideas in the texts are: the raising of school leaving age; the abolition of physical punishment; the fact that there are fewer large families; changing gender roles and sexual equality.

Ask students to talk in their pairs or groups about when and how these changes have happened in their own countries.

Structure

Perfect aspect

A

1 This question focuses on students' ability to recognise the different verb forms used in the text.

Check answers as a class.

Key

were expected	simple past passive
has replaced	present perfect
had expected	past perfect
will have outlawed	future perfect
has remained	present perfect
employed	simple past
has been declining	present perfect continuous

2

Key

has replaced, had expected, will have outlawed, has remained, has been declining

3 Ask students to consider how the perfect aspect is used in context by referring to the two texts.

Discuss answers as a class. Ask students to give examples from the texts for each of the functions.

Key

a,d and e are correct
  a All uses of the perfect aspect relate events to a later time. Past perfect is used for events before a time in the past, present perfect is used for events before now, and 'future perfect' for events before a time in the future.
  d has been declining
  e had expected, has replaced, has remained, will have outlawed

  b and c are incorrect.
  b describes only the present perfect, not perfect aspect in general. Note that 'future perfect' is a clear counterexample.
  c describes the use of past simple.

B This exercise focuses on the difference between the present perfect and simple tenses. Remind students to consider any time references made in the texts to help them choose the correct form. Remind them also that the texts mention changes that have occurred and this is reflected in the verb forms.

Check answers as a class.

Key

1	were	6	have sustained
2	has led	7	(have) created
3	finished off	8	were
4	travel	9	have become
5	began		

✚ Extra activity

Ask students which verbs reflect the changes that have occurred.

Key

'has led to children spending less time outdoors'
'children now travel further afield'
'mass entertainment has sustained a shared culture for children and created a generation gap'
'children have become consumers of'

C This exercise practises the use of the present, past and future perfect forms. Remind students to read the whole sentence and consider any time references before they complete the sentences.

Check answers as a class by asking students to read out the whole sentence.

Key

1 have met
2 will have known
3 had changed
4 has been taken away
5 will have only just got back
6 had been ransacked
7 had never had
8 has been celebrated

D This activity focuses on the use of perfect gerunds and infinitives to indicate a completed action or activity before the present time.

Check answers as a class.

Key

1 having written
2 have caused
3 Having lived
The use of the simple gerund in 1 and 3 indicates that the action of the verb is still happening. The simple infinitive in 2 indicates that something happens at any time as a general fact.

Perfect and continuous aspect

E   Ask students to consider whether the sentences refer to an activity that continued up to the present or a specified time in the past, or to something completed before the present or a particular time in the past but not specified when.

Discuss the differences in meaning as a class.

> **Key**
>
> 1 a The speaker is giving a reason why they felt hot at that time in the past by referring to the activity that led up to it.
>   b The speaker is referring to one particular occasion that occurred at an unspecified time in the past which resulted in discovering Jim was a cheat.
> 2 a This sentence refers to an activity that has continued from an unspecified time in the past until now. The activity is not finished.
>   b This refers to the result in the present of something completed at an unspecified time in the past.
> 3 a The speaker has repeatedly phoned, but without success.
>   b The speaker phoned on one occasion at an unspecified time in the past.
> 4 a This sentence refers to an activity that continued up to an unspecified time in the past. At that time Jack was still living with the speaker and had been since his arrival.
>   b This sentence refers to an activity that was over by an unspecified time in the past. At that time Jack was no longer living with the speaker.

F

> **Key**
>
> 1 have you been doing
> 2 have had
> 3 had been damaged
> 4 has changed, (has) checked, hasn't completed
> 5 had studied
> 6 had been waiting
> 7 have been meaning (non-stative use), have known (stative)
> 8 has been getting

Key word transformations   Paper 3 Part 4

G   Draw students' attention to the *Exam tip* before they begin the exercise.

When students have finished ask them to compare their answers with a partner.

Check answers as a class.

> **Key**
>
> 1 a couple communicate the happier
> 2 to bear any resemblance / relationship to
> 3 raise people's expectations of
> 4 the Taylor's marriage had run into trouble
> 5 at ease with / in the presence of
> 6 has come to be regarded as
> 7 had been down to their tolerating
> 8 has improved since he was spoken to by

Extra vocabulary

See page 176 for ideas on how to exploit this vocabulary.

transform (verb) to change the form or nature of something
implement (verb) to put an official decision into action
encounter (verb) to meet, discover or experience something
flexible (adjective) able to change to suit new conditions
erase (verb) to completely remove something written or recorded
ransack (verb) to search a place making it untidy and causing damage

Comprehension and summary

SB pages 114–115

A friend in need is a friend indeed

Draw students' attention to the title and ask them in what kinds of situation they turn to their friends for help.

Discuss the questions as a class or in small groups. Ask students what sort of support the people in the pictures give each other.

Comprehension   Paper 3 Part 5

Background notes
As both texts are about social welfare schemes that have been set up to help people in need, they contain terms relating to social services that may be unfamiliar to your students.

Text 1
A local authority flat is state-owned accommodation provided at low rent for people on low wages, with special problems.

Sleeping rough refers to being homeless and living on the streets.

A pilot scheme is one which is being tried out to see how it works.

Tenancy sustainment means encouraging people to keep up with rent payments so that they are not asked to leave their homes.

Text 2

Childcare officers are professional social workers who deal with children who have social problems.

Delinquency describes anti-social or criminal behaviour among young people.

Statutory welfare services are those services giving help and support that must be provided by the local authority by law.

Field staff and service users are terms for the professional social workers and the people they help respectively.

A probation officer deals with people who are on probation, which is a scheme whereby someone who has committed a crime is placed under supervision rather than being sent to prison.

A Ask students to read carefully through both texts and underline parts which refer to friendships or relationships between the people mentioned. Remind them not to worry about unknown vocabulary at this stage as this is dealt with in B.

Discuss answers as a class.

> **Key**
>
> Text 1
> The text mentions two kinds of friendships or relationships. First, the sense of being part of a community such as friendships formed by people sleeping rough, and second a scheme to match volunteer 'friends' with previously homeless people to help them get back into normal society.
> Text 2
> This text mentions the personal relationships formed by childcare officers and the young people they deal with.

B This activity focuses on the use and meaning of some key vocabulary items which might be tested in comprehension questions. Ask students to consider how the words are used in context.

Check answers as a class.

> **Key**
>
> Text 1
>   1 *camaraderie* is used to describe the friendships that develop between people sleeping rough
>   2 *impartial*
>   3 *non- judgemental*
>   4 *compassionate*
>   5 *conscientious*
> Words 2–5 are all qualities needed by people who become volunteer 'befrienders.'
> Text 2
>   6 *deprived* refers to the situation of the children the writer worked with
>   7 *stable* describes the lives the youngsters the writer used to work with are living now as adults
>   8 *statutory* refers to the welfare services provided by the local authority
>   9 *dreary* describes what local authority social work has become
> 10 *tenuous* refers to the relationships between social workers and the people they deal with

C Remind students to keep their answers to the comprehension questions as brief as possible.

Students compare their answers with a partner.

Check answers as a class, referring to relevant parts of the texts.

> **Key**
>
> Text 1
>   1 that they are close and supportive (This paraphrases 'being part of a community' and 'camaraderie' in the text.)
>   2 to emphasise how frightening it can be for the homeless to change their way of life (This relates back to the sense of community and camaraderie that the homeless share.)
> Text 2
>   3 it has become impersonal (This paraphrases 'dreary, mechanistic, systematic, technocratic' in the text.)
>   4 the service user

Summary writing   Paper 3 Part 5

Proof-reading a summary

Activities D and E focus on the need for accuracy in students' summary writing.

D

> **Key**
>
> Volunteers should be *unbiased* in outlook (*or* have an unbiased outlook) and be capable *of relating* to *homeless* people and their problems without *pre-judging* them. *In* addition, they should be *sympathetic* towards their predicament, *dependable*, dedicated and have good inter-personal skills.

E

> **Key**
>
> The *writer's* personal experience indicates that, in the past, excellent relationships between staff and youngsters together *with* a mutual trust led to a long-term *improvement* in the youngsters' lifestyles. *Nowadays, however,* increasing workloads imposed *on* staff have resulted in a deterioration *in* these relationships, which is having a detrimental effect on those who *feel* increasingly *alienated* by these *attitudes*.

☐ Alternative activity

Both activities D and E can be done competitively.

Ask students to work in pairs and set a time limit of about 8 minutes for them to find and correct the mistakes in both summaries.

The pair who have identified and corrected the most mistakes win.

F   Remind students to follow the steps for summary writing they used in previous units. See SB page 87 for a list of steps to follow.

> **Sample summary**
>
> Firstly, friendships formed between people sleeping rough can provide support and comfort. As well as this, volunteer 'befrienders', who can understand the problems of homeless people, can help them start a new way of life. Furthermore, friendships which develop between social workers and young people can help them overcome their problems and later improve their lives as adults. (58 words)

Extra vocabulary

See page 176 for ideas on how to exploit this vocabulary.

arrears (noun) money that is owed
integrate (verb) to become part of a group or whole
priority (noun) something more important than other things
biased (adjective) tendency to show favour for or against something
alienated (adjective) feeling of not belonging to a group or society

Listening   SB page 116

The perfect partner

Allow students about 2 minutes to make their lists individually and then ask them to compare with a partner. Encourage them to say what they agree or disagree with in their partner's list.

Round off the activity by doing a survey with the whole class to find out which qualities students considered most important and which the least.

Three-way matching   Paper 4 Part 4

A 🎧 Draw students' attention to the *Exam tip* first. Ask students to read through the six statements carefully and then play the recording.

After the second listening, check answers as a class.

> **Key**
>
> 1 S   2 S   3 D   4 B   5 S   6 B

Tapescript

PRESENTER Today we're talking about the factors which affect marriages and relationships. With me is Derek Lindhurst, a marriage guidance counsellor, and Susan Dobson, who manages an introductions agency. Now, talking about and analysing relationships is much more common today than it ever was in the past, but are we getting any better at making a success of our marriages? What makes a relationship work?

SUSAN That's a question we spend an enormous amount of time thinking about when trying to help our clients make successful relationships. Fundamentally, though, it all comes down to love and the warm, secure and fulfilling feelings love gives us, and it's these which provide the impetus to continue the partnership.

DEREK Absolutely, but there's much more to a successful relationship than love. Let's face it, the dizzy passion and excitement fade and it's what you're left with which is the most important thing.

SUSAN But *keeping those moments of romance and indulgence going in a relationship leads to a lasting intimacy* which is much closer than a partnership where love is interpreted merely as companionship.

DEREK Companionship is crucial, though. Look at the numbers of couples getting married in their 40s and 50s. They're seeking reassurance and comfort.

SUSAN I couldn't agree more, and *people of this age have developed tolerance and coping strategies. Perhaps they don't expect so much as when they were in their 20s and will be content with something which isn't the ideal they once had.*

DEREK Maybe, but they'll have the experience of having been in relationships and will know that they can survive the break-up and can operate on their own.

SUSAN I think that's being rather cynical. People enter relationships to share common interests and experiences, and they can do this at any age. You're not guaranteed long-lasting success but it's a great place to start. Coming from the same social position, education and experience makes people feel they're on common ground and can understand each other.

DEREK *Whether people stay together or not is more to do with who they are than where they've come from. It's a question of personality rather than upbringing.* Our personality's unique, but obviously, it's going to be influenced by role models to a certain extent. You see, since childhood we've developed deep-rooted ideas about what's right and wrong in a relationship, and also what's right and wrong in other contexts. We've learned this from observing our parents. *Exploring our deeper selves and finding a common code of behaviour in a relationship is a journey all couples should take – especially if they want to have confidence in the long-term survival of their relationship.*

SUSAN Don't you find that people can't always come up with the words for describing those things? We've interviewed couples we introduced who have found long-lasting happiness. We record the language they use to talk about themselves. And we present this language to the people who have difficulties in expressing their ideas about life and love, to see if they can personalise it. *It's so important for couples to find out if they have similar views.*

DEREK Actually, much of my time is spent encouraging clients to open up to each other and reveal things they may not have thought worth talking about or have hidden for years. It's so easy to assume that your partner knows exactly how you feel about an event or shared experience.

SUSAN And it's good to keep reaffirming each other, especially at the beginning of a relationship. We're all worried about how others see us, so just saying how much we like and respect the other person is going to do the world of good for the relationship. *Making an effort, being generous, and being able to laugh about something that*

didn't go too well. That's what it's all about.

DEREK *I don't think we can underestimate the importance of developing and maintaining regular communication*, not just on everyday happenings and plans, but about how you reacted to something, what the long term effect on you has been and whether your feelings have changed in any way. All this should be a regular feature of time spent together. If you bottle things up, it will almost inevitably lead to problems in the long run.

SUSAN It is such a vital area. *Clearly, the more a couple are able to communicate, in every sense, both verbally and physically, the easier it is for them.* If someone loses a job, or there's a bereavement to cope with then if you can talk together, you'll be able to work through it over time. If couples haven't learned to express their feelings before these events, it can be very difficult to overcome them.

DEREK All relationships experience stresses and strains – they're a fact of life. But if you can really listen to each other, not just hear what someone is saying, but listen to what they're getting at, it will help to find solutions to external factors and issues within the relationship itself.

PRESENTER Well, that's all we've got time for, but thank you again for that most interesting discussion.

Vocabulary

Expressions connected with communication

B Ask students to work in pairs to do the activity.

Discuss answers as a class.

Key

1 *say what you mean* may be said when one person thinks the other is not being frank
2 *eat humble pie* means that one person has to admit they were wrong and apologise
3 *get your message across* may be said when someone is not making their point clearly enough
4 *lie through your teeth* means to tell lies shamelessly
5 *talk sense into* is used when someone wants to give another person some very strong advice or a warning about what they have done or are likely to do
6 *get something off one's chest* means to confess something that has been on your mind
7 *take something amiss* means to get upset at what someone said or did, often mistakenly
8 *have a heart to heart* means to have a confidential and frank discussion about something
9 *fall out with someone* means to stop being friends usually after a disagreement or argument
10 *miss the point* means to fail to understand the most important information.

Your views

C If it could be difficult for members of the class to talk about relationships known to them, choose a couple well known through the media or entertainment, for example.

✚ Extra activity

Write these verbs on the board.

> go out with
> get together with
> look up to
> get on well with
> care about
> let someone down
> have something / nothing in common with
> break up
> fall out with
> put up with

Ask students to work in pairs and make up a brief story of a relationship using as many of the verbs as possible.

Allow them 5 minutes to make up their story.

When they have finished, ask each pair to tell their story to the class.

Photocopiable activity 8   TB page 155

Speaking SB page 117

Extended speaking Paper 5 Part 3

A Divide the class into pairs and allow students 4–5 minutes to discuss the questions.

Round off the activity by asking the class as a whole what aspects of family life they think are represented in the pictures. If any ideas come up that have not been discussed previously, ask students to add them to their notes.

Planning and speaking

B Ask students to read their prompt cards and think about the discussion in A to see what ideas they can use. Allow about a minute for this.

Before students start speaking, draw their attention to the *Exam tip*.

Now ask students to speak in turn. Remind them that they have to speak for 2 minutes in the exam.

Responding

C Students answer the questions to respond to what their partner said.

Give feedback at the end on any points of fluency or accuracy you want to deal with.

Exploring the topic

D Students discuss the four questions in small groups. Allow about 5 minutes for the discussion and then invite one student from each group to present the group's ideas for comparison as a class.

Writing SB pages 118–119

A letter Paper 2 Part 1

Understanding the task

A

> **Key**
>
> 1 and 3 are explicitly mentioned
> 2 and 4 are implied

Analysing the sample

B

> **Key**
>
> 1 The writer agrees with statements 1 and 2.
> 2 For statement 1 the writer mentions improvement in health care and the fact that due to a falling birth rate larger numbers of adults are not economically active. For statement 2 the writer mentions people's reluctance to save and the need for the government to take measures to make sure everyone has a pension plan.
> 3 The writer disagrees with statements 3 and 4.
> 4 For statement 3 the writer argues that this is a negative attitude and mentions that many old people lead active and fulfilled lives. For statement 4 the writer points out the responsibility of children to look after their parents in old age and mentions the benefits that old people can give to the family.
> 5 The sample is written in a suitably formal style for a letter to a newspaper.

Writing skills

Responding

C Ask students to refer back to the example and see how the two patterns apply to other paragraphs.

> **Key**
>
> It follows the second pattern.

D

> **Key**
>
> *I would like to take issue with your comments about* 2a disagree
> *The principal reason for this is that* 2b explain or 1b extend
> *You are entirely correct to point out that* 1a agree
> *The case of … illustrates this point exactly* 1c or 2c an example
> *There are other factors as well that are important to consider* 1b extend
>
> As regards your point about … , I agree fully / I disagree entirely.
> What we also need to consider is …
> A good example of this would be …
> This is due to … / This can be attributed to …
> This is because …
> The reasons for this are …
> There is another factor as well …

E Ask students to work in pairs to write their paragraphs. Remind them to respond using their own ideas.

When they have finished, ask them to exchange paragraphs with another pair for comparison.

Check the use of the suggested patterns and expressions.

Writing your letter

F Go through each of the stages in turn, brainstorm ideas and discuss questions as a class.

Unit 8 Overview key

SB pages 120–121

Lexical cloze Paper 1 Part 1

A

1 D	2 A	3 A	4 B	5 C	6 C
7 B	8 B	9 C	10 D	11 D	12 A

Word formation Paper 3 Part 2

B

1	relationship(s)	6	irretrievably
2	disagreements	7	resolution
3	outcome	8	unemotional
4	excessively	9	grievances
5	undesirable	10	satisfactory

Key word transformations Paper 3 Part 4

C

1 is (thought of as) the norm
2 given no resources
3 to kick the habit
4 nothing to fall back on in
5 has been turned / converted into
6 his apartment had been broken into
7 is thought to have left the country
8 was detrimental to

Vocabulary Test Unit 8 TB page 133

Progress Test Unit 5–8 TB pages 140–141

9 Money makes the world go around

▶ *See unit summary on page 4.*

Exam training in this unit

Reading	Multiple-choice questions on one text: identifying purpose and intention
Use of English	Cloze: gist comprehension of the text Comprehension and summary: paraphrasing
Listening	Multiple-choice questions on four extracts: eliminating incorrect options
Speaking	Themed discussion
Writing	Writing a proposal: describing benefits

Find out if the students know the meaning of the expression *money makes the world go round*. (The expression implies that money is so important that it's what makes the world function.) Ask students if they agree. The overall theme of the unit is money and commerce.

Reading SB pages 122–124

Supply and demand

Introduce the activity by asking if students can explain the term *supply and demand*. It's an economic term referring to the relationship between the amount of goods or services that are available and the amount that people want to buy.

Ask students to consider whether the products in the list are luxuries or necessities.

Students work in small groups to discuss the question.

Invite one student from each group to present the group's ideas for discussion as a class.

Round off the activity by asking students to suggest any other products that could be added to the list.

Multiple-choice questions Paper 1 Part 4

A This activity aims to encourage students to read the text for overall gist before looking at the multiple-choice questions.

Check answers as a class.

> **Key**
>
> It refers to a craze for buying and selling tulips which occurred in Holland in the early seventeenth century.

B Draw students' attention to the *Exam tip*.

Before students do the exercise, remind them to consider any techniques they practised in earlier units for dealing with the multiple-choice questions. See the *Exam tip* on SB page 25 and exercise B on SB page 95.

Check answers as a class.

> **Key**
>
> 1 C   2 C   3 D   4 A   5 A   6 D   7 C

Your views

C Students discuss the three questions in small groups.

Invite one student from each group to present the group's ideas to the class.

Vocabulary

Expressions connected with trade and money
Exercises D and E focus on specific vocabulary from the text.

D Ask students to go through the text and underline any words or phrases they think are specifically connected to trade and money.

When they have done this, ask them to match the words they found with the ten definitions, looking for expressions they missed, if necessary.

Check answers as a class.

> **Key**
>
> | | | | |
> |---|---|---|---|
> | 1 | merchant | 6 | judicious trading |
> | 2 | rare commodities | 7 | defaulters |
> | 3 | stock markets | 8 | penury |
> | 4 | speculators | 9 | purchaser |
> | 5 | stock-jobbers | 10 | vendor |

E Ask students to look at how the verbs are used in the text before they complete the sentences. Remind them to read through all the sentences first before they choose a suitable verb and to consider what form the verb should be in.

Check answers as a class.

Key

1	went for	5	traded
2	crashed	6	dabbles
3	spread	7	made
4	fluctuates	8	ruined

Expressions with *pick*

F In this context *pick up* means *to buy*.

Ask students to read through the sentences and discuss with a partner what each expression means, then discuss answers as a class.

Key

1 chosen
2 criticising unfairly
3 learnt
4 collect / get
5 caught
6 plays about with
7 select
8 start an argument
9 went slowly and cautiously
10 carry on with what is left

❏ **Alternative activity**

If you think the class might have difficulties with this exercise, write the explanations in the key above in a jumbled order for students to match.

G Remind students that they may need to change the form of the verb to fit the sentence and also that they should consider the meaning of the whole sentence before they choose an expression.

Check answers as a class.

Key

1	pick up	5	picked their way
2	picking on	6	pick a fight
3	pick up the pieces	7	picking at
4	pick up	8	picked out

Extra vocabulary

See page 176 for ideas on how to exploit this vocabulary.

weird (adjective) very strange
epidemic (noun) sudden, rapid increase in a disease or something bad
deem (verb) to consider, regard
outrageous (adjective) shocking and unacceptable

semblance (noun) situation of something seeming to exist
fluctuation (noun) frequent changes in amount, size or quality
substantial (adjective) large in amount or importance
lobby (verb) to influence or try to persuade a government official
bicker (verb) to argue or quarrel
null and void (expression) no longer valid
trigger (verb) to start a series of reactions or a process
undermine (verb) to weaken
astute (adjective) very clever and quick at knowing what to do
pretext (noun) a false reason or excuse

Language in use

SB pages 125–127

Selling your wares

Background notes

A flea market is a street market where second hand items or antiques can be bought cheaply.

A pawnbroker is someone who lends money at interest on the security of a person's personal property. The items may be sold if they are not reclaimed by their owner by paying back the loan (plus interest) within a certain time.

Students work in pairs to discuss their reasons.

Each pair presents their reasons for comparison as a class.

Cloze Paper 3 Part 1

A This activity aims to encourage students to read through the whole text to get a general idea of what it is about before choosing a word to fit the space.

Check answers as a class.

Key

1 It was a poor and unhealthy place to live in.
2 At first he seemed enthusiastic ('seemed like a good thing to sell') but later he found it tiring and depressing.
3 It was embarassing trying to sell to people he knew. Also, people couldn't afford the books.

B Before students do the exercise, remind them to consider techniques they practised in earlier units for dealing with cloze texts. See the *Exam tip* on SB page 11.

Check answers as a class.

Key

1 ago   2 on   3 up   4 as   5 until   6 how
7 open   8 little / bit / lot   9 the   10 from
11 would   12 worth   13 in   14 is   15 what

✚ **Extra activity**

The text is written in a very conversational and colloquial style. Write definitions 1–10 on the board and ask students to find words or phrases to match them in the text.

		Key
1	started out walking	hiked off
2	pay tuition fees	put myself through
3	large pieces of something	hunks
4	carrying with difficulty	lugging
5	contacts or connections	ties
6	selling	peddling
7	occurred or happened	went on
8	spent	went through
9	quite	pretty
10	collapsed	caved in

Structure

Reported speech

These activities are designed to revise the changes in verb form, pronouns, word order and punctuation between direct and reported speech.

C

Key

1 Change *I* to *you* and *had* to *have* in the first sentence and *sounded* to *sounds* in the second. In both sentences add speech marks and commas.
   'You have inside ties,' he claimed.
   'This book-set sure sounds great,' my hosts said.
2 She asked me if / whether I had ever sold books before.
   I asked them how many books they had sold.

Note: Draw students' attention to the difference between the two sentences with *ask*.
Point out that direct questions beginning with the auxiliary verbs *do*, *have* and *be* are reported with *if* or *whether*.
Ask can also be used with an infinitive to report a request. e.g. She asked me *to open* the window / I asked *to go* home early.
Ask can also be used with *about* followed by a noun phrase, e.g. She asked me *about* my holidays in Spain / I asked him *about* his studies at university.

D This activity focuses on reporting in past and present time and the use of modal auxiliary verbs in reported speech.

Remind students to pay attention to the tense of the reporting verb and consider how the modals are used in reported speech.

Check answers as a class.

Key

1 The president says that they are negotiating terms at the moment.
2 She said she might pop round this evening.
3 He says if he were younger, he would learn how to use a computer.
4 The teacher asked the students if they would mind not smoking in the library.
5 a 1 and 3
   b 1 and 2
   c 2 and 4

Draw students' attention to the fact that modal verbs and conditionals don't always change their form in reported speech. Also ask students to compare the use of *ask* in 4 to report a polite request using a modal verb with the other uses of *ask* in C2.

Reporting verbs

These exercises focus on the verb patterns which follow specific reporting verbs.

E Remind students that the correct choice of verb depends on the meaning of the sentence in direct speech. All the verbs, except *wonder* because it reports a question, can be followed by a construction beginning with *that*.

Check answers as a class focusing on accuracy with verb forms.

Key

The adverbs for the key to F are included in italics.
1 Paul *clearly* explained that he hadn't been able to attend the meeting because he had been away on holiday.
2 Sally *discreetly* whispered that her father had just won a lot of money.
3 The thief *grudgingly* confessed that he had stolen the car.
4 Rebecca *defiantly* announced that she was going to marry him.
5 The politician *forcibly* argued that it was imperative that taxes were reduced.
6 The Browns wondered *anxiously* how much money their holiday was going to cost.
7 Sam insisted *angrily* that he hadn't been there.
8 Mr Black made it *absolutely* clear that he wasn't going to work at the weekend.

F Remind students that the meaning of the adverbs comes from how they are used in the sentence. The sentences themselves should give them a clue as to the most suitable adverb.

Ask students to work in pairs to do the activity.

Check answers as a class using the key in E above.

Note Adverbs of manner and comment, particularly *-ly* adverbs, can generally go in mid-position and end-position.

G This is an awareness-raising activity to focus on the different verb patterns following certain reporting verbs.

Check answers as a class.

Key

1 copying   2 for forgetting   3 to let
4 not to divulge

H Suggestions for what the speakers actually said are included in the key.

Key

1	on doing	'Don't bother! I'll do it myself.'
2	to having	'Do I really have to write that report again? I haven't got time.'
3	not to cross	'Now, you mustn't cross that road by yourselves. It's dangerous.'
4	about taking	'We'd like to take an English course. Can you give us some details?'

5	to comply	'We think it would be a good idea to comply with the regulations.'
6	(to) making	'Yes, you're right. I did make a mistake with the prescription.'
7	to sue	'I'll sue you if you continue to neglect safety precautions.'
8	about having	'Why do we have to get up so early? It's not fair!'
9	to be set	'Please, please, set me free to go home to my wife.'
10	to vote	'Come on, it's vitally important to vote against this bill.'

Suggest

I

Key

1 b, d and e are possible
   a and c are not possible because the verb *suggest* is never followed by an object pronoun.
2 *Suggest* can be followed by a gerund when the speaker is included in the suggestion. This is not a hard and fast rule, however.
   e is unusual because normally *that* and *should* are used as in sentence b in British English. This use is typical of American English speech.

J Remind students to consider the answers from I when they do the exercise.

Check answers as a class.

Key

1 Peter suggested having a barbecue.
2 Tim suggested that his mother should go to the theatre.
3 Brenda suggested that we should try that new place for dinner. / Brenda suggested trying that new place for dinner.
4 The teacher suggested that I should do the essay again. / The teacher suggested I do the essay again.

K Draw students' attention to the change in the form of the verb *to be* and the use of *that* in the two example sentences.

Check answers as a class.

Key

1 a It was said *that* the Queen *was considering* abdication.
  b The Queen was said *to be considering* abdication.
2 a It is said *that* the Chairman of the Board *has absconded* with the funds.
  b The Chairman of the Board is said *to have absconded* with the funds.

You might see these sentences in newspaper reports or hear them on TV / Radio news programmes.

Extra vocabulary

See page 176 for ideas on how to exploit this vocabulary.

wares (noun) goods for sale
imperative (adjective) very important, needing immediate attention
divulge (verb) to reveal something secret
comply with (verb) to act according to rules or laws
abscond (verb) to run away usually taking something
assign (verb) to give someone a particular task

Photocopiable activity 9 TB page 156

Comprehension and summary

SB pages 128–129

Money can't buy me love!

This activity serves as an introduction to the two texts on attitudes towards work and money which follow.

Ask students if they know the song *Can't buy me love*, written and sung by The Beatles in 1964.

Conduct a class survey on what students think brings true happiness other than money.

Comprehension Paper 3 Part 5

A This activity aims to encourage students to read through the two texts to find out the main points that are made before looking at the comprehension questions.

Allow students a few minutes to read through the texts and answer the questions.

Check answers as a class.

Key

1 The majority of the population feel work is a necessity, not just to earn more money but also to prevent boredom and meet other people.
2 It shows our characters and our attitudes towards life.
3 She returned to work by using the money to start her own business.
4 He realised he needed to work for the social contact and, more importantly, to avoid getting bored.

B

Key

Text 1
 1 an unhappy workforce, despite earning well
 2 measuring success according to the standards of successive generations
Text 2
 3 working is more important than the money
 4 I'd be bored out of my mind.

Summary writing Paper 3 Part 5

Reporting comments

C Remind students to look carefully at the differences between the two paraphrases before choosing which one is best. Ask them to underline the key phrases in the original comments that are being paraphrased. These are included in the key.

Check answers as a class.

Key

1 b 'we look over our shoulders'
2 a 'knocking ourselves out'
3 a 'bored silly'
4 b 'never had very high outgoings'
5 a 'missed the social interaction'

D Remind students of the steps they followed for previous summaries. See SB page 87.

Listening SB page 130

Big spender!

Introduce the activity by drawing students' attention to the picture and ask them what aspect of shopping it represents. Ask them if they enjoy shopping.

Allow students a few minutes to discuss the three questions in pairs and then ask each pair in turn to present their views for comparison as a class.

Round off the activity by asking students what they understand by the phrase *good value for money* and if they can give any examples of this.

Multiple-choice questions Paper 4 Part 1

A 🎧 Draw students' attention to the *Exam tip* before they begin the listening task.

Ask students to read the questions and options for Extract 1 and then play the recording. Students mark either what they think the correct option might be or what they think can't be correct.

Continue to play the recording for them to check or confirm their choices from the first listening. Repeat this procedure with each extract in turn.

Check answers as a class at the end of each extract.

Key

1 C   2 B   3 C   4 A   5 B   6 B   7 B   8 C

Tapescript

Extract 1

WOMAN Let me explain the 10-point plan, which operates on a scale of one hour.

MAN A plan for selling, you mean?

WOMAN Well, it's more than that. It's a complete strategic approach to the whole business really. If you follow all the points in the plan, *you can almost guarantee a sale in an hour*. The important thing is preparation. First, identify your customer and make sure you prepare all the necessary paperwork. You can't make any kind of successful sale without it. Find out exactly where the customer lives – and before you go, check your appearance.

MAN Sort of smart but casual?

WOMAN Exactly! No way-out, scruffy clothes but not too prosperous either, if you see what I mean! Then – the kit – you must take all the equipment you need for the demonstration … and you must look enthusiastic and smile! *Spend the first two minutes greeting the occupants of the house. This greeting stage is crucial.* And don't prejudge what kind of people they might be. You'd probably be wrong. Of course, you'll hear the usual objections at the door, but just introduce yourself politely and remember to keep smiling.

MAN Fine. I think I've got that!

Extract 2

MAN People are getting bored with trainers. Until a few seasons ago, they were just smelly shoes for sport. But with fashion moving towards formal wear, not just for men, but for women too, *trainers have had to shape up and look luxurious.* This season my collection includes a plush, leather trainer to wear with a suit. The leather soles are wafer-thin, and toes are shaped to a narrow point. Men want an essential style that fits in across the board, from casual to formal. Even the sports trainer isn't what it used to be. This year one well-known sports giant is launching its latest technological revolution. Their new system has thrown out the air pocket altogether and replaced it with four sprung supports in place of a conventional sole. The influence of the trainer among fashion's new shoes still remains strong. You could say that ready-to-wear designers have had their eyes on the trainer ever since it became cool to wear trainers to the office. But with so many designers moving into the futuristic footwear market, *the top sports brands might just have reason to worry!* That's why shoe specialists with the right amount of technical know-how are fighting back!

Extract 3

WOMAN Over the last year or so, many booksellers have sprung up on the Net. The buying is done in a matter of minutes – the time it takes to activate the search engine and make your choice. *Yet surprisingly few readers actually make use of this consumer tool.* It's all the more surprising when you consider the sheer wealth of titles available online. If the book you want is out of print, some firms will consult their network of retail suppliers or their stockists of old titles for you. In 50% of the cases, they'll track it down for you within two months. Whereas your average high street retailer is limited by shelf-space to, say, some 100,000 titles, most Internet sites stock nothing but lists. The book you've ordered is then picked up from the relevant publisher or distributor. 'Are online booksellers a threat to traditional bookshops?' I hear you ask. Not yet. Their weak point is their delivery service. Things have speeded up tremendously recently, however. But like most forms of electronic commerce, book-buying on the Web looks appealing but is not very convincing in practice. For the serious reader, *nothing replaces the pleasure of opening a book at random and falling under the spell of its first few lines*!

Extract 4

MAN My latest song's just succeeded in climbing the charts throughout the world. The scale of this success is a hundred times greater than anything I could have dreamed of. When I first went solo, I bought a few items of basic equipment and started my own studio.
Almost immediately, things started to look up. I was asked to do two songs for the soundtrack of a new film, and the equipment gave a new momentum to my song writing. But only 18 months ago, being on tour meant seven of us in a van, with me taking my turn driving and helping to lug the gear in and out of halls. Now, I've sold out an entire US tour, and it means several trucks, two buses and a crew of more than 30. It's difficult to get my head around – and that's before the financial rewards start to come through, as soon they will. But don't expect to hear songs about how tough it is to be a rich, multi-million-selling star on my follow-up album, which is due later this year. *My feet are still very much on the ground. It's not so long since money was really tight for me,* and nobody much was listening to my music. I haven't forgotten how that felt.

Vocabulary

Homonyms

B Encourage the use of dictionaries for this activity if you wish.

Ask students to consider the meaning of each word as it is used on the recording first. These are marked 🎧 in the key.

Discuss answers as a class.

> **Possible answers**
>
> *smart* well-dressed (adjective) 🎧; clever (adjective); to feel pain (verb)
> *stage* a point or period in a process (noun) 🎧; raised platform on which actors, musicians, etc. perform (noun); to put on a play or perform (verb); to organise and carry out a demonstration or protest (verb)
> *sole* undersurface of foot or shoe (noun) 🎧; the only one (adjective); a type of fish (noun)
> *cool* fashionable (adjective) 🎧; fairly cold (adjective); calm, not friendly (adjective)

charts list of best selling records (noun) 🎧; sea maps (noun); diagram of statistics (noun)
gear equipment (noun) 🎧; mechanism for changing speed in a vehicle (noun); special clothing (noun); possessions (noun)
point Extract 1: a particular stage in a process or time (noun); Extract 2: the thin, sharp end of something (noun); Extract 3: a characteristic or quality of something (noun). Other meanings of *point* are: a particular fact, idea or opinion (noun); to show with a finger (verb); the meaning, purpose or reason of something (noun); the most important part of what is being said (noun); a particular place, position or moment (noun); a single mark in some games or sports (noun);

Business expressions

C Ask students to work in pairs to complete the expressions.

Check answers as a class.

As a follow up, students stay in their pairs and write sentences of their own using four of the expressions.

> **Key**
>
> 1 a good buy   5 out of stock
> 2 to shop around   6 it goes bankrupt
> 3 to break even   7 to buy on credit
> 4 to buy in bulk

Extra vocabulary

See page 176 for ideas on how to exploit this vocabulary.

versatile (adjective) having many different uses or skills
wary (adjective) cautious
trace (verb) to find something by careful looking
accessible (adjective) easily reached, entered, used or understood
envisage (verb) to imagine what will happen in the future
immerse (verb) to become completely involved in something; to put something into a liquid so it is completely covered

Speaking SB page 131

Themed discussion Paper 5 Part 2

A Allow students about 3 minutes to discuss the questions in pairs.

Speculating

B Allow students a few minutes to discuss their responses in their pairs.

Ask each pair to present their views for comparison as a class.

➕ Extra activity

Write these adjectives on the board.

memorable
informative
witty
eye-catching
original
subtle
dramatic
persuasive
appealing

Ask students to work in pairs and choose three of the adjectives to describe what they think a good advertisement should be and say why that adjective is appropriate, e.g. 'A good advertisement should be *subtle* because if it is too obvious people will react against it.'

Allow 5–10 minutes for this and then ask each pair to present their ideas for comparison as a class.

Evaluating

C Remind students to use appropriate phrases for expressing their opinions and politely disagreeing with each other. See the functions boxes on TB pages 21–22.

Explain to students if they are not sure that a *corporate image* is one that a company develops so that people associate that image with the company's products.

Allow students approximately 3 minutes to discuss the pictures in their pairs.

Ask each pair to present their views for comparison as a class.

D Ask students to discuss the meanings of the expressions first and why they might be appropriate or inappropriate as a slogan.

Ask each pair to choose one of the expressions and present to the class why they think it would be the most suitable. Take a vote as a class on the best one if you wish.

Round off the activity by asking students if there are any other expressions with time that they know of which might be suitable. See exercise E, Expressions with time on SB page 26.

Exploring the topic

E Allow students a few minutes to discuss the statements in their pairs.
When they have finished, conduct a class survey on the pros and cons of advertising by asking pairs to present their views and putting them on the board under the two headings.

Writing   SB pages 132–133

A proposal   Paper 2 Part 2

Understanding the task

A

Analysing the sample

B

Writing skills

Describing benefits

C

Writing your proposal

D It might be useful to refer back to the proposal in Unit 1 of the Student's Book, pages 20–21. Ask students to consider what is different and what is similar between this proposal and that in Unit 1. **Possible answer:** the proposal in Unit 1 requires outlining a current situation and making recommendations. This

proposal requires outlining a project and describing the benefits. Both proposals require a formal and impersonal style and should be organised into sections with appropriate headings including an introduction and a conclusion.

Go through each of the stages in turn, discuss questions and brainstorm ideas as a class.

Unit 9 Overview key

SB pages 134–135

Vocabulary Test Unit 9 TB page 134

10 Taking liberties

▶ *See unit summary on page 4.*

Exam training in this unit

Reading	Multiple-choice questions
Use of English	Key word transformations
	Comprehension and summary: avoiding repetition
Listening	Multiple-choice questions
Speaking	Themed discussion
Writing	An essay: organising paragraphs

Ask students what they understand by the expression *taking liberties*. Explain that the expression means behaving in an excessively familiar way or doing something you are not authorised to do. The overall theme of the unit is civil liberties and the law.

Reading SB pages 136–138

Rights and wrongs

Ask students what play on words is used in this title. The *rights and wrongs* of an issue are the moral questions associated with it. In the context of the unit theme, *rights* has the meaning of a moral entitlement.

1 Allow students a few minutes to decide which of the three rights they consider to be the most important.

Compare choices as a class.

Conduct a class survey, if you wish, to find out which rights students consider to be the most important and which the least.

Ask students why they consider some of these rights to be more important than others.

2 Elicit examples from students as a class. Ask them why people have been deprived of some of these rights and whether it is ever justifiable.

Multiple-choice questions Paper 1 Part 2

A This activity aims to encourage students to read through the four texts to get a general idea of the overall theme or topic that connects them.
Allow students a few minutes to read through the texts.

Discuss answers as a class.

Ask them to consider whether the texts refer to a national or international situation and whether they represent a personal or collective view.

> **Key**
>
> All four texts relate to the theme of oppression or freedom from oppression.

B Before they begin the exercise remind students that a careful reading of both the question stem and the options is required (see SB page 25).

Check answers as a class.

> **Key**
>
> 1 C 2 A 3 C 4 D 5 A 6 A 7 D 8 B

Comprehension

C Remind students that an understanding and an awareness of the purpose and style of the texts is important, as this is one of the skills tested in the multiple-choice questions.

Ask them to find examples of the styles in each text.

Discuss answers as a class.

> **Key**
>
> 1 Text 1
> The purpose of the text is to make people aware of the situation and to explain the intentions of Amnesty International.
> The style is neutral and direct, almost like a list, and suitable for presenting the information clearly, e.g. 'Some are imprisoned because', 'Some are arrested because'
> Text 2
> The purpose of the text is to give a vivid description of the loss of basic human values in extreme circumstances.
> It is written in a narrative / descriptive style and expresses the writer's personal feelings, e.g. 'you were concentrating on yourself and your own survival', 'How fast man changes!', 'a parade of the selfish and the dying'
> Text 3
> The purpose of the text is to create a positive picture of human cooperation and a sense of optimism.
> The style is descriptive and personal and involves the reader in the events, e.g. 'It was an intensely intimate state of almost childlike marvel', 'I doubt if

any of us will ever be privileged enough to experience something like that again'

Text 4
The purpose of the text is to give a legal definition of universal human rights.
The style is very formal and suitable for an official document which has authority in law, e.g. 'proclaims', 'rights and freedoms set forth', 'to secure their universal and effective recognition and observance'

2 Text 1 describes injustice and repression and promotes opposition to it.
Text 2 depicts human cruelty and selfishness when faced with the need to survive.
Text 3 gives a sense of shared experience and a capacity to overcome oppression peacefully.
Text 4 advocates human cooperation and mutual respect.

Vocabulary

D This activity focuses on the meaning of the words in context.

Check answers as a class.

Key

1	publicise	5	repression
2	diverse	6	dim
3	hobbled	7	strive
4	sheds	8	jurisdiction

Expressions with *free*

E Check answers to the matching exercise before students complete the sentences.

Key

1 i 2 b 3 f 4 a 5 g
6 j 7 h 8 e 9 d 10 c

Ask students to read through the sentences before they choose the correct expression.

Check answers as a class.

Key

1	free of charge	6	free-for-all
2	free from	7	given free rein
3	free and easy	8	made free with
4	in free fall	9	Free speech
5	free as a bird	10	free with her criticism

Extra vocabulary

See page 176 for ideas on how to exploit this vocabulary

proclaim (verb) to publicly and officially tell people about something important
endowed (adjective) born with or naturally have a particular quality
entitled (adjective) to have the right to do or have something
scrawny (adjective) unattractively thin, skinny
atrocious (adjective) very bad or unpleasant
insolence (noun) rude behaviour showing a lack of respect
intimate (adjective) close friendly relationship, very private and personal
mainstream (noun) the normal and accepted ideas and opinions
ultimate (adjective) final, main, most important

Language in use

SB pages 139–141

The jury's out

The expression *The jury's out* means that the jury have left the court and that their decision is being awaited. However, it is often used in other contexts to suggest that a conflict of opinions has not been resolved. Before you begin the activity, make sure students know what each of the crimes are.

Key

blackmail	demanding money from a person by threatening to reveal secrets about them
manslaughter	the crime of killing someone illegally but not intentionally
libel	a false statement that damages someone's reputation
arson	the crime of deliberately setting fire to something in order to cause damage
reckless driving	driving in such a way that other people's lives are threatened
fraud	deceiving someone in order to obtain money or goods illegally
forgery	the crime of making a copy of something in order to deceive people

In small groups, students discuss the questions. Explain that, for question 1, they can decide on how long a jail sentence should be and how much a fine should be.

Compare answers as a class.

To extend the discussion, ask students what crimes appear regularly in the media. This may vary from country to country. If students are all from the same country, ask them why certain crimes feature in the media more than others.

Structure

Gerunds and infinitives

A Students read the text, then discuss the questions with their partners.

After some discussion, refer them to SB page 180.

Ask them if they found anything surprising in the jury's decision.

> ❏ **Alternative activity**
> Before students refer to SB page 180, you can conduct a class survey, with students voting *yes* / *no* or *guilty* / *not guilty* on questions 1 and 2, giving their reasons based on what they read in the text.

B This activity requires students to identify the use of gerund forms in a variety of contexts. Ask students to underline the examples in the text.

Check answers as a class.

> **Key**
>
> 1 without reporting
> 2 not stopped driving
> 3 his shooting

C This activity requires students to identify the use of infinitive forms in a variety of contexts. Ask students to underline the examples in the text.

> **Key**
>
> 1 could not get over
> 2 Owen let the event take over
> 3 unable to lead a normal life
> 4 Owen claimed to have fired
> 5 advised them to concentrate on
> 6 any intent to kill

D This exercise practises the different gerund or infinitive structures identified in B and C.

Check answers as a class and refer to structures in B and C.

> **Key**
>
> 1 giving (gerund after a preposition)
> 2 to see (infinitive after a verb)
> 3 trying (gerund after an adjective)
> 4 stay (infinitive without *to* after verb + object)
> 5 to use (infinitive after verb + object)
> 6 travelling (gerund after a verb)
> 7 to see (infinitive after an adjective)
> 8 to develop (infinitive after a noun)
> 9 to improve (infinitive after a noun)
> 10 singing (gerund after adjective and/or possessive pronoun)

E Discuss answers as a class.

> **Key**
>
> 1 to ensure   2 only to discover

F Remind students that they can use *only to do* or *to do* as in the examples in E. Ask them to consider whether they want to express a purpose or a result.

Students compare sentences in pairs.

Ask for a few example sentences from the class. Accept any answers that seem reasonable.

> **Suggested answers**
>
> 1 We came back from our two week holiday, only to find that that our house had been burgled.
>   We came back from our two week holiday to help care for our ill grandparents.
> 2 She studied hard, only to discover that the exam was cancelled.
>   She studied hard to pass her exams.
> 3 He entered parliament at the age of 19, only to be voted out before he reached 25.
>   He entered parliament at the age of 19 to represent the people of Northampton.
> 4 I phoned the airline to find that the offices were closed.
>   I phoned the airline to confirm my flight.
> 5 Emily opened the letter to discover that it was from her boyfriend.
>   Emily opened the letter to find out whether she had won the competition.

G This exercise focuses on the change of meaning between using a gerund or an infinitive after certain verbs.

Students put the verb in each sentence into the right form first.

Check the answers and discuss the changes in meaning as a class.

Key

1. a to say
   I regret to say is used as a formal way of breaking bad news.
   b saying
   I regret doing something indicates that the speaker wishes that he/she hadn't done it.
2. a to win
   When you *try to do something* it implies that achieving that action is the objective.
   b cleaning
   If you *try doing something* it implies that it might help you achieve another final objective, in this case, starting the car.
3. a seeing
   If you *remember doing something*, you have a memory of something that happened before.
   b to send
   If you *remember to do something*, first you realise that you need to do it, then you perform the action.
4. a to talk
   To go on to do something means to do something after completing something else.
   b talking
   To go on doing something means to continue doing it.
5. seeing
   If you *never forget doing something*, then you always have a memory of what happened.
   b to lock
   If you *forget to do something*, then you don't do it, even though you should.
6. a to have
   If you *stop to do something*, then you end an activity to do something else.
   b going out
   If you *stop doing something*, then the action stopped and did not continue.
7. a to think
   I dread to think is an expression used to indicate that the consequences of something are too horrible to imagine.
   b having
   If you *dread doing something*, then you are not looking forward to doing it.
8. a to send
   If you *mean to do something*, then you have an intention to do it.
   b being away
   If an event *means doing something*, then it implies that the event brings about an obligation to perform certain actions.

Key word transformations   Paper 3 Part 4

H   Some infinitive and gerund structures are practised in this exercise.

Check answers as a class by asking students to read out the whole sentence.

Key

1. is no point in appealing
2. intention of giving up the fight
3. paid no attention to what
4. prevented the jury (from) reaching
5. the last patient / the last patient to be called / the last to be called
6. showed no remorse for
7. put a stop to the games
8. to keep on campaigning against the delivery

Extra vocabulary

See page 176 for ideas on how to exploit this vocabulary.

revert (verb) to return to a former state
curtailment (noun) a limitation or restriction of something
contravene (verb) to go against a law
portray (verb) to give a picture of something, describing in a particular way
verdict (noun) a decision made in a court of law
remorse (noun) feeling of regret or being extremely sorry
stubborn (adjective) determined not to change your opinion
pre-meditated (adjective) thought about or planned beforehand
entail (verb) to involve something that cannot be avoided
condolence (noun) an expression of sympathy over a death

Comprehension and summary

SB pages 142–143

Behind bars

Ask what the expression *behind bars* is intended to suggest. The expression is used to describe being in prison and alludes to the fact that windows in prisons are often made more secure with metal bars.

Allow students a few minutes to discuss the questions in small groups.
Ask each group to present their ideas for comparison as a class.

You could extend the discussion by asking them also to consider what the purpose of prison is, whether it should be for punishment or for rehabilitation.

Comprehension Paper 3 Part 5

Background notes

The Court of Appeal is a special court where a formal request to change a judgement or decision is made.

The High Court is the highest court of law which covers all civil and some criminal cases. The court has 80 or so judges who make decisions on cases individually without a jury.

A *ruling* is a decision made by a judge or court that has the force of law.

Lord and *Mr Justice* are titles held by High Court judges.

The *Home Office* is the government department that deals with the administration of the law.

A *solicitor* is a person trained in legal matters who advises clients on their cases and often acts for them in court.

Tagging refers to an alternative punishment to jail in which the convicted person has to wear a small electronic device, known as a tag, so that their movements can be monitored.

A This activity aims to encourage students to read through both texts to get an overall idea of their content before attempting the comprehension questions.

When students have read through both texts, check answers as a class.

> **Key**
>
> Both texts mention court cases in which mothers have won the right to keep their children with them in prison beyond the age of 18 months. Both texts discuss the rights and wrongs of this situation.

B Remind students that they should keep their answers as brief as possible.

Check answers as a class.

> **Key**
>
> Text 1
>   1 to emphasise the possibility of large numbers of similar cases occurring as a consequence
>   2 stringent, rigid
> Text 2
>   3 unprecedented
>   4 alternative punishments, specifically tagging.

C Students discuss the question from both the point of view of the child's welfare and the mother's rights. Allow a few minutes for discussion.

Ask each pair to present their views to the class for comparison.

Summary skills Paper 3 Part 5

D Remind students that it is important that they consider how the phrases are used in the text before paraphrasing as the meaning is often dependent on the context. Ask them to consider what the phrases refer to.

Students compare their paraphrases with a partner.

Check answers as a class.

> **Key**
>
> Text 1
>   1 change its attitude towards
>   2 went against their entitlement
>   3 protecting the well-being
>   4 not dealt with strictly enough
>   5 have not been discussed or considered
> Text 2
>   1 won a case
>   2 monitored
>   3 given special favours
>   4 picking up prison slang
>   5 possibly damaging

E Draw students' attention to the *Exam tip* before they begin the activity.

Ask them to underline the repeated information first.

> **Key**
>
> Repeated information: separating children from their mothers, producing catastrophic ~~effects~~ results

Students rewrite the paragraph in pairs or compare their own rewrites with a partner.

> **Sample answer**
>
> Firstly, separating children over the age of eighteen months from their mothers would go against the mothers' entitlements under the European Convention on Human Rights. Secondly, taking a baby from either its mother or main carer for any length of time can have seriously damaging effects on the welfare of both. (51 words)

G Remind students of the steps they followed for previous summaries (see SB page 49).

Sample summary

Firstly, allowing mothers involved with drugs to keep their children in jail would give the public a false impression that the jail system is not strict enough. Furthermore, it may cause resentment among other prisoners who feel the mother is getting special favours. Finally, it is harmful to the children because they become aware of their surroundings and start to learn prison slang. (63 words)

Listening SB page 144

A fair trial?

Background notes
The statue in the picture represents justice and is part of the Old Bailey, a famous court in London.

1 Elicit suggestions from students. The scales represent fairness and equal treatment for all and the sword represents punishment or retribution.

2 If possible, put students from different countries together and ask them to explain their legal systems to each other. If students are all from the same country, ask them to work in small groups to consider how they would explain their legal system to a foreigner.

Allow a few minutes for this and then compare answers as a class.

3 Students discuss this question in small groups. Ask them to explain why they feel confident or not.

Multiple-choice questions Paper 4 Part 3

A 🎧 Before they begin the listening task, remind students to read through the questions and the options carefully before they listen. Remind them also to use the second listening to change or confirm their initial answers.

After playing the recording the first time, allow students some time to think about their answers.

Continue to play the recording a second time.

Ask students to compare answers with a partner.

Check answers as a class.

Key

1 B   2 A   3 A   4 C   5 D

Tapescript

INTERVIEWER Today in the studio we have Dr Lafford from the Forensic Science Service, who is here to tell us a little more about forensic science …

DR LAFFORD Good morning.

INTERVIEWER Now, I think most people have a fairly good general picture of the kind of work you do – in many ways it's a development of Sherlock Holmes and his magnifying glass, isn't it?

DR LAFFORD Yes, you could put it that way, although we've come a long way since then of course, but Holmes was very much a detective of the modern age – of course he was an intelligent man and his medical knowledge often seemed better than that of his companion Dr Watson, and certainly his observations were always very detailed … but what sets him apart is that *Holmes provides us with a good model – a very good model in fact – of the kind of approach – psychological approach – that a forensic scientist should have, and that is that the forensic scientist is absolutely impartial.*

INTERVIEWER So, you're not strictly speaking part of the police force … ?

DR LAFFORD No, we are quite separate.

INTERVIEWER Could you tell us a little about your work and what it is you do?

DR LAFFORD Well the basic principle behind forensic science is that every contact leaves a trace. Wherever we go, whatever we touch, material is transferred both ways. The shoe that leaves a mark on the ground also picks up traces of dirt, and the hand that makes a fingerprint also carries away particles from the object that was handled … and things like hair or carpet fibres are easily passed from one person to another.

INTERVIEWER *I see, so it's not just that the suspect leaves clues at the scene of the crime, the scene of the crime leaves clues on the suspect …*

DR LAFFORD Absolutely, and that is normally the most compelling evidence – not just when you have a fingerprint, for example, but also where you've found traces of, say, the carpet at the scene of a crime on the suspect's clothing, and that, of course, can be very hard to explain away.

INTERVIEWER Is your work fairly straightforward – a question of seeing whether various samples match up?

DR LAFFORD No, no, no, not at all … *forensic science is often a very painstaking task – and very time-consuming – much more so than previously, in fact, because the range of tests has mushroomed* … for example, we might be given some pieces of a headlight swept up after a hit-and-run accident and asked to identify the car, so we would fit the thousands of pieces together like a vast jigsaw, and might be able to identify the number embossed on the back of the glass ... that would help us identify the model of the car, the make, the age, and so on, making it easier to search for the suspect ... and then, once the car was located, we could tell whether the lights had been on at the time of the accident by examining the light bulb, because there would be minute pieces of molten glass on the metal filament in the bulb ...

INTERVIEWER So you need some fairly sophisticated equipment as well as patience ...

DR LAFFORD Indeed. Now, the electron microscope is invaluable in our line of work – and it basically does two things – it gives us a fantastically detailed image, so, for example, you can tell whether a piece of hair has been broken, or cut with a pair of scissors or a knife. And *it can also give you the chemical composition of a sample*, so that you can take, perhaps, a tiny flake of paint on a suspect's clothing and match it with paint at the scene of the crime.

INTERVIEWER Are you at the stage then where you could say that the evidence that you provide is foolproof?

DR LAFFORD No, not foolproof. There is always room for human error and there's nothing that can be done about that ... *forensics is not an absolute science* – I mean, let me give you an example. Now, Sherlock Holmes might have found a strand of hair at the scene of a crime, perhaps black and two inches long, that would have helped him identify the murderer on the basis that the hair matched the murderer's. Now, we also examine hair ... but in the example I gave you, perhaps one person in twenty has black hair two inches long, so we need to improve on this analysis to narrow down the number of suspects. So, we would analyse the strand of hair ... using the electron microscope, as I was saying earlier ... look at its chemical composition, whether it came from a man or a woman, see how it was cut, whether it showed any traces of particular chemicals and so on, and in that way, instead of saying that one person in twenty had hair like that, it might be one person in 500,000 or a million. *That would be just about as far as we could go. Now there's no such thing as certainty ... just a balance of probability, even with the most advanced techniques of genetic fingerprinting.* The evidence we provide is there to be interpreted, and that's very important.

INTERVIEWER Well, Dr Lafford, thank you very much. We'll take a break now, but stay with us and we'll be back ...

Vocabulary

Expressions connected with the law

B Remind students to read the sentences first and then choose an expression that they think best fits in with the meaning of the sentence as a whole.

Check answers as a class.

> **Key**
>
> 1 the letter of the law
> 2 lay down the law
> 3 above the law
> 4 the law of the jungle
> 5 take the law into his own hands
> 6 a law unto himself

➕ Extra activity
Write the following phrases on the board.

> to be acquitted
> to be put on trial
> to be found guilty
> to be arrested
> to be found innocent
> to be accused of
> to be sentenced to
> to be charged with
> to be convicted

Ask students to work in pairs to describe the legal process by putting the phrases in the right order.

Remind them to use the nouns *crime* and *prison*, and link the stages with *first*, *then*, *following this* and *if*.

Allow them 5 minutes to do this and check answers by asking each pair to read out its description.

Key
First you are arrested and then charged with a crime. Following this, you are put on trial where you are accused of the crime. If you are found innocent, you are acquitted but if you are found guilty, you are convicted and sentenced to prison.

Speaking SB page 145

Themed discussion Paper 5 Part 2

A Before students begin the activity, elicit examples of laws connected with civil liberties and put them on the board. If students have difficulties, refer to the list on SB page 136.

Allow students a few minutes to discuss the questions in their pairs. Ask them to consider in what circumstances laws on civil liberties could be changed.

Ask each pair to present its ideas to the class for comparison.

Speculating

B Allow students a few minutes to discuss the question in pairs.

Each pair presents its views to the class for comparison.

Evaluating images

C Allow each pair a few minutes to discuss the pictures and then ask them to compare their ideas with another pair.

Finish the activity by getting a class consensus on the effectiveness of the images.

◻ Alternative activity
Write these phrases on the board and encourage students to use them during their discussion
very / quite effective in that
gets / doesn't get its message across well
not really very effective at all because
it makes a point about … very well

Suggesting alternatives

D Ask students to remain in their pairs and to agree on at least two additional images. Remind them that they can use ideas from their discussion in part A.

See TB page 21 for phrases students can use for making suggestions.

Allow a few minutes for discussion, then ask each pair to present its ideas to the class for comparison.

Exploring the topic

E Students discuss the question in small groups. Ask students to consider whether there are circumstances in which laws on civil liberties may be suspended. Ask them to give examples, e.g. *There are cases where …, In the event of …, In certain circumstances …*

Compare opinions as a class.

Photocopiable activity 10 TB page 156

Writing SB pages 146–147

An essay Paper 2 Part 1

Understanding the task

A Ask students to read the sample question and then decide which of the two formats are required.

> **Key**
>
> Format 2
> Remind students that the first format was dealt with on SB pages 176–177.

Analysing the sample

B Check the questions as a class.

> **Key**
>
> 1
> | | |
> |---|---|
> | Paragraph 1 | Introduction |
> | Paragraph 2 | Analysis of the causes |
> | Paragraph 3 | Suggestions for solutions |
> | Paragraph 4 | Conclusion |
>
> 2
> Lead sentence: This states the necessity of finding out the causes of the rise in crime.
> Cause 1: A poor social environment can lead to feelings of alienation, frustration and anger.
> Cause 2: Inadequate education can lead to feelings of failure and boredom and the possibility of being open to bad influences.
> Cause 3: The absence of loving parents may lead to a child not developing a sense of responsibility and consideration.
>
> 3 There is a lead sentence which introduces an overall solution followed by specific solutions to causes 1, 2 and 3 in the same order as they are presented in the second paragraph.
>
> 4
> | | |
> |---|---|
> | Paragraph 2 | Firstly, Secondly, Finally |
> | Paragraph 3 | First of all, In addition, And lastly |

✚ Extra activity
Elicit from students other phrases they could use to sequence their points in the paragraphs.

Possible answers
To begin with …
Besides this, …
Another factor to consider is …
Furthermore …

Writing skills

Organising paragraphs

C Ask students to work in pairs to do the activity. Check the arrangement of notes before they write out the sentences in full, making sure the suggested solutions in the second paragraph follow the same order as the problems mentioned in the first. Encourage the use of the linking phrases from question 4 in B and remind students that they will need to add to the notes to expand them into full sentences.

Key

First paragraph

Lead sentence	Truancy a complex problem – different causes.
Problem 1	Students lack parental support – communication problems between parents and school.
Problem 2	Students bored – curriculum not relevant or stimulating.

Second paragraph

Lead sentence	How to combat truancy? – solve underlying causes
Solution 1	Encourage parental participation – parent's evenings, more communication, homework.
Solution 2	Make lessons more relevant, interesting etc; more resources and teacher training.

Sample paragraphs

Truancy is not something new and nowadays has become a complex problem which has several different causes. Firstly, students often lack proper parental support, and this has led to communication problems between the parents themselves and schools. Secondly, students are becoming bored at school largely because the curriculum they are obliged to follow is no longer relevant or stimulating to them.

The answer to the question of how to combat truancy lies in finding solutions to the underlying causes. First of all, parents should be encouraged to participate as much as they can in their children's schools. This can be done through organising parents' evenings, which will encourage more communication between teachers and parents, and by asking parents to take an interest in helping their children with their homework. In addition, lessons could be made more interesting and relevant to the students by investing in more resources for the school such as up-to-date books and videos, and by developing teacher training so that teachers can motivate the students better.

Writing your essay

D Ask students to read through the exam question first.

Go through each of the stages in turn and discuss questions or brainstorm ideas as a class.

Draw students' attention to the *Exam tip*. Ask them to refer to the sample essay for examples of an impersonal style.

Unit 10 Overview key

SB pages 148–149

Lexical cloze Paper 1 Part 1

A

1 A	2 D	3 A	4 C	5 B	6 B
7 D	8 C	9 B	10 C	11 C	12 D

Word formation Paper 3 Part 2

B

1	essentially	6	unnatural
2	tendency	7	pairing
3	intrusion	8	dramatic / dramatised
4	distinctly	9	intellectual
5	namely	10	accessible

Key word transformations Paper 3 Part 4

C

1 it will mean leaving early
2 there was no point in trying
3 was unwilling to lend me
4 has no intention of resigning
5 died without finishing
6 forget seeing the Pyramids for
7 have been in free fall
8 seemed to show / have no remorse over / about

Vocabulary Test Unit 10 TB page 135

11 That's entertainment

▶ *See unit summary on page 4.*

Exam training in this unit

Reading	Gapped text
Use of English	Gapped sentences: finding the missing word from different possibilities
	Comprehension and summary: understanding the force of lexical items, eliminating irrelevance
Listening	Sentence completion: spelling
Speaking	Extended speaking: exploring the topic
Writing	A review: creating interest

The overall theme of this unit is entertainment and leisure.

Reading SB pages 150–152

The silver screen

The silver screen is a term used to refer to the cinema in general.

1 Students discuss the statements in pairs. Allow a few minutes for this, then compare opinions as a class.

Extend the discussion by asking what other influences may have been stronger on people's lives, what the advantages of video might be over the cinema, and what examples could be given of a decline in the quality of films.

2 Discuss students' interpretation of the phrase as a class. *A slice of life* refers to films being a short representation of real life whereas *a piece of cake* refers to something being very easy to do. The quotation plays on the words *slice* and *piece*.

Gapped text Paper 1 Part 3

A Remind students to look for referencing pronouns and phrases in both the article and the 7 paragraphs that can help them decide where in the article the paragraphs should go. Paragraph A can be used as an example. Students find words and phrases that refer to something mentioned before ('A *further* blow') or which indicate the time ('after the war').

Check answers as a class.

> **Key**
>
> 1 G 2 C 3 D 4 A 5 H 6 B 7 E

B Students work in pairs to find information in the article that will answer the two questions.

Check answers as a class.

> **Key**
>
> 1 Competition from foreign films and television.
>   Falling audiences due to demographic changes as people moved away from the cities.
>   Government legislation to reduce the monopoly the studios had on distribution.
>   The cost of new technology.
> 2 Building new cinemas such as drive-ins and multiplexes to serve the needs of people who had moved away from the cities.
>   Investing in new technology such as Technicolour, widescreen effects and multi-track stereo sound to make their films more spectacular.

Your views

C Discuss the two questions as a class.

Extend the discussion by asking students to describe some films recently made in their countries and to say how successful they have been and by asking them to give examples of how computer technology has changed the cinema.

Vocabulary

Complementation

D Students match words 1–12 with their complements a–l first, then check with the text.

Check answers as a class.

> **Key**
>
> 1 f 2 h 3 b 4 g 5 d 6 e 7 c 8 a
> 9 i 10 j 11 l 12 k

E Students find the adjectives in the text first and try to guess the meaning from the context before they use a dictionary.

Check answers as a class.

Expressions with colours

F Check answers as a class, focusing on the explanations.

➕ Extra activity

Ask students what expressions with colours exist in their language and what their meanings are. Ask students what emotions they associate with the colours red, blue and green.

Extra vocabulary

See page 176 for ideas on how to exploit this vocabulary.

usurp (verb) to replace by taking away power

prestige (noun) status gained through respect and admiration

outlay (noun) money spent in starting a new project, investment

up in arms (expression) expressing angry opposition to something

culmination (noun) the highest point or end of something

watershed (noun) a crucial point in the development of something

oblivious (adjective) completely unaware of something

surge (verb) to suddenly and forcefully move

Language in use

SB pages 153–155

Don't stand on ceremony!

Don't stand on ceremony is a phrase used to request that somebody behave in a relaxed and informal manner.

Background notes

Annual university balls are held at universities in Britain either in the spring or at the end of the academic year. Students are required to wear very formal dress for the occasion and purchase a ticket, which is often very expensive.

DJ is short for dinner jacket, a black jacket with silk lapels worn with black trousers and a black bow tie on formal occasions.

Structure

Uses of *have* and *get*

A Students read the text and discuss their answers in groups.

Compare answers as a class.

On the board, write a list of preparations for the formal events they mention in response to question 2.

The causative use of *have* and *get*

B

Other uses of *have* and *get*

C

D   Remind students that all the forms discussed in B and C above are practised in this exercise.

Check answers as a class.

E   Ask students to make a list of preparations using *have / get* for each of the three situations.

➕ Extra activity

Students look back at their answers to *Don't stand on ceremony* question 2 and try to express their ideas using the structure *have / get something done.*

Inversions

F

G

H This exercise practises the use of inversions with negative adverbials.

Check answers as a class, focusing on accuracy with word order.

Gapped sentences Paper 3 Part 3

I Remind students to read all three sentences for the context and to decide what type of word fits into the space. This will always be the same part of speech.

Draw students' attention to the *Exam tip* and the example and then apply the same procedure to each of the sentences in the exercise.

Check answers as a class.

Extra vocabulary

See page 176 for ideas on how to exploit this vocabulary.

frayed (adjective) worn around the edges
infuriating (adjective) extremely annoying
dreadful (adjective) extremely bad
abrasion (noun) damage to surface caused by rubbing

Photocopiable activity 11 TB page 157

Comprehension and summary

SB pages 156–157

The perks of the job

The perks of a job are something extra you receive in addition to your wages. These could include free flights for people who work for an airline company or a free car for company executives. If your students work, ask them whether their jobs include any perks.

The pictures show different forms of corporate entertainment. Students discuss the questions, then compare answers as a class.

Other examples of corporate entertainment include: meals at expensive restaurants, tickets to major sporting events, cocktail parties or lavish receptions, and weekend holidays.

Ask students whether they approve or disapprove of such expensive forms of corporate entertainment.

Comprehension   Paper 3 Part 5

Background notes

PR is an abbreviation for public relations, the department of a company that deals with its public image.

Journos is a colloquial abbreviation for journalists.

A *freebie* is a colloquial expression for something given away free of charge.

The Cairngorms are a mountain range in Scotland.

The Channel refers to the English Channel, an area of sea between Britain and France.

The *Solent* is a part of the English Channel near the Isle of Wight.

A   This activity focuses on students' understanding of style.

Allow students a few minutes to read both texts.

Discuss answers as a class. Ask students to give examples from the texts.

Key

Both texts are written in an informal, conversational style, which is often humourous or ironic. Both use a lot of descriptive language to convey the writers' feelings and reactions and are highly personal.

Understanding the force of lexical items

B   This activity focuses on how writers choose particular expressions to indicate their attitude. This is often tested in the comprehension questions.
There are two activities on connotation in Unit 6 (See SB page 87)

Remind students to consider how the phrases are used in the texts and what they refer to. Stress that they have to explain the impression created by the use of these phrases, not just what they mean.

Discuss answers as a class.

Key

Text 1
1   This refers to the flight and creates an impression of ease and comfort.
2   These two verbs describe the light on the sea and the snow and create an impression of a clear, bright day.
3   This refers to how the writer was eating the food and creates an impression of eating large amounts of it with a sense of pleasure.
4   This refers to the food itself and creates an impression of it being delicious and a pleasure to eat.

Text 2
5   The writer uses a nautical metaphor to create an impression of other people being willing to take the writer's place on the trip. A 'wake' is the track left in the water's surface by a moving boat.
6   This refers to the writer's initial attempts at sailing and creates an impression of inexperience or lack of skill.
7   This refers to how the boat was sailing and creates an impression of effortless, smooth movement.
8   This refers to the meal and creates an impression of enjoyment and satisfaction.

C   Remind students that they should keep their answers as brief as possible.

Check answers as a class.

Key

Text 1
1   how shall I put it?
2   to be ironic about his / her total change of attitude towards the trip

Text 2
1   to indicate that the writer's reservations were short-lived
2   There's no sense of mystery or adventure any more.

D   Discuss the question as a class.

Key

In order to engage the reader on a more personal level. It creates a sense that they are speaking directly to the reader.

Summary writing Paper 3 Part 5

Eliminating irrelevance

Ask students to consider whether parts of the summary refer directly to the writers' reactions.

When they have finished, ask them to compare what they have crossed out with a partner.

Check answers as a class.

> **Sample summary**
>
> Despite some initial reluctance, based on jealousy and a suspicion of unnecessary extravagance, both writers seemed either flattered or eager to accept the corporate hospitality they were offered. Although neither writer professed to be an expert in the activities they were invited to take part in, they were both aware that they would never have experienced these activities otherwise. (59 words)

✚ Extra activity

Ask students to look back at the two texts on corporate entertainment again and find the following nouns being used as verbs:
thread spoon crew mirror
Discuss with students how the meaning of the noun is reflected in its use as a verb in each context.
Write these common nouns on the board:
pencil picture table pocket handle plant label chair ship scale

Students work in groups to write examples of how these nouns can be used as verbs. Allow 5 minutes for them to write as many examples as they can. Encourage the use of dictionaries. This can be done competitively with the pair or group finding the most examples winning.

Possible answers

to pencil a date in your diary or to pencil in a provisional arrangement
to picture something in your mind
to table a motion at a meeting
to pocket some money in order to keep it for yourself
to handle or deal with a difficult situation or person
to plant a bomb or a suspicion in someone's mind
to label someone as something, e.g he was labelled as a liar
to chair a meeting, e.g to act as a chairman
to ship goods, meaning to transport them
to scale the heights of success or to scale something down, i.e. to reduce it

Extra vocabulary

See page 176 for ideas on how to exploit this vocabulary.

soothing (adjective) relaxing and comforting
renowned (adjective) well-known
alacrity (noun) great willingness or enthusiasm
deft (adjective) skillful and quick

Listening SB page 158

Sugar and spice and all things nice

According to a nursery rhyme, girls are made of *sugar and spice and all things nice*, while boys are made of *frogs and snails and puppy dogs' tails*.

Draw students' attention to the pictures and ask them whether they have eaten Indian food and what they thought of it.

When students have finished discussing the questions in pairs, compare answers as a class.

If students are all from the same country, ask them to describe what they consider to be their national dishes.

Sentence completion Paper 4 Part 2

Background notes
Chicken tikka masala is a type of curry dish.
Tandoori is an Indian method of cooking meat on a metal rod in a clay oven.
The *Raj* refers to the period of colonial occupation of India by the British.
The subcontinent refers to the Indian subcontinent which includes Bangladesh, Bhutan, India, Nepal, Pakistan, and Sri Lanka.

A 🎧 Draw students' attention to the *Exam tip* before they begin the listening task.

Remind students that they should read through the sentences carefully before they listen and try to predict what might fit in the gaps.

After playing the recording the first time, allow students some time to think about their answers.

Continue to play the recording a second time.

Ask students to compare answers with a partner.

Check answers as a class.

Tapescript

PRESENTER In Britain we spend £26 million a week in Indian restaurants and eat 25 million portions of chicken tikka masala a year. Pat Chapman, author of the Cobra Good Curry Guide and founder of the Curry Club, is the presenter of our food programme today.

PAT CHAPMAN *When Emperor Napoleon failed to capture the British Isles, he dismissed us as a nation of shopkeepers.* Were he around today, he might observe that we are now a nation of curry-house keepers. *Curry is now a national obsession.* But, surprisingly, it wasn't until the twilight of the Raj that Britain's first Indian restaurant, Veeraswamy, opened in 1926 in London's Piccadilly. Such is the popularity of curry that it is still there, but this was very nearly not the case. By 1950, there were just six curry restaurants in the whole of Britain. Curry hadn't really caught on, and it might never have done so *had it not been for the chronic labour shortage caused by the nation's new-found, post-war prosperity.* It was solved by bringing in immigrant labour from the West Indies and the subcontinent. *The Indians, finding Britain to be a spice desert, soon made arrangements to import their beloved spices and foodstuffs.* It wasn't long before enterprising Indians invested in restaurants to offer Indian food to the indigenous British population. It was a revelation to a nation who considered garlic a suspicious item. *Not only was curry addictive but it was, above all, affordable.* In just four decades, Britain became besotted with curry. Today, there is scarcely a town without its 'Indian'. The total in the UK is a staggering 8,000 and they still continue to open and expand. We still, erroneously, refer to our curry restaurants as 'Indian'. In fact, over 85% are Bangladeshi-owned, with only 8% run by Indians and *8% by Pakistanis.* Interestingly, many of our 'Indian' restaurants still operate to a formula that was pioneered in the late 1940s. A way had to be found to deliver a variety of curries from order to table, without unreasonable delay. *Authentic Indian recipes require hours of cooking in individual pots, and there was no guarantee that they would ever be ordered.* So, cubed meat, chicken or potatoes and vegetables were lightly curried and chilled, and a large pot of thick curry gravy, a

kind of master stock, was brewed to medium strength. *To this day, portion by portion, on demand, these ingredients are reheated by pan-frying them with further flavourings.* In this way, one cook can knock up several dishes within minutes. *Rice is pre-cooked, breads and tandoori items made to order by a different specialist,* and, hey presto, your order! The menu can be very long, and any dish is available with meat, poultry, prawns, king prawns and most vegetables, too. This is still the formula of the standard British curry house. However, it is clear that, judging by the many new restaurants which seem to appear almost daily, and the selection which appear in the Good Curry Guide, – curry is a-changing!

Vocabulary

Expressions connected with food, drink and eating

B Introduce the activity by asking students whether there are any expressions connected with food and eating in their language. Ask them to explain to the class what they mean.

Students read through the nine sentences first, trying to guess the meaning of the expressions, before they choose an appropriate one from the list.

Check answers as a class. The expression *a finger in every pie* is illustrated.

> ❏ **Alternative activity**
> To round off the activity ask students to choose 2 of the expressions they like best and use them in sentences of their own.

Spelling

C This activity focuses on several aspects of English spelling that often give students difficulties. Students work in small groups to find the errors and correct them.

Check answers as a class.

Extra vocabulary

See page 176 for ideas on how to exploit this vocabulary.
cliché (noun) a phrase or idea that has been overused
chronic (adjective) a bad condition that lasts for a long time
besotted with (adjective) obsessed with
erroneously (adverb) wrongly

Speaking SB page 159

A Students discuss the questions in pairs.

Compare answers as a class.

Ask why some of the programmes in question 2 are popular and whether they serve any useful purpose.

Find out if there are any other similar types of programmes they know of to add to the list.

Extended speaking Paper 5 Part 3

B Check students have understood what to do by asking one or two students to explain the instructions to you.

Remind students of the importance of giving fluent and coherently linked responses to the prompts. Students should respond politely to their partners. Draw students' attention to the *Exam tip* and remind students that the prompts are to help them start talking. They do not need to talk about only these prompts.

Allow 7 minutes in total. While students are speaking, go round the class and monitor their progress. Give feedback at the end on any points of fluency or accuracy you want to focus on.

Exploring the topic

C Students remain in their pairs to discuss the questions. Allow 4–5 minutes for this.
Finish the activity by choosing two or three questions for discussion as a class.

Writing SB pages 160–161

A review Paper 2 Part 2

Understanding the task

A The questions are designed to help students understand what is required in this type of writing task.

Check answers as a class.

Analysing the sample

B Before students look at the questions, ask them to read through the review and decide whether in general it is favourable or unfavourable. Ask them which of the two books mentioned the writer seems to prefer.

Students read the review again and answer the questions. For question 4, ask them to find phrases which describe plot, characters and the writer's impression of the books.

Check answers as a class.

Key

1 paragraph 1 the success of the Harry Potter books in general
   paragraph 2 the character and plot of *Harry Potter and the Philosopher's Stone*
   paragraph 3 the attraction of *Harry Potter and the Philosopher's Stone*
   paragraph 4 the limitations of *Harry Potter and the Philosopher's Stone* when compared to *A Wizard of Earthsea*
   paragraph 5 The writer's recommendations
2 It meets the readers' needs well. It gives just enough information about each book to arouse the readers' curiosity without giving away important information. It makes both books seem worth reading.
3 The review is written in a semi-formal style. It is not too academic and there are some examples of informal language e.g. 'Mum and Dad will enjoy it too.'
4 A range of vocabulary is used to give the writer's opinions and describe characters and plot. The choice of vocabulary shows how favourable the review is about these aspects of the book and creates interest.
5 The actions or plot are described in the present tense.

Writing skills

Creating interest

C This activity is designed to encourage students to use a range of descriptive vocabulary in their writing.

Ask students to read through the whole review before replacing the words in italics.

Remind them that they may need to change the form of the word they have selected according to the structure of the sentence. They may also need to add appropriate prepositions.

Students compare their new texts in pairs.

Check answers by reading the text aloud and stopping at the italicised words to elicit possible replacements from students.

Possible answers

interest	obsession with, passion for
old	faded, ancient
says	claims
old	undisturbed, ancient
tried	attempted
called	entitled
very interested	fascinated by, gripped by
find out	reveal, unravel
strange	eerie, unexpected, startling, chilling
interesting	gripping, startling, life-changing
old	ancient
new	modern, contemporary
difficult	life-changing, major, unexpected
big	tough, major
horrible	chilling, startling, eerie, unexpected

Writing your review

D Go through the stages in turn and discuss questions and brainstorm ideas as a class.

Unit 11 Overview key

SB pages 162–163

Lexical Cloze Paper 1 Part 1

A

1 B	2 D	3 A	4 B	5 A	6 C
7 B	8 A	9 B	10 D	11 C	12 D

Open cloze Paper 3 Part 1

B

1 of 2 In 3 since 4 as 5 on 6 where
7 but 8 hand 9 first 10 their 11 However
12 with 13 to 14 age 15 under

Gapped sentences Paper 3 Part 3

C

1 led 2 proved 3 issued 4 tempt 5 blame
6 process

Vocabulary Test Unit 11 TB page 136

12 All in the mind

▶ *See unit summary on page 4.*

Exam training in this unit

Reading	Lexical cloze: complementation
Use of English	Word formation: changing verbs to nouns
	Comprehension and summary: identifying information
Listening	Three-way matching
Speaking	A complete test
Writing	A report: giving explanations

Ask students to suggest when they might use the expression *all in the mind*. The expression is normally used to suggest that a feeling, memory or experience is imagined and not real. The overall theme of the unit is the mind and psychology.

Reading SB pages 164–166

The secret self

Introduce the activity by asking students whether they have ever taken a personality test and what personality tests they know about or have heard of.

When students have done the test, ask them to work in pairs to discuss the five questions. Allow a few minutes for this and then compare answers as a class.

Finish by asking the class whether they take after or have anything in common with any members of their families and in what way. Elicit from students any experiences they can think of that might change someone's personality.

Lexical cloze Paper 1 Part 1

A This activity aims to encourage students to read through the texts to get a general idea of the content before they attempt the multiple-choice gap-filling exercise.

Discuss answers as a class.

> **Key**
>
> All three texts are concerned with the functions of the mind and its effect on our well-being.

B Remind students of the importance of reading around the gap before choosing one of the four options. The answer may depend on complementation, collocation, verb patterns, set phrases, idioms, phrasal verbs or simply the correct word in context.

Check answers as a class.

> **Key**
>
> Text 1
> 1 A   2 D   3 A   4 B   5 A   6 A
> Text 2
> 7 C   8 B   9 A   10 D   11 A   12 B
> Text 3
> 13 B   14 B   15 D   16 D   17 C   18 B

C Students discuss answers with a partner.

Discuss answers as a class.

> **Key**
>
> 1 It implies that the commonly held view was that the mind was rational and people had control over their actions.
> 2 It suggests that the mind's functions are connected to our physical well-being.
> 3 In the first paragraph, the description of the seasonal changes shows an understanding of the predicament, and the use of phrases like 'consequences can be severe' and 'those who suffer' suggests sympathy.
> 4 Mental processes can be influenced by internal factors, such as the unconscious, and external factors, such as stress and climatic changes.

Vocabulary

Complementation

D Students work in pairs to find other examples in the texts. Allow a few minutes for this.

Discuss answers as a class.

E This activity focuses on the use of dependent prepositions, a form of complementation. Students choose a word for each sentence first, then check by referring back to the texts.

Check answers as a class.

Key

1 barren   2 doubts   3 control   4 suffers
5 effect   6 cure

F This activity focuses on verb patterns, another instance of complementation.

Check answers as a class.

Key

1 e   2 a   3 b   4 c   5 d

G Ask students to consider why one of the verbs does not fit into the pattern as they are doing the activity.

Check answers as a class.

Key

1 demanded The structure *demand someone to do* is impossible. This could be corrected to *He demanded that I do the work* (verb + object).
2 assisted The structure *assist to do* is impossible. This could be corrected to *She assisted them in challenging the status quo* (verb + object).
3 told We normally *tell somebody something*. This could be corrected to *I told him that I had made a mistake* (verb + indirect object + direct object).

4 arrange The structure *arrange you a place* is impossible. This could be corrected to *I'll arrange a place for you when I get to the cinema* (verb + object).
5 behave The structure *behave particularly happy* is impossible. This could be corrected to *He doesn't behave in a particularly happy way* (verb with no object).
6 resolve The structure *something will resolve* is impossible. This could be corrected to *I'm sure that some problems will resolve themselves* (verb + object).
7 approve The structure *approve that something happened* is impossible with this sense of the word. This could be corrected to *I don't approve of what has happened* (verb with no object).
8 agree The structure *agree something to be* is impossible. This could be corrected to *Experts agree that the painting is an original* (verb + object).

❏ **Alternative activity**
Ask students to rewrite the original sentence using the verb that *doesn't* fit. Examples are given in the explanations to the key.

Expressions with *head* and *heart*

H Introduce the activity by asking students if there are any metaphorical uses of head or heart in their languages.

Check answers as a class. Focus on the whole expression in the sentences given.

Key

1 to have a *head* for heights
2 to take something to *heart*
3 something comes to a *head*
4 to break someone's *heart*
5 to keep one's *head* above water
6 one's *heart* isn't in something
7 in my *heart* of hearts
8 to let something go to one's *head*
9 to be *head* over heels in love
10 to lose *heart*

❏ **Alternative activity**
Ask students to choose the three expressions they like best and write sentences of their own. Students then exchange sentences and the class decides on the three most popular expressions.

✚ Extra activity

Use this activity to revise / practise adjectives describing personality.

Ask students to imagine that their house is on fire but they have just enough time to rescue five treasured possessions from the flames. Ask them to write down these five treasured possessions on a piece of paper. Remind them not to put their names on the piece of paper.

When they have finished, collect the pieces of paper and redistribute them around the class making sure that each student doesn't get his or her own list.

Ask students to describe the personality of the person who wrote the list based on what is contained in it. If the class know each other well, they can guess who wrote it.

If you have a large class, the activity can be done in groups of 4–5 students.

Extra vocabulary

See page 176 for ideas on how to exploit this vocabulary.

primal (adjective) the earliest origins of life, very basic
outrageous (adjective) shocking and unacceptable
dysfunction (noun) a state of not working properly
overcast (adjective) covered with clouds
blustery (adjective) very windy
barren (adjective) not fertile or productive
banish (verb) to make something / somebody go away, order someone to leave a place
resolve (verb) to find a satisfactory solution to a problem

Language in use

SB pages 167–169

Just the job

Introduce the activity by explaining to students that the phrase *just the job* is used to describe something that is perfect for the situation.

Ask students to work in pairs to discuss the two questions. If students find it difficult to come up with ideas, ask them to consider what qualities are needed for each of the jobs illustrated and how they could find out whether candidates possessed these qualities.

Compare answers as a class.

Key

2 CVs, application forms, interviews, practical work-based tests, psychometric tests, selection days, a probationary period of employment, auditions.

Word formation Paper 3 Part 2

A Remind students that each set of verbs uses the same suffix.

Check answers as a class. Note spelling.

Key

1 justifi*cation*	modifi*cation*	gratifi*cation*
2 appear*ance*	resembl*ance*	assist*ance*
3 dismiss*al*	referr*al*	renew*al*
4 announce*ment*	embarass*ment*	develop*ment*
5 indica*tion*	reitera*tion*	separa*tion*

B Remind the students to read through the whole text first to get an idea of what it is about before deciding what form of the word fits each space. Whether a negative or positive form of the word is required will depend on the context.

Check answers as a class.

Background notes

DIY stands for do-it-yourself and is used to describe the type of store or shop where items for doing home improvements can be bought.

Key

1 impressively	6 notification
2 psychological	7 unsuccessful
3 applicants	8 assurances
4 relationships	9 dismissal
5 productivity	10 extraordinarily

C Allow students a few minutes to discuss the questions in pairs. Compare answers as a class.

❏ Alternative activity

Ask students to read the text and discuss the questions in pairs before they do the word formation exercise. This will encourage them to read the whole text for gist first.

Structure review

The following activities provide revision of all the grammar structures practised in each unit.

Sentence structures

D   Remind students to consider the structure of the whole sentence in the text before choosing an option. Ask students to match the correct option to one of the sentence structures in the list. These are included in the key.

Check answers as a class.

Key

1   have uses of *have* and *get*
2   can one predict inversion
3   for which relative clause
4   It cleft sentence
5   have uses of have and get
6   what cleft sentence
7   whose relative clause
8   not only inversion
9   but also part of same inversion
10 what cleft sentence

Verb forms

E

Key

1   will have been waiting
2   don't imagine
3   has been working
4   sounds
5   still hadn't been built / was still being built
6   is leaving
7   have read
8   is being

F   Draw students' attention to the example and check that they have understood what to do.

Check answers as a class.

Key

2   h   Why was I the last to be told?
3   f   Do you mind if I smoke in here?
4   a   He is known to have applied illegally for a passport.
5   e   She apologised for causing so much trouble.
6   c   There's no point in trying to make her change her mind.
7   d   I regret to say that we cannot give you the job.
8   b   She warned the children not to go near the cliff edge.

Modal and conditional forms

G   Draw students' attention to the example and check they have understood what to do.

Check answers as a class.

Key

1   anyone want to know
2   the car not been fitted
3   might have told
4   cannot possibly have predicted
5   must have been driving
6   needn't have bought
7   must have been taken
8   had had

Photocopiable activity 12 TB page 157

Extra vocabulary

See page 176 for ideas on how to exploit this vocabulary.

reiterate (verb) to repeat something already said for emphasis

overrule (verb) to change / reject an official decision

dissonance (noun) lack of agreement or a harsh combination of musical notes

refined (adjective) made pure by having other substances removed, or polite, well-educated and able to judge quality

lucrative (adjective) producing large amounts of money

lay off (verb and noun) become redundant, not needed for work any longer

inundated (adjective) so many things that you are unable to deal with them

vague (adjective) not precise, unclear

futile (adjective) no chance of success

gratify (verb) to satisfy a wish or please somebody

Comprehension and summary

SB pages 170–171

Subversive shrinks

Draw students' attention to the title and explain that *shrink* is a colloquial and slightly derogatory expression referring to psychiatrists and psychoanalysts. Allow students a few minutes to discuss the three questions in pairs.

Compare answers as a class.

> **Possible answers**
>
> 1 The essential difference between the two professions is that a psychiatrist has been trained as a medical doctor first and treats clients who have a mental illness. A psychoanalyst deals with clients who are not necessarily ill but need help to overcome emotional problems.
> 2 A psychiatrist may use drugs as well as therapy in treating clients. A psychoanalyst, as the name suggests, uses various forms of therapy based on an analysis of the client's emotions, past experiences and possibly dreams. These aspects of psychoanalysis are mentioned in the two texts which follow.

A Discuss answers as a class.

Ask students whether any of their ideas from the discussion in *Subversive shrinks* are mentioned in the texts.

> **Key**
>
> 1 Both texts could be found in articles from magazines or journals on the subject of psychology.
> 2 Text 1 entertaining, sceptical
>   Text 2 entertaining, sceptical, admiring

B Remind students that they should keep their answers as brief as possible.

Check answers as a class.

> **Key**
>
> Text 1
>   1 to show that their unhappiness is only interesting to them and not anyone else
>   2 refuge
> Text 2
>   3 The writer is not convinced of its effectiveness.
>   4 to emphasise that Adam Phillips has undermined psychoanalysis

C Ask students to consider how the phrases are used in context and how they connect to the overall idea expressed in both texts.

Discuss answers as a class.

> **Key**
>
> Text 1
>   1 This suggests that psychoanalysis cannot do the impossible despite what some people believe.
>   2 It gives the impression that the man could easily give a list of things he would like to do without even thinking about it.
> Text 2
>   3 This gives the impression that we may be able to do something about it by ourselves.
>   4 This reinforces the idea that there is no easy and sudden solution to the problems.
>   5 A couch is typically associated with a psychoanalyst and the writer wants to make it clear that Adam Phillips is different.
>   6 This suggests that psychoanalysis is not a precise science.

Summary writing Paper 3 Part 5

Remind students to underline the key words in the exam question first as this will help them decide which of the statements are relevant to the summary, i.e. 'the dangers of psychoanalysis'.

Check answers as a class. The parts of the texts which relate to the relevant statements are included in the key.

Finish the activity by discussing with students why statements 2, 3, 7 and 8 are not relevant to the summary.

Possible answers

Statement 2 is not relevant because text 1 says 'We organise our lives around fears.' This does not mean that psychoanalysis makes people afraid.
Statement 3 is not relevant because text 2 says 'being sad is part of what it means to be happy', which suggests that psychoanalysis acknowledges that it cannot provide happiness.
Statements 7 and 8 are not relevant because they do not refer to the *dangers* of psychoanalysis.

E See SB page 49 for guidelines for you and your students on what to consider.

Sample summary

Psychoanalysis can prevent you from facing up to and engaging with the world by encouraging you to think too deeply about yourself. Such introspection can be a futile and time-wasting effort. Moreover, it can give you false ideas about who you are and can result in further damage being caused by forcing you to think about the negative aspects of your life. (63 words)

Listening SB page 172

Lend me your ears!

The title is part of a famous quotation from *Julius Caesar* by William Shakespeare: *Friends, Romans, countrymen, lend me your ears. I come to bury Caesar, not to praise him.* It is intended as a request for people to pay attention to a speech.

This activity serves as an introduction to the listening task which follows. Ask students to tick the statements individually first and then compare them with a partner.

Conduct a class survey by finding out which of the statements are true for most of the class, some of the class and a few of the class.

Finish the activity by asking students what types of things they enjoy listening to and what things they have to listen to but don't particularly enjoy.

Three-way matching Paper 4 Part 4

A 🎧 Ask students to read through the six statements carefully before they listen to the tape. Remind them that the speakers will not use exactly the same words as in the statements.

After playing the recording the first time, allow students some time to think about their answers.

Continue to play the recording a second time.

Ask students to compare answers with a partner.

Check answers as a class.

Key

1 J   2 B   3 B   4 M   5 J   6 J

Tapescript

PRESENTER The subject of our afternoon 'Let's talk' slot is hearing ability and with me in the studio are teachers Mark Jones and Judy Watson, who have been part of a government team conducting research into the ability of pupils to hear and listen in class. So, what has been the result of the research? Have we found out anything new?
MARK Well, we've certainly known for a long time that the ear is the most remarkable musical instrument ever devised. It enables the brain to duplicate the sound of every other instrument, and can even replay entire

symphonies. We decided to delve even deeper into its amazing powers.

JUDY I couldn't have put it more succinctly! Its capacity is truly astounding: It can discriminate between millions of nuances in sound. Between the outer layer of the eardrum and your receiving brain, there are tens of thousands of interdependent structures. *But what we were really looking at was why our listening habits are so poor. We wanted to try and find out how we can improve them, particularly at a young age and use them to the advantage of our memory and other senses.*

MARK What we were finding was that some of our students were easily distracted in class. Now, you know as well as I, that it's impossible to feel completely motivated and involved in every lesson you attend. *I think we would all agree, looking back to our childhood, that that particular scenario is nothing short of utopian!*

JUDY Speak for yourself! But, joking apart, *I am quite ready to admit that not everyone would be totally riveted by each and every lesson* – especially on a hot Friday afternoon. But the interesting thing about distraction is that it comes in two guises: first there's the external environment, and then, there's our own internal thoughts.

MARK Actually, it's a combination of these two factors that leads to most distraction. *On the other hand, what I find really fascinating is how the mind can reject sounds around us that we're not interested in.* We can sort of switch off to the sounds that don't concern us and concentrate on those that do.

JUDY But there's always an exception to the rule! A screaming child is one noise that nobody can blot out – even if you aren't the mother! There's no doubt, though, that being aware of this ability to blot out certain sounds will help your powers of concentration. *For example, if you're in a crowded gathering, most people can train themselves to ignore things they hear but don't want to listen to.* If you try it, you'll find that you're able to pay attention, despite the surrounding noise, to the person you're interested in.

MARK But to come back to a lack of concentration – *take boredom, for instance. This usually occurs in a situation where we are 'obliged' to pay attention*, but in which our interest is not completely engaged. And the result is a fairly immediate wandering of the mind, and an almost total loss of what is being said.

JUDY Well, an interesting sideline to that is how it can be tackled. There is one technique for highly boring situations, and I take your point about being under pressure to listen. I don't think anyone would take exception to that! *But the thing to do is adopt the position of a strongly opposed critic.* You can lean forward 'all ears', even when listening to something boring. This means that your attention is directed to a complex, constructive criticism of all that you are hearing.

MARK And we mustn't forget - one last point about forgetting what you have been listening to, or should have

been listening to. This can be extremely embarrassing both for the listener and the speaker, and a waste of time – your time as well as the speaker's. There are actually three very good tried and tested techniques you can use for improving your listening ability: self-motivation, setting yourself to listen, and key selection, which means connecting key words and images to each other.

JUDY Now that's actually vital in all this, isn't it? All of these are among the most tried and tested methods of improving any mental performance. Self-motivation is very closely related to willpower. *And setting yourself to listen can be practised by creating your own individual listening exercises, in which you actively set out to hear more of what goes on around you – at work, while travelling. You can give yourself little personal tests* for detecting differences between, say, the songs of different birds, and the general noise level at work or school at different times of the day. And to help you remember, you can connect key words and images to one another. This will help you first of all visualise, then remember what you have heard.

PRESENTER Thank you for that and now …

Your views

B Introduce the activity by asking students what they can remember from the listening and refer them to the six statements.

Students work in pairs to discuss the three questions and ask them to note down their suggestions for remembering and concentrating. Allow five minutes for this.

Compare suggestions as a class.

If you wish, write students' suggestions on the board and discuss as a class which ones they think would be most effective.

Vocabulary

Expressions with *ears*

E The expression *lend an ear* is depicted in the illustration

Key
1 b   2 e   3 g   4 c   5 f   6 h   7 a   8 d

❏ Alternative activity
Ask students to use three of the expressions to describe something from their own experience.

Speaking SB pages 173–175

This section provides a complete speaking test to be used for exam practice.

Before starting the activity, ask students to close their books and elicit from them what each of the three stages of the speaking test are. Also elicit what speaking activities they have practised in previous units.

If possible, students should work in groups of three. Before they begin, establish who will take which role (The Examiner/Observer, Student A and Student B), and that these roles will change.

Explain that each student should follow the instructions in the appropriate column of each table. While students are speaking, monitor and make notes on any points of fluency and accuracy you want to focus on in a feedback session at the end of the activity. Feedback can be given at the end of each activity or at the end of this Speaking section.

Introduction Paper 5 Part 1

A 🎧 Play the recording. Students listen to the answers and how the candidates give full responses.

Tapescript

INTERVIEWER Good morning. My name's Petrina Cliff and this is my colleague Thorkild Gantner. And your names are ...?

MURIEL Muriel Carbonet.

XAVIER Xavier Laurent.

INTERVIEWER Xavier. Thank you. Could I have your mark sheets please?

XAVIER Of course. There you are

INTERVIEWER Thank you. Now first of all, it would be nice to find out something about each of you. Where are you from Muriel?

MURIEL I am from Paris.

INTERVIEWER And you, Xavier?

XAVIER From Paris as well.

INTERVIEWER Do you live in the city centre?

MURIEL Right now you mean? No I live in the Buckinghamshire County. I live in a place called Prestwood. It's after Amersham, yes.

INTERVIEWER And how do you travel to school, Xavier?

XAVIER Well, it's easy for me because I am living in the school premises. The classroom is on the first floor and I'm living classroom on the fifth floor. So I just have to travel by lift.

INTERVIEWER OK. Could you tell us what you remember most about your childhood?

XAVIER ... Maybe the boarding school, or ... some holidays I spent here for exchange in family - in families in Great Britain. In Sussex and West Sussex, you know near Brighton and in Bognor Regis.

INTERVIEWER OK and could you tell us the main reasons why you are learning English Muriel?

MURIEL Yes, of course. I – I came to England to improve my English in view of getting a better job when I go back. Yes.

INTERVIEWER OK. Thank you. Now we'd like to ask you what you think about one or two things. If you could study another language apart from English, which one would you choose?

MURIEL I would - I would choose Chinese, because I think the economy of China is booming and I think it might be useful to learn Chinese to get a better job and also to travel in China.

XAVIER I think I would learn Spanish, because ... while China is ... undergoing a - an economical improvement, I think that the South of America or the south of the continent will be the next region in the world to ... to improve its economy.

INTERVIEWER Thank you. And Xavier, how important do you think it is to be ambitious in life?

XAVIER I think it's important because ... ambition helps you to have goals in life. If you are not ambitious sometimes, you don't need anything, so you don't see why you would have to work or to earn a living or I don't mean judging people only with their wages or salary – it's like judging a book by its cover – but I think it's important to be ambitious because it helps you. ... Yes.

INTERVIEWER Thank you.

B Confirm that each student knows precisely which role they will take and that 'the Examiner/Observer' is looking at SB page 175.

After 3 minutes, stop the activity.

Themed discussion Paper 5 Part 2

C Confirm that each student knows precisely which role they will take and that 'the Examiner/Observer' is looking at SB page 175.

Draw students' attention to the exam tip before they begin.

After 4 minutes, stop the activity to allow 'the examiner' to give feedback.

Extended speaking Paper 5 Part 3

D Confirm that each student knows precisely which role they will take and that 'the Examiner' is looking at the appropriate page. Each student should now have played the role of 'Examiner/Observer'.

After 8 minutes, stop the activity to allow 'the Examiner' to give feedback.

E   Students can stay in the same roles for this activity. Draw students' attention to the exam tip before they begin.

Writing SB pages 176–177

A report Paper 2 Part 2

Understanding the task

Background notes

Continuous assessment is an alternative to assessment based on marks or grades given for a single exam taken at the end of term or of a course. It consists of marks or grades being awarded for a series of assignments, projects and short tests given to students throughout the term or course. The final mark or grade is based on an average of all the marks or grades awarded.

A

> **Key**
>
> 1   The benefits of the scheme, the drawbacks and recommendations for improvements.
> 2   The name of the school, when the experiment took place, who took part in the scheme, and how the scheme was organised, i.e. what type of continuous assessment was used.
> 3   The students' reactions to the scheme, the benefits and drawbacks, and ideas for improvements, as well as the information mentioned in 2.
> 4   Brainstorm ideas on possible *benefits* and *drawbacks* to a continuous assessment scheme as a class. Use the notes in the *Background* above if necessary. Brainstorm possible ideas to overcome the drawbacks.

Analysing the task

B   Students use their answers and ideas from the questions in A as a checklist.

C

> **Key**
>
> 1   The writer has answered the question well by covering the three specific areas mentioned in the question and by providing the necessary additional information. The writer has also used a formal, impersonal style suitable for a report of this type. The report is also well-organised with clear sections and appropriate headings.
> 2   Both the benefits and the drawbacks of the scheme have been clearly stated by the writer along with reasons and explanations.
> 3   The writer's recommendations are clearly stated in the conclusion which includes a brief summary of the students' reactions although 'some safeguards' seems rather vague.

Writing skills

Explaining

D   The aim of this activity is to focus students' attention on using appropriate linking words to make their writing more fluent. Remind students to consider how the link words function within the sentence as a whole and to look at verb forms and punctuation in the sentence.

E   Draw students' attention to the example and remind them that they should link the *ideas* expressed in the two sentences. This may mean changing the order and choice of words.

> **Possible answers**
>
> He worked hard, and as a consequence of this, he did well in the exams.
> He worked hard because he wanted to do well in the exams.
> Doing well in the exams would mean him working hard.
> Working hard resulted in him doing well in the exams.
> His success in the exams stemmed from the fact that he worked hard.
> He wanted to do well in the exams and therefore he worked hard.

Writing your report

F   Go through each of the stages in turn and discuss questions or brainstorm ideas as a class.

Unit 12 Overview key

SB pages 178–179

Lexical cloze Paper 1 Part 1

A

1 A	2 A	3 B	4 B	5 C	6 C
7 B	8 D	9 B	10 B	11 D	12 A

Word formation Paper 3 Part 2

B

1 authoritative
2 influential
3 therapeutic
4 abnormal
5 manifestations
6 innovative
7 invariably
8 extraordinarily
9 implications
10 controversial

Key word transformations Paper 3 Part 4

C

1 gave me an assurance that he would
2 insisted on my being
3 was anxious not to be
4 fed up with being treated
5 up to my ears in work so
6 were in favour of changing the system
7 stemmed from the fact that
8 made such an impression on the judges

Vocabulary Test Unit 12 TB page 137

Progress test Units 9–12 TB pages 142–143

Vocabulary Test Unit 1   Name _____

A   Complete each sentence with a word from each box.

rolling	new	wet	nosy
couch	stuffed	fair-weather	

broom	potato	parker	shirt
blanket	stone	friend	

1 Jeff's a .... – he's never really supportive when things are going wrong.
2 Frank is always moving from one town to another, never settling down – he's a real ....
3 Veronica is a .... – she never stops trying to find out what's happening in other people's lives.
4 Don't be such a .... – by not joining in, you're spoiling everyone else's fun.
5 Belinda has been a .... since she got the job – she has made so many changes for the better.

(5 marks)

B   Fill each gap with one or two words.

1 After spending so much time in preparation for the match, the team found it hard to come .... with their defeat.
2 Schools have come .... a lot of criticism for failing to provide education on the dangers of smoking.
3 At the moment, she's won't agree to our plans, but I think she'll come .... if you keep trying to persuade her.
4 The government intends to come .... heavily on hospitals that are performing badly.
5 Jenny often comes .... words that I've never heard before – she can be really difficult to understand.
6 The doctor came straight to .... – either I eat healthier food or I can expect health problems in the future.
7 Kate has had terrible luck with her health – no sooner had she recovered from her sore throat than she came .... with a case of the flu.
8 The anaesthetic used in the operation was very powerful, and it took nearly twelve hours for John to come ....
9 After weeks of deliberation, the committee came .... with a solution that would satisfy both nurses and patients.
10 I eventually came .... to the idea of moving to a new city.

(10 marks)

C   Underline the word which collocates correctly in each of these sentences.

1 I noticed an ad for a demonstration of the 'Quit now' hypnotherapy technique – it was *taking / giving / having* place at my local health centre.
2 Poor health can damage your emotional *safety / well-being / comfort*.
3 Smoking can *take / make / have* long-term effects that won't emerge until the distant future.
4 After yesterday's victory, the champion can now take his *honorary / rightful / valid* place amongst the greatest heroes of boxing.
5 I decided not to join the luxury health club – it was *ridiculously / hysterically / crazily* expensive.

(5 marks)

D   Complete the missing word in each of the following sentences.

1 Many people are still very c................ about alternative medicine: they don't really trust its effectiveness.
2 The new fitness system requires no p................ experience – even an absolute beginner can use it.
3 You should never exceed the recommended d................ with these pills as it could be dangerous.
4 The hike through the mountains was so physically demanding that I felt completely d................ of energy by the end.
5 I felt very a................ about my dentist's appointment – I was convinced something bad would happen.
6 I always experience a tremendous feeling of e................ at the moment when I take off in an aeroplane.
7 I find a hot, relaxing bath the best way to s................ aching and tired muscles.
8 At this time of year nearly everyone s................ from a cold or some kind of flu.
9 As his business crumbled, Jim realised that all his previous achievements had not been real but i................ .
10 After two weeks in solitary confinement, the prisoner p................ with the guards to be allowed out.

(10 marks)

Vocabulary Test Unit 2   Name _____

A Match an adjective from the box with each of the definitions below.

catastrophic	extraordinary	systematic
skeletal	alarming	baffled
abundant	defunct	

1 .... confused or failing to understand something
2 .... more than enough, in great supply
3 .... no longer in use
4 .... highly disastrous
5 .... done according to a plan
6 .... unusual or remarkable
7 .... liable to cause fear or concern
8 .... very thin

(8 marks)

B Replace the phrase in brackets using either a book expression or an expression with *time*.

1 Only (*the future can reveal*) ....
.........whether interstellar travel will be a reality.
2 Can't it wait until after lunch as I'm a bit (*in a rush*)
.... ?
3 I think you should (*do what your brother does*)
....
and spend more time on your studies.
4 I'm in (*favour with Jack*) ....
at the moment because I helped him with his biology assignment.
5 It's essential that you are (*punctual*) ....
.... for the lecture as the professor gets angry with latecomers.
6 The bored expression on his face during the lessons (*said a great deal about*) ....
.... his attitude towards the subject.
7 Now's (*not the best moment*) ....
to tell me you're afraid of flying as we're just about to board the plane!
8 In the interests of safety, all experiments in the laboratory must be carried out (*in strict accordance with the regulations*) ....

9 As the deadline for presenting the report is on Monday we'll have to find a good excuse in order to (*gain a few more days*) ....
10 Even (*in good circumstances*) ....
.... I find working on the computer difficult, but with this new programme it's become impossible.

(10 marks)

C Complete each sentence with the correct form of the word in brackets.

1 Due to his .... with the equipment we nearly had a nasty accident. (*care*)
2 I think it's .... to expect us to complete the project in such a short period of time. (*real*)
3 Government proposals for the .... of some previously banned drugs have caused a great deal of controversy. (*legal*)
4 Some predictions by early science fiction writers about the future of electronic communication have turned out to be .... accurate. (*ordinary*)
5 Having thought he had eliminated all traces of it, the sudden .... of the computer virus mystified the technician. (*appear*)
6 The words *close* and *shut* are completely .... in most circumstances. (*change*)
7 Sarah tried ballroom-dancing, but she found she was too .... to be good at it. (*coordinate*)

(7 marks)

Vocabulary Test Unit 3   Name _____

A Underline the correct word in italic.

1 I could hear the bottles of wine I bought at the supermarket *clinking / crashing / smashing* in the bag as I walked along the street.

2 Simon really shouldn't be so *averse / antagonistic / reluctant* towards people who don't share his views.

3 In many silent movies the heroine is always *salvaged / recovered / saved* from some terrible fate at the last moment.

4 The Prime Minister has unexpectedly *declared / decreed / assumed* his support for the new safety measures at all football stadiums.

5 In the final seconds of the match, the Albion defender disastrously *deflected / detracted / diverted* the ball into his own goal.

6 Only officers are permitted to use a car from the army vehicle *pool / bank / lake* for their personal use.

7 She felt so *finished / drained / dry* of emotion after her long ordeal on the lifeboat that she could hardly speak.

8 There was a terrible *reek / aroma / scent* of burning plastic coming from the kitchen.

9 There is *overcoming / overbearing / overwhelming* evidence that the thief escaped through the window.

10 With an impending sense of *fate / destiny / doom*, the passengers on the Titanic realised the ship was sinking.

11 Some of the soldiers were taken to *shock / task / blame* by the General for falling asleep on duty.

12 High wire artists at the circus always use a safety net to *break / gather / take* their fall if they make a mistake.

13 The safety officer resigned because he could not *take / admit / face* the prospect of being held responsible for the fire.

(13 marks)

B Complete each sentence with the most suitable verb from the box, making any changes necessary.

peep	glimpse	stare	wink
peer	gaze	glance	

1 The short-sighted Police Inspector .... closely at the photograph in an effort to identify the tiny figures in the background.

2 I quickly .... through the newspaper to see if it contained any news about the accident.

3 Arnold secretively .... out through the gap in the living room curtains to see what his neighbours were up to.

4 As the train sped through the station, I .... someone on the platform with a gun.

5 During the exam, I wasted too much time .... absent-mindedly out of the window at the people strolling in the park.

6 I knew our secret was safe when she .... knowingly at me from across the table.

7 Sue's eyes opened wide, and she .... in astonishment as the film star walked across the bar towards her.

(7 marks)

C Fill each gap with one or two words.

A friend of mine recently asked me to do him a (1) .... His room had been neglected and was in an awful condition and he wanted someone to do it (2) .... for him as he was planning to sell the house. He tried to persuade me that a bit of manual labour would do me (3) .... and that I might even enjoy a break from my usual routine. I replied that he should get in some professionals who could, as the saying goes, do it with (4) .... closed, as they have much more experience at it. Besides, knowing my friend, he would probably be giving intructions and taking it easy while I did all the (5) ....

(5 marks)

Proficiency Masterclass © Oxford University Press **Photocopiable**

Vocabulary Test Unit 4   Name _____

A Rewrite each sentence using the word given in italic. Do not change the word.

1 When our flight was delayed, we had to accept the idea of spending the night in the airport. (*resigned*)
....
....

2 The idea of travelling across the Sahara in an old coach didn't appeal to Mark at all. (*unattractive*)
....
....

3 Travelling alone is not just a matter of taking a good guidebook with you. (*more*)
....
....

4 A performance of traditional dance is scheduled for this evening in the village square. (*take*)
....
....

5 The backpackers underwent three hours of interrogation by the border guards. (*subjected*)
....
....

6 Not only was our last holiday expensive, it was also a disaster. (*besides*)
....
....

7 Paul never took other people's feelings into consideration. (*insensitive*)
....
....

8 For Miriam, the long journey up river was an adventure. (*regarded*)
....
....

(8 works)

B Fill each gap with a suitable word from the box.

weary	optimistic	affected	infested
afraid	dejected	disillusioned	

The drawbacks of independent travel in tropical climes can leave even the most (1)................ of travellers feeling (2)................ . Even if you survive the cheap hotels (3)................ with bugs, insects or other tiny creatures, you will certainly be (4)................ by the heat and humidity, which can make you feel so (5)................ that you lack the energy to make the most of your trip.

Some are left feeling so (6)................ by the experience that they wonder why they ever set off in the first place and are often (7)................ to ever attempt such an adventure again.

(7 marks)

C Fill each gap with one or two words.

1 The extravagant meal in the restaurant meant that we ran .... money and couldn't take a taxi home.

2 It's a little bit arrogant of you to look down .... at other people.

3 After spending two hours in the pouring rain, Steve looked like a ....

4 Don't look a .... in the mouth: take the chance of a free holiday when it's offered to you.

5 The thief was caught .... when the police burst in just as he was opening the safe.

(5 marks)

D Unscramble the letters to make a suitable word. The first letter is given in bold.

1 After hacking our way through the thick undergrowth for five hours, we eventually .... (*erdemge*)into a clearing in the forest.

2 A .... (*uageucoors*)person is one who shows great strength of character in the face of opposition.

3 Many areas of Africa are dusty and .... (*idar*)places with very little rainfall.

4 The travel agency has a worldwide .... (*tenorkw*) of branches.

5 As the house had been empty for some months, there was a .... smell when we arrived. (*ysmut*)

6 As the sides of the valley were extremely steep, we had to .... (*ablermc*) up on our knees.

7 Helen has become so .... (*sdeobses*)with the idea of visiting Tibet that she can think or talk about nothing else.

8 Jim got a .... (*veseerpr*) pleasure from setting off the hotel fire alarm and annoying all the guests.

9 Despite the actors' professional status, their performance was so .... (*maasteurih*) that most of the audience left early.

10 Mike showed how .... (**r**efuerocsul) he was by repairing the car with a few spare tools.

(10 marks)

Vocabulary Test Unit 5   Name _____

A Complete the collocation in each sentence with a word from the box.

stage	reach	throw	call
harsh	grave	raise	vast
drastic	run	tremendous	controlled

1 The chemical factory was closed down because it was pumping .... amounts of toxic liquid into the river.
2 The zoo management committee have decided to .... a meeting to discuss falling visitor numbers.
3 Phil managed to .... the alarm as soon as he saw smoke coming from the heater.
4 Animal rights groups are planning to .... protests outside shops selling fur and leather products.
5 Unless .... action is taken soon to reduce the volume of traffic in the cities, pollution levels will become intolerable.
6 We decided to .... a party to celebrate winning a government grant to set up a bird sanctuary.
7 Many species of tiger are in .... danger of extinction due to the destruction of their natural habitats.
8 Chinese zoologists are trying to get giant pandas to breed by keeping them in a strictly .... environment.
9 The .... realities of life in the wild are in stark contrast to the idealised picture we get from television.
10 The Green Party is going to .... an advertising campaign to raise the public's awareness of environmentally friendly products.

(10 marks)

B Replace the phrase in brackets with a suitable animal expression.

1 We had a (*really good time*) ....
on safari, with parties every night and stunning landscape to see during the day.
2 Farmers in some developing countries can barely produce enough food to (*survive*)
....
3 I tried to convince John that the environment was in danger, but I soon realised that I was (*wasting my time*) ....

4 She wasn't really upset when I lost my job – they were only (*false tears*) ....
5 The public inquiry into noise pollution is very slow – it's proceeding at a (*very slow speed*)
....

(5 marks)

C Replace the phrase in brackets with a suitable expression using the words *light* or *dark*

1 Fresh evidence about how the dinosaurs became extinct has recently (*been discovered*)
....
2 After spending months on her school project, Anne began to see (*that this difficult period was nearly over*) ....
3 The City Council is trying (*not to tell us anything*) .... about their plans for redeveloping the parkland areas.
4 Jenny must have been tired – when she went to bed, she (*went to sleep immediately*) ....
....
5 No one knows anything about Carol – she's a bit of a (*mysterious person*) ....

(5 marks)

D Fill each gap with a suitable adverb from the box.

deeply	blissfully	perfectly	greatly
fully	seriously	bitterly	highly

1 All the wardens working in the wildlife park have been .... trained.
2 The minister was .... offended by the bad language used by protesters during his speech on the environment.
3 All workers in the safari park have to be ....
insured in case of accidents while on duty.
4 The revellers carried on with their party, ... unaware that they were disturbing all of the neighbours.
5 Despite the high daytime temperatures, it can get .... cold at night in the desert.

(5 marks)

Vocabulary Test Unit 6   Name _____

A Complete the missing word in each of the following sentences.

1 Oscar's remarks are so w................. – he uses words in such a clever and amusing way.
2 Don't be c................. ! Only a five-year-old would cry over a broken toy.
3 I tried to convince Pippa that it's in her interests to go, but she's too s................. to see the facts.
4 Smith's solution was i................. , amazing his colleagues with its cleverness and originality.
5 Carl's manner immediately struck her as c.............. –so pleasant, polite and sophisticated.
6 When the islands were discovered, the natives treated the explorers with a sense of c................. innocence and generosity.
7 With his blond hair and blue eyes, Gina thought he was really c................. .
8 Phil's a c................. character – he deliberately tricked us into paying for his meal.
9 I think the book has quite an a.............. storyline. There were times when I couldn't help laughing.
10 Tina is a very d................. person – once she sets her mind on something, there's no stopping her.

(10 marks)

B Replace the phrase in brackets with a suitable expression related to words and reading.

1 The actor read through his part in the scene over and over until he (*knew all the lines by heart*) ....
2 The actual words in the text are quite simple and straightforward, but, if you (*look closely at what is implied*) .... , you'll realise that it has a much deeper meaning.
3 The student's essay on Dickens was failed by his tutor because he had copied it (*in exactly the same words*) .... from an article in a literary journal.
4 The journalist was told by his editor, (*very briefly*) .... , that his article was rubbish.
5 Victor was so upset and surprised by his wife's sudden announcement that he was (*unable to find anything to say*) ....

(5 marks)

C Add the appropriate negative prefix to each of these adjectives.

1 .... agreeable   9 .... reverent
2 .... coherent   10 .... auspicious
3 .... mortal   11 .... honest
4 .... authorised   12 .... biased
5 .... violent   13 .... understood
6 .... capable   14 .... enthusiastic
7 .... plausible   15 .... logical
8 .... literate   16 .... just

(8 marks)

D Fill each gap with the correct form of the word given.

1 The theory that some of Shakespeare's plays were written by someone else has been .... false by new evidence. (*prove*)
2 In romantic novels the handsome hero .... falls in love with the heroine and they live happily ever after. (*vary*)
3 The painting had a very innocent .... quality that many people admired . (*child*)
4 After gaining access to the computer, Bond succeeded in .... the encrypted enemy information. (*code*)
5 There are ....writers trying to get their work published these days. (*number*)
6 What makes him .... is his easy-going and open manner. (*like*)
7 The film is .... because of its amazing photography and powerful acting. (*memory*)

(7 marks)

Vocabulary Test Unit 7   Name _____

A Complete the missing word in each of the following sentences.

1 The Prime Minister has come in for heavy c................. in the press for his failure to deal with the economic crisis.

2 Staying in luxury hotels, throwing expensive parties and taking exotic holidays are just a few aspects of the e................. lifestyle that people are tempted into after winning the lottery.

3 In her newspaper article, the journalist perfectly c................. the mood of the ordinary people on the subject of unemployment.

4 The market in computer software is very l............... at the moment, with some companies making huge profits in a short space of time.

5 Some museums are considering returning ancient art treasures to their country of origin as they are regarded as part of that country's h................. .

6 The dictator d................. of all his political opponents by either having them imprisoned or deported.

7 This particular l................. was chosen for the new youth centre as it is close to the housing estate where most of the kids live.

8 My old, battered dictionary finally d................. when I dropped it on the floor and all the pages fell out.

9 Being o............... means that you can spot small details in a scene that most people don't even notice.

10 What caused the famine and starvation in the country was the fact that many international organisations had failed to realise the g............... of the situation beforehand.

(10 marks)

B Fill each gap with one word.

1 The Rennaisance in Italy is often described as the golden .... of art and literature.

2 There's plenty of beer in the fridge; help .... to whatever you want.

3 The golden .... when taking an important exam is not to stay up revising until the early hours the night before.

4 Although William lost his job, he was given a substantial redundancy payment, which just goes to show that every cloud has a silver ....

5 On his retirement he was given a golden .... of a fat cheque and an engraved watch in recognition of his many years of loyal service to the company.

6 Watch out for Pete, he's so silver-................. that he can persuade anyone to do anything!

7 If you can't manage moving flat on your own, ask Richard, he's always willing to lend a helping ....

8 What really showed that Silvie had a .... of gold was how she gave up her free time to help orphaned children.

(8 marks)

C Underline the correct word in italic.

1 If you're planning a general knowledge quiz, encyclopedias are a *wealthy / rich / affluent* source of information.

2 One aspect of sociology is the study of how humans have *interacted / interfaced / intersected* with each other in different communities at different times.

3 The development of the internet and satellite TV has meant that mass communication is no longer *contracted / confined / constrained* by geographical factors.

4 The whole community was in the *grip / clasp / grasp* of fear when they heard that there was a killer on the loose.

5 All the people in the village were given vaccinations to prevent the *extension / growth / spread* of the disease to other areas.

6 I wonder if you could help me *over / out / through* with my course assignment, I'm a bit stuck for ideas at the moment.

7 The decision by the college authorities to reduce the number of places available in the halls of residence *bore / grew / bred* discontent among the students.

(7 marks)

Vocabulary Test Unit 8   Name _____

Total: _____
25

A Replace the phrase in brackets with a suitable expression using the word *fall.*

1 Dick's car is so old that it's beginning to (*have parts come off it*) ....
2 It's always best to have some money saved which you can (*use when you need it*) ....
3 Many families have (*failed to keep up with*) .... the payments on their loans due to the downturn in the economy.
4 All my plans for a holiday in the Bahamas (*came to nothing*) .... when the tour company I had booked with went bankrupt.
5 The money the charity organisation raised (*didn't reach*) .... the amount they needed to set up the drug rehabilitation centre.
6 The gang members (*attacked*) .... their rivals with clubs and chains and the police were called to break up the fighting.
7 We had been worried that the months of planning and preparation for the school concert would come to nothing but, fortunately, everything (*came together*) .... just at the right moment and it was a huge success.
8 Paul's mother became worried when the principal of the school informed her that he thought Paul had (*become involved with*) .... a group of football hooligans.

(8 marks)

B Fill each gap with one or two words.

1 I've been thinking a lot about something recently, and I want to tell you about it – I really need to get it off ....
2 I can't take any more of his attitude – I'm going to tell him what I think and have it .... with him once and for all.
3 John and Emma's relationship improved after they had their heart .... – such a frank and confidential discussion can really clear the air.
4 Be careful what you say to Dave – he often takes people's comments ....
5 Alison's always doing the wrong thing – it's time someone sat her down and talked some .... into her.
6 I had to admit my mistake and apologise – I really had to eat ....

7 The police knew what Collins was saying wasn't true, but he persisted in lying through his ....

(7 marks)

C Fill each gap with a verb and a preposition from the box, making any changes necessary.

wind	track	tip	accuse
fall	drop	walk	

off	out	of	up
away	down	in	

1 Jack .... of university in order to become a rock musician.
2 A group of students from the high school were .... stealing cassettes from the local record shop.
3 My mother always warned me that if I didn't study hard enough at school I would .... in a dead-end job with no prospects.
4 Someone .... the police that a bank robbery was going to take place the following day.
5 The police eventually .... the escaped criminal living under a false name in Malaga.

(5 marks)

D Underline the correct word in italics in each sentence.

1 The movie actually *carries / bears / shows* no resemblance to the original novel on which it is supposed to be based.
2 After two years living in central Africa, it came as no surprise to Jim when he *fell / came / lay* victim to a bout of malaria.
3 I've never felt entirely at *comfort / ease / leisure* with the new director as he has a manner which I find somewhat intimidating.
4 The rise in adolescent crime rates has been *given / put / fallen* down to a lack of proper parental control.
5 I don't want to *raise / lift / expand* your expectations too high, but it's quite likely you'll get a promotion soon.

(5 marks)

Vocabulary Test Unit 9   Name _____

A Fill each gap with a suitable word from the box, making any changes necessary.

spread	speculate	fluctuate	ruin	make
crash	break	go	dabble	trade

It has become almost fashionable these days to
(1) .... in the stock market. Most
people who do are not professionals who
(2) .... vast sums of money, but
ordinary people hoping to (3) .... a
profit by (4) .... in stocks and shares.
At worst they expect to (5) .... even and
get back the money they invested.
However, there are always risks – stock prices can
(6) .... , going up or down according to
the economic or political climate. The most extreme
example of this occurred in October 1929, when the
stock market in the USA (7) ....
dramatically causing a severe and lasting economic
crisis. Confidence in the market disappeared
overnight and panic quickly (8) .... with
people desperate to sell their shares as prices
plummeted. Many ordinary people were financially
(9) .... when their stock holdings
became worthless and even some major companies
(10) .... to the wall, leading to
widespread unemployment.

(10 marks)

B Complete these sentences with an appropriate expression with *pick*.

1 She was .... from among a
   dozen applicants for the job.
2 Even though I know my work is as good as anybody
   else's, my boss keeps .... me.
3 I managed to........................... some Spanish
   during the six months I was working in Madrid.
4 It's easy to .... some bargains in
   the end of season sales.
5 After the business went bankrupt, we had to
   .... and start again.
6 It's possible to .... an unpleasant
   illness when travelling in the tropics.
7 We had to .... through the
   items at the auction as we didn't want to knock
   anything over and have to pay for the damage.
8 As Jack finishes work earlier than me, I've asked
   him to take the car and........................... the
   children from school.

(8 marks)

C Complete the missing word in each of the folowing sentences.

1 In legal contracts involving the sale of property the
   person buying is referred to as the p................. .
2 ... and the person selling is known as the
   v................. .
3 When buying household items, people often buy
   on c................. rather than use cash.
4 Many companies buy in b................. rather
   than order smaller quantities, which cuts down
   on costs.
5 I'm afraid the item you want is out of s...............
   at the moment – we'll be receiving a new order next
   week.
6 If you're buying a new hi-fi then it's a good idea
   to s................. around to find the best value
   for money.
7 When the stock market collapsed, many financiers
   were reduced to p................. and some even
   ended up begging on the streets.

(7 marks)

D Write a word which fits both sentences.

1 Susan was the .... beneficiary of her
   uncle's will as she was the last remaining member
   of the family.
   Why does the .... of my left shoe always
   wear out before the right?
2 Geoff looked very .... in a new Italian
   suit.
   It was a very .... business move to buy
   up some of their smaller competitors and gain a
   larger share of the market.
3 At this .... in the financial year, the
   company will need to review its accounts.
   Their failure to guarantee delivery on time was the
   weak .... of the company and led to its
   eventual collapse.
4 From the sales .... you can see that the
   company's profit has increased slightly.
   The band's new single went straight to the top of
   the .... within a few days of its release.
5 Hundreds of workers made redundant by the closure
   of the factory .... a demonstration
   outside parliament.
   The amateur dramatics society .... a
   production of Shakespeare's Hamlet at the local
   theatre in aid of charity.

(5 marks)

Proficiency Masterclass © Oxford University Press **Photocopiable**

Vocabulary Test Unit 10 Name _____

A Fill each gap with one or two words.

1 Jim is always negative about other people's work – he is far too free with ....

2 The right to free .... is fundamental to democracy.

3 Life as a student can be very free and ...., without any of the stress and responsibilities of working for a living.

4 Members are not required to pay an admission fee and can get tickets to all matches free of .... at the club office.

5 When she was released by the new government after spending ten years in jail as a political prisoner, she finally felt as free as ....

6 Susan was given free .... in choosing her staff for the advice centre, without having to get approval from the board.

7 What started as a polite disagreement soon became a complete free-................., with everybody shouting at the same time.

8 At last, Denise was free .... her mother's interference in her personal life.

9 While his father was away, Tony .... free with his father's car.

10 The price of the company's shares has been in free .... since they lost the important defense contract.

(10 marks)

B Replace the phrase in brackets with a suitable expression using the word *law*.

1 Rachel is a (*person beyond anyone's control*) .... , as she never takes any notice of the office regulations and comes into work whenever she likes.

2 No one, not even the Prime Minister, can be (*beyond the legal system*) .... – we all have to accept responsibility for our actions.

3 Sid beat up the man who had stolen his car, so the police arrested him for taking (*his own steps to get justice*) ....

4 According to the (*strict legal rule*) .... , parking her car outside the hospital entrance was an offence, but the police let Mia off because it had been an emergency.

5 In politics, the (*survival of the strongest*) .... applies – only the most ruthless get to the top.

(5 marks)

C Rewrite each sentence using the word given.

1 You would be wasting your time taking this case to court. (*point*)
....
....

2 The former dictator gave no indication that he was sorry for his crimes. (*remorse*)
....
....

3 The police ended the fighting between the two gangs by arresting the leaders. (*put*)
....
....

4 I didn't listen very carefully to the lecture on forensic science. (*pay*)
....
....

5 The students voted to continue the protest against government education cuts. (*keep*)
....
....

6 The defence lawyer felt he had won the battle when his client was cleared of all charges. (*scored*)
....
....

7 When the players turned up late for training, the coach decided to get strict. (*lay*)
....
....

8 I do not intend to spend my weekend writing up these reports. (*no*)
....
....

9 The company couldn't open a new office owing to a lack of funds. (*prevented*)
....
....

10 I would rather not imagine what might happen if we forget our passports. (*dread*)
....
....

(10 marks)

Vocabulary Test Unit 11 Name _____

A Fill each gap with a verb from the box. Make any changes necessary.

split	lead	undergo	oblige	blame
attack	fight	prove	demonstrate	
flourish	add	create	adjust	

The music scene in Jamaica (1)................. a major transformation during the period from the mid-sixties to early seventies with the emergence of reggae. The music industry had difficulty (2)................. to the new conditions, and the sheer volume of the music (3)................. too loud for most dance hall owners. In response, enthusiasts organised their own open air dances, which (4)................. to a loss of revenue for the entertainment companies who were eventually (5)................. to sell off many of the dance halls. An increase in drug abuse was (6)................. on these events, and many older residents of Kingston complained about the noise, (7)................. to the pressure on the new music. However, independent record producers such as King Tubby and Lee Perry (8)................. hard against the domination of the major record companies in an effort to get their music played to a wider audience. Eventually, the record industry giants (9)................. some of their companies in two in order take advantage without having their established labels associated with 'rebel' music. In later years, reggae (10)................. and spread beyond Jamaica, especially when Bob Marley became an international star .

(10 marks)

B Underline the correct word in italic.

1 In recent years, there has been a *slide / drift / flow* away from the big cities.

2 The use of computer-enhanced images has brought about *wide / profound / absolute* changes in film production.

3 The clerk had a long *column / pillar / pile* of figures to add up at the end of the day.

4 Because of its innovative techniques, the film was hailed by many critics as a *significant / serious / special* achievement in modern cinema.

5 The director's temper became a little *unrelaxed / frayed / stressed* during the rehearsal.

6 The early morning sunlight *sparkled / speckled / glittered* on the waves, which created a delightful effect.

7 During the thirties, Hollywood produced many *luxurious / lavish / luscious* musicals with huge casts and elaborate sets.

8 This new home entertainment centre comes as a(n) *kit / gear / outfit* which you assemble yourself.

9 Wearing his headphones, Lee could sit back and listen to the music, *unaware / oblivious / ignorant* to the world around him.

10 Because it was his first time sailing, the journalist spent a long time awkwardly *fidgeting / fumbling / frolicking* with the ropes that operated the sails.

(10 marks)

C Fill the gaps in each sentence with a word from the box.

wine	blood	beans	tape	belt
sheet	biscuit	pie	cake	tie
pancake	milk	towel	carpet	tea

1 Well that really takes the .... ; I've never seen such an awful movie in my entire life !

2 Operating the new projector is such a piece of .... that even a beginner can do it.

3 Applying for a license to hold an open-air concert involved so much red .... that the organisers felt it wasn't worth the effort.

4 As writer, director and leading actor in the play, Steven seems to have a finger in every .... with this production.

5 Her face turned as white as a .... when she realised that she had broken the camera.

6 James bought a house in a green .... area outside the city, surrounded by open fields and woodland.

7 Details about the surprise ending to the film must be kept a secret, so please don't spill the ....

8 Deborah's joke about the dog and the goldfish fell as flat as a .... – no one laughed.

9 It's no good crying over spilt .... – you can't change what has been done.

10 Jonathan can truly claim to have blue .... – his grandfather was related to the royal family.

(10 marks)

Vocabulary Test Unit 12 Name _____

Total: ____ / 30

A Fill each gap with a verb from the box. Make any changes necessary.

cast	border	near	treat	deal
restore	resolve	come	approve	gave
expect	demand	assist	expose	disappear

1 The United Nations has .... that all troops be removed from the occupied zone immediately.

2 Losing a major contract because he'd overlooked some important details .... doubts upon Jack's ability to do the job.

3 The team's star player pulled a muscle five days before the big final, which .... a severe blow to his chances of playing in the match.

4 I don't think we need to make any changes as this problem with the new system is only temporary and will .... itself in due course.

5 The doctor said that Susan's illness had .... about as a consequence of stress and overwork.

6 These instruments contain very delicate parts and should be .... with care as they can very easily get damaged.

7 Mark's behaviour at the staff party .... on the outrageous, although most people were prepared to excuse him as he'd had too much to drink.

8 It was Ruth's hard work and meticulous preparation that .... in getting us the contract to carry out the research.

9 Some of the technicians at the nuclear power station were given thorough medical examinations as it was feared that they had been .... to harmful radiation.

10 I think you should try and work out your personal problems yourself as I don't really .... of spending so much money for a private therapist's advice.

(10 marks)

B Complete each gap with one or two words.

1 All the tutor's advice about preparing for the exams fell .... ears – they ignored him completely.

2 I know it's time-consuming sorting out all these files but don't .... heart now – we've only got a few more to do.

3 When his girlfriend criticised the story he'd written, Bill .... to heart – he was very upset.

4 The long period of tension and quarrels between them .... a head – the crisis came when Jill told her husband she wanted a divorce.

5 Everyone around the dinner table was .... ears – we paid great attention as he told us about his adventures travelling up the Amazon.

6 Jim's still a little bit .... the ears – he is very naïve.

7 When Sheila told Pete their relationship was at an end, it really .... his heart – he was devastated.

8 Your success in getting your story published is only the first step, so don't let it .... your head – don't get conceited.

9 You can't really prepare in advance for the questions the interviewer will ask you, so you'll just have to .... by ear – see what happens as you go along.

10 He'd only agreed to take on the project when a colleague turned it down, so his heart wasn't really .... – he had no real enthusiasm for it.

(10 marks)

C Write the noun form of each of these verbs.

1 justify ....
2 resemble ....
3 indicate ....
4 notify ....
5 renew ....
6 announce ....
7 produce ....
8 assure ....
9 refer ....
10 apply ....

(10 marks)

Progress Test Units 1–4 Name _____

A Word formation

For questions 1–10, read the text below. Use the word given in capitals below to form a word that fits in the space.

The often dull realities of life aboard a space station, with its long periods of (1)................., seem a far cry from the thrill and sensation of science fiction movies. But this was (2) .... disproved by the incident which occurred on the Mir space station on 26th June 1997 during the docking of a supply vessel.

The sudden (3) .... from view of the vessel during the final stages of the docking (4) .... gave the crew on the station the first indication that something was wrong. When it turned up again, it collided with a science module attached to the station. The ensuing situation quickly became (5) .... for the crew. With air rapidly escaping from the hole caused by the (6) ...., the station was heading for disaster. A catastrophe was averted by the quick-thinking and (7) .... of the crew in isolating the damaged section.

Although no claims that the station was (8) .... had been made by the technicians, they were still shocked at just how vulnerable it was shown to be. One factor that (9) .... contributed to the near tragedy was the station's age. Nevertheless, the crew themselves said they didn't feel (10) .... with the mission and all agreed that the new International Space Station should go ahead.

1	ACTIVE	6	COLLIDE
2	DRAMA	7	RESOURCE
3	APPEAR	8	DESTROY
4	PROCEED	9	ARGUE
5	NIGHTMARE	10	ILLUSION

(10 marks)

B Comprehension questions

Answer these questions about the text in A.

1 In the first paragraph, what image of life on a space station does the writer create?

....

2 Which word in paragraph 3 highlights the fact that the space station was a disaster waiting to happen?

....

(4 marks)

C Key word transformations

For questions 1–8, complete the second sentence so that it has a similar meaning to the first sentence, using the word given. Do not change the word given. You must use between 3 and 8 words, including the word given.

1 Susan's ability to be optimistic about being stuck in this deserted town is something I envy.
   bright
   I wish I could ....
   like Susan about being stuck in this deserted town.

2 It was impossible for him to have seen distinctly who was involved in the incident from that distance.
   out
   From that distance, he ....
   .... who was involved in the incident.

3 My father has allowed me to use his car as a temporary measure while mine is being repaired.
   time
   For .... , I'm using my father's car while mine is being repaired.

4 It's only because a magazine advertisement attracted my attention that I took this adventure holiday.
   eye
   Had a magazine advertisement ....
   ....,
   I wouldn't have taken this adventure holiday.

5 The climbers seemed unharmed by having to spend two nights on the mountain in a blizzard.
   worse
   The climbers seemed ....
   .... having to spend two nights on the mountain in a blizzard.

6 I only managed to see the tennis star for a brief moment through the crowd.
   glimpse
   I only succeeded ....
   .... the tennis star through the crowd.

7 I was very grateful to him for being so kind as to help me carry the luggage to the taxi.
   did
   He very...
   ....by carrying the luggage to the taxi.

8   Some medicines make you feel worse than you did
    before.
    do
    Some medicines ....
    .... than good.

(16 marks)

D Gapped sentences

For questions 1–6, find one word only which can be used appropriately in all three sentences.

1   Any breach of discipline in the army could result in
    you having the .... thrown at you.
    The experiment must be carried out by the .... ,
    otherwise we may face accusations of professional
    misconduct.
    I think you should take a leaf out of Jim's ....
    and take up some form of exercise.

2   It will take the team's star player time to
    .... his form after being out so long
    through injury.
    It was difficult for the emergency services to
    .... any bodies from the buildings in the
    aftermath of the earthquake.
    She needed several weeks to .... from the
    illness she picked up in the tropics.

3   We found a quiet, secluded .... by the
    river for our picnic.
    We realised we were in a tight .... when the
    border guards pointed their guns at us.
    Although running on the .... is recommended
    as good exercise, I find it rather boring.

4   Customs officials will .... down heavily
    on anyone smuggling illegal goods into the
    country.
    We were a bit worried as it took her a few minutes
    to .... round after being knocked on the head.
    He has a tendency to........ out with some strange
    expressions he learnt from a old phrase book.

5   The captain sounded the .... when the
    ship began swaying in the high seas.
    The doctor said there was no cause for .... as
    the pain would soon go away.
    Jane felt a growing sense of .... when the
    children hadn't returned from the boating trip.

6   I have a feeling we have made the wrong decision
    but only .... will tell.
    The police arrived in the nick of .... to prevent
    the robbery.
    Now's a fine .... to tell me that you are going to
    be an hour late!

(12 marks)

E Writing

Write your answer to one of the following writing tasks.

1   The extract below is part of a magazine article you
    read on the effects of recent technological advances
    on our lives. You have decided to write a letter to be
    included in the Reader's Letters section of the
    magazine responding to the issues raised and
    expressing your own views.

> **It's a sad fact** that nowadays more and more people
> are being persuaded to part with money they don't
> really have on fashionable technological devices. A
> mobile phone may be very handy for someone such as
> a doctor, who needs to be contacted in an emergency,
> but I can't see the necessity for most people. And what
> damage is being done to the eyesight of all those
> people who spend hours glued to a computer screen
> surfing the internet? If you ask me, these are two
> technological advances we could well do without.

Write your **letter** in 300-350 words.

2   The authorities at the college where you are
    studying are considering a complete ban on
    smoking anywhere on the premises. As a member of
    the student welfare committee, you have been asked
    to write a **proposal** for the authorities outlining
    alternatives to the ban and suggesting ways in which
    greater awareness of the health risks can be
    promoted. Write your **proposal** in 300 – 350 words.

(20 marks)

Progress Test Units 5–8 Name _____

67 _____ %

A Cloze

For questions 1–15, read the text below and think of the word which best fits each space. Use only one word in each space.

When Isaac Newton walked along the beach and bent down to pick up seashells, (1)................. did he realise that the vast ocean of undiscovered truth that lay before him would contain such scientific wonders. He probably was (2)................., like everyone else of his generation, to foresee a time when science would unravel the secrets of life, the atom and the mind. Today, the ocean has yielded (3)................. a wealth of secrets that it is now a wondrous source of scientific possibilities and applications. Perhaps in (4)................. lifetime, we will see many of these marvels of science unfold (5)................. our very eyes, for we are no (6)................. the passive observers of the dance of nature that we (7)................. to be; we are (8)................. the process of becoming active choreographers. With the basic laws of the quantum, DNA and computers discovered, we are now embarking on a (9)................. greater journey, one that ultimately promises to take us to the stars. (10) .... our understanding of the fourth pillar, space-time, increases, this opens up the possibility in the distant future of being able to become masters of space and time. Barring some natural catastrophe, such as war (11)................. environmental collapse, we are on our (12) .... to becoming a truly planetary society. And what will (13)................. this possible is the power of these three revolutions. Ultimately, we will fulfil our destiny, and (14)................. our rightful place among the stars. The harnessing of these scientific revolutions is the (15)................. step towards making the universe truly our backyard. Others will follow.

(15 marks)

B Comprehension questions

Answer these questions about the text in A.

1 Explain in your own words why the writer has chosen to use the expression 'becoming active choreographers' in the second paragraph.

....

2 What exactly does the phrase 'these three revolutions' (paragraph 3) describe?

....

(4 marks)

C Key word transformations

For questions 1–8, complete the second sentence so that it has a similar meaning to the first sentence, using the word given. Do not change the word given. You must use between 3 and 8 words, including the word given.

1 Do you think you could assist us in this difficult situation?
   out
   Would you object ....
   ....in this difficult situation?

2 It's a pity we hadn't saved enough money to cope with just such an emergency.
   fall
   If we had saved more money, we would have had enough ....
   ....in just such an emergency.

3 You'll feel better after telling me what you think.
   chest
   If you ....
   .... , you'll feel better.

4 An able politician is one who is able to convey his point of view effectively.
   across
   An able politician can get ....
   .... everyone.

5 Tigers will become extinct unless something is done quickly.
   under
   Tigers are ....
   ....and something must be done quickly.

6 After a year in prison, it eventually dawned on Clive how wrong he had been to commit a crime.
   light
   After a year in prison, Clive eventually ....
   ....
   and decided that committing crime was wrong.

7 Although the manager said little, it was obvious to everyone how he felt.
   lines
   Everyone was able to ....
   ....although the manager said little.

8 Our last holiday was the best we've ever had.
   whale
   We...
   ....on our last holiday.

(16 marks)

Proficiency Masterclass © Oxford University Press **Photocopiable**

D Gapped sentences

For questions 1–6 find one word only which can be used appropriately in all three sentences.

1 Taking on extra staff was a leap in the ....
as we had no idea how many people we needed.
Brian's a bit of a .... horse as he never seems to
confide in anyone about his private life.
Please don't keep me in the .... about what's
really happening at work.

2 I don't take very kindly to people who ....
my ideas.
I'm such a bad cook I can't even .... an egg!
People who .... in this area of the river will be
prosecuted.

3 The house is situated on the .... road
into the town, which is extremely noisy.
Could you explain exactly what your .... reason
for wanting the job is?
The railway that runs through Newcastle-on-Tyne
is the .... line to Scotland.

4 William is a good talker; he's never ....
for words!
If you want to get your umbrella back, you can try
the .... and found office at the station.
It's easy to get .... in a big city like London.

5 Some people say that the 1950s were the ....
...... age of Hollywood.
When Mr Thomas left the firm he was given a
.... handshake by his superiors.
The .... rule about crossing a road in Britain is
to look right, left, then right again.

6 The bird .... its wings and flew
gracefully over the river.
The news of the victory .... quickly round the
city.
The soldiers .... out and started to walk
towards the wood.

(12 marks)

E Writing

Write your answer to one of the following writing tasks.

1 A magazine for young people has been running a series of articles about family life in different countries. You have read this extract from an article written by a student who lived abroad for a year. The same magazine has asked you to write an **article** reponding to the question of which style of family is best, and supporting your arguments with examples from your own experience.

> **WHEN I FIRST ARRIVED**, I was shocked by the deeply traditional family structure that still survived. Like many others in this country, the Ohaya family was very large. There were 11 children aged between 3 and 17, and two elderly grandparents and an aunt living in the same house. The Ohayas were like a small tribe with a complicated network of supporting relationships, but little privacy. I couldn't help comparing this with my own country where modern families are small and isolated, but independent and mobile. I still can't make up my mind which is best.

Write your **article** in 300–350 words.

2 You are working for a sports camp that organises two-week sports training courses for teenagers during the summer. You have been asked by your employers to think about how you will recruit and assess the trainers who will teach on the course. Write your **proposal**.

(20 marks)

Progress Test Units 9–12 Name_____

A Lexical cloze

For questions 1–12, read the two texts and decide which answer (A, B, C or D) best fits each gap.

REAL FAKES

When the artist and restorer Tom Keating (1)............ that he had produced and sold thousands of fake paintings, panic immediately (2)................. throughout the art world. Many of Keating's works, supposedly by famous painters, had (3)................. vast sums of money at auction houses around the world. They had suddenly become worthless overnight, leaving some galleries and private collectors facing financial (4)................. . Keating was prosecuted for (5)................., but charges against him were dropped on grounds of his ill health, and he never had to serve a prison (6)................. . Ironically, since his death, the value of genuine Keating fakes has soared, and some of them command even higher prices than those of the artists he copied.

1 A confessed   C acceded
   B declaimed   D affirmed
2 A poured   C filled
   B stretched   D spread
3 A gone to   C gone for
   B gone on   D gone with
4 A crash   C desolation
   B ruin   D destruction
5 A forgery   C libel
   B arson   D blackmail
6 A time   C period
   B stretch   D sentence

PRODUCING THE MAGIC

In a world that is still dominated by the (7)............... productions of major Hollywood studios, and in which all too many European films fall as (8)................. as a pancake, producer Tim Bevan seems to have found the magic touch. As the co-founder of Working Title Films, he has to his credit over 40 of the most critically and commercially acclaimed releases of the last two decades and he has had (9)................. no disasters. His close working relationship with scriptwriter Richard Curtis has (10)................. to some spectacular successes – *Four Weddings*, *Notting Hill* and

Bean accumulated over a billion dollars between them, enough to make most of his rivals (11)................. with envy. But Bevan has not let his success go to his (12)................. , and remains sensitive to the needs of the people he works with.

7   A imprudent   C lavish
    B oblivious   D inordinate
8   A badly   C flat
    B poor   D dull
9   A scarcely   C barely
    B hardly   D virtually
10 A caused   C created
    B resulted   D led
11 A blue   C red
    B green   D yellow
12 A ears   C eyes
    B heart   D head

(12 marks)

B Comprehension questions

Answer these questions about the texts in A.

1 Exlain why the writer of the first text has chosen to use the word 'soared'.
   ....

2 Why does the writer of the second text choose to use the phrase 'the magic touch'?
   ....

(4 points)

C Key word transformations

For questions 1– 8, complete the second sentence so that it has a similar meaning to the first sentence, using the word given. Do not change the word given. You must use between 3 and 8 words, including the word given.

1 My mother refuses to allow anyone to smoke in the house.
   have
   My mother won't ....
   ....in the house.

2 Unfortunately someone stole his passport on the train.
   had
   Unfortunately he ....
   ....on the train.

3 I'm concerned about her new boyfriend – he smokes and he drinks too.

only

I'm concerned about her new boyfriend –not ....as well.

4 Of course he was shocked - nobody has ever spoken to him like that.

anyone

Of course he was shocked - never .... like that.

5 He thinks that learning the piano would be utterly boring.

remotely

He is ....learning the piano.

6 In the end, the party was much more interesting than I had expected.

turned

In the end, the party ....much more interesting than I had expected.

7 Don't worry about the test – it'll be really easy for you.

cake

Don't worry about the test – it .... for you.

8 I'm afraid I'll be home late – I've still got lots of work to do tonight.

ears

I'm afraid I'll be home late – I'm .... tonight.

(16 marks)

D Gapped sentences

For questions 1–6 find one word only which can be used appropriately in all three sentences.

1 The new commander arrived at the base to take .... of the army.
  The radio works OK, but there's something wrong with the volume ....
  I'm not saying she's a bad mother, but she seems to have very little .... over how her son behaves.

2 Do you know where I can .... this suit dry-cleaned?
  I'll .... my secretary to fix up a meeting some time next week.
  I'm not sure exactly what they earn, but I know they .... paid a lot more than me.

3 The prosecution will attempt to .... that you were at the scene of the crime.
  We all doubted her abilities, but she was determined to .... us wrong.
  This problem is very complicated and may .... to be impossible to solve.

4 Everyone knows that you are .... to wear a seat belt in this country.
  I asked him to pass the ball and he duly ....
  Thank you so much for your help – I am much .... to you.

5 It takes a long time to learn to play a musical instrument well and it's all too easy to lose ....
  The cottage is in the .... of the village, opposite the green.
  I didn't have the .... to tell him he would probably never be good enough to join the team.

6 The psychiatrist concluded that the patient had a .... personality.
  John and Sue aren't going out any more – they .... up a few weeks ago.
  Let's drive across to France and we can .... the petrol.

(12 marks)

E Writing

Write your answer to one of the following writing tasks.

1 You have read this extract from a letter to a newspaper about equal pay and opportunities. You decide to write to the newspaper, responding to the points that are raised in the letter and giving your own views.

I do believe that we need to look beyond the laws that have been brought in, welcome as they are, and ask some further questions. Why, for example, are women so over-represented in low-paid (or even unpaid) careers, and why are so few of the highest earners women? Why are so few career paths designed for women who want to take some years off and then return part time or full time later? Is there a case for positive discrimination?

Write your **letter** in 300–350 words.

2 You were asked by a local newspaper to visit two different institutions for young offenders. The first was extremely strict and laid particular emphasis on punishment, while the second aimed to rehabilitate and educate. Write an **article** about the visits, comparing and contrasting the institutions and saying which approach is the most beneficial.

(20 marks)

Key to the Vocabulary Tests

Unit 1

A
1 fair-weather friend
2 rolling stone
3 nosy parker
4 wet blanket
5 new broom

B
1 to terms
2 in for
3 round
4 down
5 out with
6 the point
7 down
8 round
9 up
10 round

C
1 taking
2 well-being
3 have
4 rightful
5 ridiculously

D
1 cynical
2 previous
3 dose
4 drained
5 apprehensive
6 exhilaration
7 soothe
8 suffers
9 illusory
10 pleaded

Unit 2

A
1 baffled
2 abundant
3 defunct
4 catastrophic
5 systematic
6 extraordinary
7 alarming
8 skeletal

B
1 time will tell
2 pressed for time
3 take a leaf out of your brother's book
4 Jack's good books
5 on time
6 spoke volumes
7 a fine time
8 by the book
9 buy time
10 at the best of times

C
1 carelessness
2 unrealistic
3 legalisation
4 extraordinarily
5 reappearance
6 interchangeable
7 uncoordinated

Unit 3

A
1 clinking
2 antagonistic
3 saved
4 declared
5 deflected
6 pool
7 drained
8 reek
9 overwhelming
10 doom
11 task
12 break
13 face

B
1 peered
2 glanced
3 peeped
4 glimpsed
5 gazing
6 winked
7 stared

C
1 favour
2 up
3 good / no harm
4 their eyes
5 donkey work

Unit 4

A
1 When our flight was delayed, we were resigned / resigned ourselves to the idea of spending the night in the airport.
2 Mark found the idea of travelling across the Sahara in an old coach unattractive.
3 There's more to travelling alone than taking a good guidebook with you.
4 A performance of traditional dance will take place this evening in the village square.
5 The backpackers were subjected to three hours of interrogation by the border guards.
6 Besides being expensive, our last holiday was a disaster.
7 Paul was insensitive to other people's feelings.
8 Miriam regarded the long journey up river in a small boat as an adventure.

B
1 optimistic
2 dejected
3 infested
4 affected
5 weary
6 disillusioned
7 afraid

C
1 out of
2 your nose
3 drowned rat
4 gift horse
5 red-handed

D

1 emerged
2 courageous
3 arid
4 network
5 musty
6 clamber
7 obsessed
8 perverse
9 amateurish
10 resourceful

Unit 5

A

1 vast
2 call
3 raise
4 stage
5 drastic
6 throw
7 grave
8 controlled
9 harsh
10 run

B

1 whale of a time
2 keep the wolf from the door
3 flogging a dead horse
4 crocodile tears
5 snail's pace

C

1 come to light
2 the light at the end of the tunnel
3 to keep us in the dark
4 went out like a light
5 dark horse

D

1 highly
2 deeply
3 fully
4 blissfully
5 bitterly

Unit 6

A

1 witty
2 childish
3 stubborn
4 ingenious
5 charming
6 childlike
7 cute
8 crafty
9 amusing
10 determined

B

1 word perfect
2 read between the lines
3 word for word
4 in a word
5 lost for words

C

1 disagreeable
2 incoherent
3 immortal
4 unauthorised
5 non-violent
6 incapable
7 implausible
8 illiterate
9 irreverent
10 inauspicious
11 dishonest
12 unbiased
13 misunderstood
14 unenthusiastic
15 illogical
16 unjust

D

1 proven/proved
2 invariably
3 childlike
4 decoding
5 innumerable
6 likeable
7 memorable

Unit 7

A

1 criticism
2 extravagant
3 captured
4 lucrative
5 heritage
6 disposed
7 location
8 disintegrated
9 observant
10 gravity

B

1 age
2 yourself
3 rule
4 lining
5 handshake
6 tongued
7 hand
8 heart

C

1 rich
2 interacted
3 confined
4 grip
5 spread
6 out
7 bred

Unit 8

A

1 fall apart
2 fall back on
3 fallen behind with
4 fell through
5 fell short of
6 fell on
7 fell into place
8 fallen in with

B

1 my chest
2 out
3 to heart
4 amiss
5 sense
6 humble pie
7 teeth

C

1 dropped out
2 accused of
3 wind up
4 tipped off
5 tracked down

D

1 bears
2 fell
3 ease
4 put
5 raise

Unit 9

A

1 dabble
2 speculate
3 make
4 trading
5 break
6 fluctuate
7 crashed
8 spread
9 ruined
10 went

B

1 picked out
2 picking on
3 pick up
4 pick up
5 pick up the pieces
6 pick up
7 pick our way
8 pick up

C

1 purchasor
2 vendor
3 credit
4 bulk
5 stock
6 shop
7 penury

D

1 sole
2 smart
3 point
4 charts
5 staged

Unit 10

A

1 his criticism
2 speech
3 easy
4 charge
5 a bird
6 rein
7 -for-all
8 from
9 made
10 fall

B

1 law unto herself
2 above the law
3 the law into his own hands
4 letter of the law
5 law of the jungle

C

1 There's no point in taking this case to court.
2 The former dictator showed no remorse for his crimes.
3 The police put a stop to the fighting between the two gangs by arresting the leaders.
4 I didn't pay much attention to the lecture on forensic science.
5 The students voted to keep (on) protesting against government educations cuts.
6 The defence lawyer felt he had scored a victory when his client was cleared of all charges.
7 When the players turned up late for training, the coach decided to lay down the law.
8 I have no intention of spending my weekend writing up these reports.
9 The company was prevented from opening a new office by a lack of funds.
10 I dread to think what might happen if we forget our passports.

Unit 11

A

1 underwent
2 adjusting
3 proved
4 led
5 obliged
6 blamed
7 adding
8 fought
9 split
10 flourished

B

1 drift
2 profound
3 column
4 significant
5 frayed
6 sparkled
7 lavish
8 kit
9 oblivious
10 fumbling

C

1 biscuit
2 cake
3 tape
4 pie
5 sheet
6 belt
7 beans
8 pancake
9 milk
10 blood

Unit 12

A

1 demanded
2 cast
3 dealt
4 resolve
5 come
6 treated
7 bordered
8 assisted
9 exposed
10 approve

B

1 on deaf
2 lose
3 took it
4 came to
5 all
6 wet behind
7 broke
8 go to
9 play it
10 in it

C

1 justification
2 resemblance
3 indication
4 notification
5 renewal
6 announcement
7 production
8 assurance
9 referral
10 application

Key to the Progress Tests

Progress Test   Units 1–4

A

1	inactivity	6	collision
2	dramatically	7	resourcefulness
3	disappearance	8	indestructible
4	procedure	9	arguably
5	nightmarish	10	disillusioned

B

1 a boring, idle, uncomfortable life
2 vulnerable

C

1 look on the bright side
2 couldn't have made out
3 the time being
4 not caught my eye
5 none the worse for
6 in catching a (brief) glimpse of
7 kindly did me a favour
8 do (you) more harm

D

1	book	4	come
2	recover	5	alarm
3	spot	6	time

E

1 The letter should take up the specific points made in the extract: whether technology is harmful or useful, and whether its popularity is a matter of fashion. It can agree or disagree with the view expressed. The writer's views should be clearly expressed. The letter should be rhetorical in tone.
2 The proposal should suggest some alternatives to a ban and ways of raising awareness about the health risks. It should lead to a recommendation. The proposal will be formal or neutral, with clear headings and paragraphs.
See TB page 9 for the Writing General Mark Scheme.
Note: As an approximate guide, the following marks should be given out of twenty: band 0 = no marks, band 1 = 1–3 marks, band 2 = 4–7 marks, band 3 = 8–12 marks, band 4 = 13–16 marks, band 5 = 17–20 marks.

Progress Test   Units 5–8

A

1	little	9	much / far
2	unable	10	As
3	such	11	or
4	our	12	way
5	before	13	make
6	longer /more	14	take
7	used	15	first
8	in		

B

1 to show we are now able to control nature or the 'dance of life'
2 quantum, DNA, and computers

C

1 to helping us out
2 to fall back on
3 get things off your chest
4 get his/her message across to
5 under (the) threat of extinction
6 saw the light
7 read between the lines
8 had a whale of a time

D

1	dark	4	lost
2	poach	5	golden
3	main	6	spread

E

1 The article should talk about the writer's preferred family structure with examples. The article should be fairly informal, as the readership is made up of young people. The reader's interest should be aroused by the article and the opinions and examples expressed.
2 The proposal should include a detailed plan for the recruitment and assessment of trainers, with an explanation of why this procedure is being recommended. The proposal should be formal or neutral, and should have clear headings and paragraphs. The reader should be persuaded that the suggestions are appropriate.
See TB page 9 for the Writing General Mark Scheme.

Progress Test   Units 9–12

A

1 A   2 D   3 C   4 B   5 A   6 D
7 C   8 C   9 D   10 D   11 B   12 D

B

1 to emphasise how quickly the price of the
   paintings has risen
2 to give the impression that Bevan has a talent
   that guaranteees success

C

1 have anyone smoking
2 had his passport stolen
3 only does he smoke, but he drinks
4 has anyone spoken to him
5 not remotely interested in
6 turned out to be
7 will be a piece of cake
8 up to my ears in work

D

1 control   4 obliged
2 get   5 heart
3 prove   6 split

E

1 The letter should take up the specific points
   mentioned in the extract: why women receive lower
   pay, why there are fewer career paths for women,
   and whether positive discrimination is a good idea.
   It can agree or disagree with the proposal that
   action is needed. The writer's view should be
   clearly expressed. The letter should be rhetorical
   in tone.
2 The article should compare and contrast details of
   each institution based on the writer's experience
   of them. It should lead to a conclusion in which
   the writer's opinion is expressed. The article
   should be neutral in tone. The reader should be
   interested in the writer's experience and know
   what their conclusions are.

See TB page 9 for the Writing General Mark Scheme.

Photocopiable Activities

Teacher's notes

Activity 1.1

Aim
Students practise comparing, contrasting and persuasion while talking about sports.

Preparation
Photocopy page 158, one per student.

Procedure
Students read through the sample paragraph. Ask what the words in italic are expressing (comparison).

Divide the class into pairs or small groups.

Assign a different sports association to each pair or group.

Allow students 8–10 minutes to prepare what they are going to say to promote their sport. They can use some of the cues given for their sport and their own ideas. They can also say why other sports are not so good. Encourage the use of structures in the sample to compare their sport with the ones their colleagues will promote.

When they are ready, a student from each pair/group tries to persuade the rest of the class to join their association. Encourage other groups to ask questions.

The class can take a vote on the most persuasive.

Follow-up
Students write a paragraph for the university brochure about the sport that they are promoting.

Activity 1.2

Aim
Students practise forming complex sentences using relative clauses and reduced clauses.

Preparation
Photocopy page 159, one per student.

Procedure
Students read the instructions.

Ask them to find the relative clauses and reduced clauses in the first paragraph.

Key
Originally founded in 1954 by Mr F. E. Kayshus with money donated by charity … (reduced clause)

… donated by charity (reduced clause)

… which is the largest sports and leisure organisation in the country (relative clause)

Students work in pairs to write sentences from the notes in each section. Remind them to use the handwritten guidelines to help them.

Ask them to compare their sentences with another pair.

Compare sentences as a class by asking each pair in turn to read out what they have written for each section.

A vote can be taken on the best answer for *Our Motto*.

Key

Facilities
The centre, (which is) situated in pleasant countryside within easy reach of the city, boasts excellent facilities, including a gym, a sports shop and a sauna. There is also a canteen where a wide range of healthy dishes, based on dietary advice from professional nutritionists, is available.

The Gym
Designed to our own specifications, the gym, which is fully air-conditioned and contains the latest training equipment, is the largest in the area. Highly qualified instructors, who are on duty at all times, are available for advice on personal training programmes.

Aerobics Sessions
For those not wanting a heavy workout in the gym, there are twice-daily aerobics sessions (which are) aimed at enhancing flexibility and suppleness.

Specialised Training Centre
Widely regarded as one of the best of its kind in the country, the centre was originally set up by James Grigorus, the sprinter, whose portrait hangs in the entrance lobby. Many local athletes, some of whom have gone on to win medals in major championships, have benefited from its facilities.

Sauna and Jacuzzi

Located in the newly-opened extension, the sauna and jacuzzi, which are open all day, offer the chance to unwind and soothe aching muscles.

Sports Shop

Members making purchases in the sports shop can take advantage of a 10% discount on all items.

Our Motto

Our aim is that sense of well-being so essential to everyone whose lives are hectic and stressed.

Activity 2

Aim

Students practise use of the continuous aspect.

Preparation

Photocopy Version A on page 160 for half your students and Version B on page 161 for the other half.

Procedure

Divide the class into pairs. In each pair, one student should receive a copy of Version A, the other Version B.

Give each student a few minutes to read the paragraph which is complete on their sheet.

Student A dictates their version to student B.

Student B fills the gaps in their version with student A's words, or a different phrase if they think student A is incorrect.

Repeat this procedure with student B dictating.

When they have finished, students compare their versions and discuss whether they agree on the form of the verb used.

Give each pair a copy of the correct version on page 162 to check their answers, or display this on an overhead projector.

Follow-up

Ask students who they think the narrators are in each passage and what they think has happened or is going to happen. Encourage them to speculate.

There is no correct answer. Discuss students' ideas based on the text.

Activity 3.1

Aim

Students practise using modals for deduction and speculation about the past, and for expressing possibility, necessity and obligation.

Preparation

Photocopy page 163, one per student.

Procedure

Divide the class into pairs.

Students look at the first story *A bit of mystery*. To find a solution, students make deductions based on the evidence and then speculate about what happened. Students should make a note of their ideas.

Allow students about ten minutes for discussion.

When they have finished, ask each pair to read out their solutions.

Follow the same procedure for *Tired of waiting*.

This time, students should decide what they are going to say to their friend.

Follow up

You can take a class vote on the best suggestions.

Possible answers

A bit of mystery,
Dave can't have been working because the shop closes at 4 p.m., so he should have been home by 5 p.m. .
He must have left in a hurry as the door was open and the keys were on the table.
He can't have taken the dog for a walk as its lead was still on the table.
The window must have been broken from the outside as the glass is on the floor inside and he must have cut himself picking up the pieces.
He must have had a visitor because there are two cups of coffee on the table.
He must have remembered about the cinema as there is a ticket on the table.
It can't have been Dave on the phone as he would have replied.

Suggested solution
Someone could have thrown something through the window from the street outside and Dave might have

been angry about it, which accounts for the shouting the neighbour heard. This could have frightened the dog, who knocked over the furniture. Dave could have left the door open when he went outside to see who had broken the window and the dog may have run out and Dave had to chase after it. The phone call could have been burglars checking to see if anyone was at home. The visitor can't have been his girlfriend as she is on holiday.

Tired of waiting
We needn't have arranged to meet so early.
You might / could / should have phoned.
I needn't have left the party so early.
I could have stayed longer at the party.
I needn't have got up so early.
I could have got up later.
I could have gone to the shops.
I could have had some breakfast.
I might not have felt so hungry.
I needn't have waited in for you.
I could have done some work for my English class.
I shouldn't have believed you would be here on time.
I could have gone with someone else.

Activity 3.2

Aim
Students practise paraphrasing and eliminating irrelevance.

Preparation
Photocopy page 164, one per student.

Procedure
Divide the class into pairs or small groups.

Allow them around 10 minutes to discuss how to reduce the sentences and say the same thing within the least number of words.

When they have finished, each pair or group presents its solutions. Compare them as a class.

Follow-up
Each pair or group thinks of something simple to say, then writes an overelaborate paraphrase of it. The paraphrases are read out to the class who have to guess what the real meaning is.

Possible answers
1 Some people use more words than they need.
2 I don't like going to the dentist.
3 Take care crossing the road – you might get run over.
4 I didn't do my homework.
5 The English can't speak other languages.
6 I don't know.
7 My team lost / The other team won.
8 I'm not looking forward to the exams.

Activity 4.1

Aim
Students practise expressions and reading for gist with short texts.

Preparation
Photocopy page 165, one per student.

Procedure
Students read the articles, then work in pairs to decide which title belongs with which article.

Compare answers as a class.

Discuss the questions below the articles as a class.

Follow-up
In pairs, students write their own article using one of the headlines that did not match with an article. Alternatively, this could be set as a homework task.

Key

A	A close shave
B	Looking on the bright side
C	Never look a gift horse in the mouth
D	Caught red-handed
E	Package ordeals

Activity 4.2

Aim
Students practise a variety of conditional forms.

Preparation
Photocopy page 166.

Cut it up to make one set of 12 challenge cards.

If you have a large class you may need two or three sets.

Procedure
Divide the class into pairs or small groups.

A student from the first pair or small group takes a card and reads out what is written on it, together with the cue word in brackets.

All pairs or groups then have one minute only to write a conditional sentence starting with the cue word.

Each pair or group reads out their answer. If their answer is correct, they get one point. Use the key to check their answers.

A student from the second pair or group then takes the next card and reads it out and so on until all the cards have been used.

The pair or group with the most correct sentences wins.

Key

1	Should you change your mind about the trip, get in touch with me as soon as possible.
2	Were it not for the pile of work I have to do, we could get away for the weekend.
3	Should you misplace your passport, contact your embassy immediately.
4	But for our tight schedule, we would have had more time to explore the old quarter of the city.
5	Provided you don't let the local wine go to your head, you'll have a great time at the village carnival.
6	Had it not been for your insistence on taking the scenic route, we wouldn't be hopelessly lost now.
7	Had we been able to understand the guidebook, we might have been spared the embarassment of finding ourselves on a nudist beach.
8	Unless you show consideration for their customs, local people won't take kindly to you.
9	Had we taken our language lessons seriously, our attempts to communicate with local people would have met with more success.
10	Were you to find yourself penniless and stranded in a foreign city, what would your first course of action be?
11	But for the hospitality of the local people, our stay on the island would have been a nightmare.
12	Had I known it was private event, I wouldn't have come.

Activity 5

Aim
Students practise verb + noun collocations.

Preparation
Photocopy page 167, one per pair or group. Cut up the worksheets as indicated.

Procedure
Divide the class into pairs or small groups.

Give each pair or group one set of cut up verbs and one set of noun phrases.

Students in their pairs or groups match the verbs with the correct noun phrases.

Set a time limit and do the activity as a race if you wish.

Encourage them to make guesses about any they are not sure of.

Check each pair or group's answers using page 167 as the key.

Follow-up
In their pairs or groups, students use ten of the verb + noun collocations in sentences of their own. Encourage the use of dictionaries for any of the collocations that may be unfamiliar to them. Alternatively, this could be set as a homework task.

Activity 6.1

Aim
Students practise cleft sentences for emphasis

Preparation
Photocopy page 168, one per student.

Procedure
Students read the speech to find all the cleft sentences used in it for making emphasis. Ask them what adjectives and phrases the speaker has used to be more forceful (outrageous, unacceptable, annoying, unnecessary, unreasonable, take exception to, draw the line at, goes without saying.)

Students choose one of the items from the list to give a speech. If you have a large class, this can be done with pairs or small groups preparing a speech together.

Allow students 10 minutes to prepare their speech. Encourage the use of cleft sentences along with the adjectives and phrases to make their speeches more emphatic. Remind them that they can add anything they want to their speeches and should try and make them humorous.

When students give their speeches, check for accuracy with cleft sentences and give feedback if necessary at the end.

Encourage students to agree or disagree with the opinions presented by other groups.

Activity 6.2

Aim

Students practise writing complex sentences. Use of *only*, *much*, *just* and *even* in adverbial phrases and *so* / *such* as modifiers.

Preparation

Make one copy of the worksheet on page 169 for each group of students.

Procedure

Divide the class into pairs or groups. Explain that owing to a computer error, the sentences in their homework have been scrambled. Students work together to unscramble their sentences. You may wish to make the activity into a race.

As a hint, remind them that a sentence always begins with a capital letter and that they can put the parts of the sentences together first and add *just*, *even*, *much* and *so* / *such* afterwards.

When they have finished, ask each group to compare their sentences with another group. Check each group's sentences. Some variations are possible.

Key

The Babel fish
Sentence 1
Although / it is / a small creature, / the Babel fish is / so / effective in removing / barriers to communication / that it has / even / been held responsible for / causing wars.

Sentence 2
Nevertheless, / understanding / even / the most obscure languages / can easily be achieved / just / by putting one in your ear, / something which is / much / appreciated by travellers.

Charles Dickens
Sentence 1
Despite being / much / admired as a writer, / Dickens was / only / able to find fulfilment / in his work, / as his personal life was / so / empty and disappointing.
Sentence 2
Even / though some of his novels are not / so / widely read, / Dickens is / just / as popular now, / if / only / because of the characters he created, / as he was / during his lifetime.
or
Even / though some of his novels are not / so / widely read, / Dickens is / just / as popular now / as he was / during his lifetime, / if / only / because of the characters he created.

An arts festival
Sentence 1
The festival / was packed with / such / a variety of events / that it was / just / impossible to decide, / even / with the help of the programme, / which ones to see.
or
The festival / was packed with / such / a variety of events / that it was / just / impossible to decide / which ones to see, / even / with the help of the programme.
Sentence 2
Some of the events, / which had been / much / publicised in the press, / proved to be / so / popular that we could / only / get tickets / by queuing for two or three hours.

Activity 7

Aim

Students practise the use of the passive in news articles.

Preparation

Photocopy page 170, one per student.

Procedure

Take the first sentence as an example. Key: **New**

measures standardising the size of sausages throughout member states *were approved* by the European Parliament yesterday.

Students work in pairs to read through the three articles and rewrite them using the passive.

Students do not need to rewrite the whole article. When they have finished, ask them to compare their rewrites with another pair.

Check answers as a class.

Follow-up
Students choose one of the headlines under *Other News* and write a brief news report using their own ideas. Remind them to use passive forms where appropriate.

Key

The Euro Sausage
New measures standardising the size of sausages throughout member states were approved by the European Parliament yesterday, which will undoubtedly cause widespread controversy. This trend for standardisation has been going on for some time now but it is the prospect of all sausages having to conform to a standard size that has been most severely criticised. The decision to introduce a 15cm standard sausage has been denounced as going too far by some politicians.

'It's absolutely outrageous,' said Bill Blanket, M.P for North Yorkshire, home of the famous Grandma Batty's Pork Sausage. 'What is really annoying to many people is the fact that they may be forced to consume 15 cm sausages even if they want larger ones.'

From January next year all shops selling over or under sized sausages will be heavily fined. Unannounced checks will be carried out by special teams of sausage inspectors from the local Public Health Department.

Revels turn into riot at wedding reception
The village of Sourbottom in the Wold was still recovering yesterday in the aftermath of a violent fight that broke out between two families at a wedding reception that was being held in 'The Queen's Head' hotel.

According to one guest, the whole thing started when the bride's mother, Mrs Eileen Stoat, was told to shut up while she was making a speech before the cutting of the cake. Friends of the bride immediately set upon members of the groom's family and when the bride's father, farmer Mr Ted Stoat, tried to intervene his jacket and shirt were ripped off and flung at the band, who had been hired for the occasion.

'They had been drinking all day,' said another guest. 'Lumps of wedding cake were hurled across the room, and tables and chairs were overturned as everyone joined in the mayhem.'

The police were summoned but by the time they arrived the fighting had spilled out into the street and reinforcements had to be brought in from nearby Mevesham.

'It was supposed to have been the happiest day of my life,' sobbed the bride, Tracy Bracken. 'But it never crossed my mind that both my new husband and my father would end up in jail.'

Six men and two women are still being detained at Mevesham Police Station and a spokesperson at Mevesham General Hospital said that nearly twenty people had been treated for minor injuries.

Albion lose again!
Mevesham Albion were defeated 3 – 0 by Avalon United last night in the local derby match.

All three goals were scored by United striker Owen Fleetfoot and Albion's captain Vinnie Viles was sent off for the third time this season. This is Albion's twelfth defeat in a row and the manager Ron Atwick is expected to be sacked if results don't improve.

Activity 8

Aim
Students practise compound character adjectives and speaking.

Preparation
Photocopy page 171, one per student.

Procedure
Students read the instructions at the start.

Students work in pairs to create two appropriate compound adjectives from the words given in A and B for each person in the profiles.

Next, students match each description with an appropriate partner for a date.

Check answers as a class, asking students to give reasons for their choice of adjective and pairing.

Follow-up

Students find any other word combinations from boxes A and B that they didn't use. Encourage the use of dictionaries.

Alternatively, students choose adjectives for other members of the class. They may wish to write a small paragraph about themselves or a colleague for a dating agency.

Key

Ron	self-opinionated and quick-tempered
Rick	warm-hearted and easy-going
Ryan	mild-mannered and good-humoured
Tina	self-centred and single-minded
Tricia	strong-willed and thick-skinned
Tracy	outgoing and broad-minded

Other possible combinations are good-natured, good-hearted, self-confident, bad-mannered, bad-tempered, narrow-minded and weak-willed.

Activity 9

Aim

Students practise speaking and various reporting verbs.

Preparation

Photocopy page 172, one per two students. Cut the page in two as indicated.

Procedure

Organise the students into pairs, students A and B.

In each pair, give each student the appropriate half.

Check that the students undersand the situation explained on the handout.

Allow a few minutes for each student to read the salesperson's comments and decide which reporting verb is appropriate for each one.

Each student then reports to their partner to explain what they were told in the shop.

Remind them that they do not need to report the exact words the salesman said, just the key idea.

When they have finished, they should decide which hi-fi they would prefer to buy.

Check answers as a class.

Key

The Sonic Sound System
The salesman *claimed* that it was the best system on the market and assured me it wasn't as expensive as it looked. He *explained* that it was such good value because there were no import costs. He *inquired* about what sort of price range I was considering but then *apologised* for being so inquisitive. He *insisted* on giving me a demonstration and *admitted* that it was rather complicated to use. Finally he *warned* me not to turn the volume up too high in case the neighbours complained.

The Hightone Hi-Fi
Before we began he *made it clear* that it was a very expensive piece of equipment. He *suggested* trying it out to appreciate its subtle tone and quality. He *pointed out* how easy it was to use and *urged me* to listen for a while. He *denied* it was overpriced and then *complained* about people wasting his time. He *promised* to give me a reduction if I was really interested in buying but then *objected* to me touching it.

Activity 10

Aim

Students practise presenting views, considering options, and agreeing and disagreeing.

Preparation

Photocopy page 173, one per student.

Procedure

Divide the class into small groups.

Allow a few minutes for students to read through the details of each candidate.

Each student in the group should present their views on which candidate should be awarded the prize. The group should reach a decision on one candidate. Encourage students to defend their point of view.

Ask each group in turn to present their decision to the rest of the class for discussion.

Invite the other groups to agree or disagree and ask students to reach a decision on one candidate as a class.

Activity 11

Aim
Students practise structures using *have* and *get* and inversions with negative adverbs.

Preparation
Photocopy page 174, one per student.

Procedure
Students look at the complaints and underline all the inversions or structures using *have* or *get* they can find.

Divide the class into pairs or small groups of 3–4 students.

Each pair or group writes down as many complaints as they can using the list and any ideas of their own. Students read out their complaints or hand you a written list.

The pair or group with the most of accurate complaints wins the refund.

Check for accuracy with word order and the verb forms after *have* and *get*.

Key

> A   I *had* hot coffee *spilt* all over my trousers in the bar. The waiter shouted at me in front of everyone, saying it was all my fault. *Rarely have I felt* so embarrassed. Then I had to *have* my suit *cleaned*/ had to *get* someone *to clean* my suit.
>
> B   *Little did I realise* when I bought the tickets to the dinner and dance how awful it would be. The musicians were so bad they *had* everyone *throwing* bread rolls at them. *Not only was the food* tasteless, but it was also undercooked.
>
> C   There is a rock star staying in the room next to me. *Hardly had I* got into bed and switched the light off *when* the music started /*No sooner had I* got into bed and switched the light off *than* the music started. *Not only was it* extremely loud but it went on to 4 a.m. . When I went to complain I *had* beer *thrown* at me and was told I was too old. *Never before have I* been so insulted.
>
> D   We waited over an hour to be served in the restaurant. *Not until* I mentioned it to the head waiter, *did someone* come to our table. Then the waiter brought us the wrong order, so I had to *get* someone else *to serve* us. *Rarely have I* experienced such bad service.

> E   When I switched on the TV in my room, I could only get the children's channel. *Not until / Only when* the porter came with the operating instructions *could we* get it working properly. *Hardly* had I settled down to watch the match *when* it exploded / *No sooner had I* settled down to watch the match *than* it exploded.
>
> F   The brochure said there were breathtaking views of the surrounding countryside. *Little did I* realise when I booked the room that this included a power station and an oil refinery!
>
> G   When I arrived I couldn't *get* anyone *to help* me with my luggage so I had to drag it to the lift myself. *No sooner had I* stepped into the lift *than* the fire alarm went off / *Hardly had I* stepped into the lift *when* the fire alarm went off. This *had* everyone *rushing* around in panic. *Only when* I started shouting *did someone* come to help me.

Activity 12

Aim
Students revise grammatical structures studied throughout the course.

Preparation
Photocopy page 175, one per two students. Cut up page 175 as indicated.

Procedure
Give half the class copies marked Student A, the other half copies marked Student B.

Students work in pairs with colleagues who have the same sheet as they do.

Students decide whether the sentences on their worksheet are correct or not and correct any errors they find.

Make new pairs in which one student should have the sheet marked Student A, the other Student B.

Students work together to compare their sentences and decide on correct sentences between them.

Check answers as a class.

Key

1 A	2 A	3 B	4 B	5 A	6 B
7 A	8 B	9 B	10 B	11 A	12 A

Why not take up **jogging?**

It's just the thing for you. It's *nowhere near as* competitive *as* soccer or golf and is *nothing like as* expensive *as* fishing. You can go jogging *whenever* you want, *wherever* you like, within reason. True, it may be rather solitary but it's *a great deal* better for your heart and lungs than any of the other activities, and *the more* you do *the fitter* you feel. So why not come and join us. It's *far and away the best* option for you!

Student Sports Associations

The Joggers
- Costs nothing, except for the price of trainers.
- Good for the heart and lungs.
- Can be done anywhere, at any time, within reason.
- Energetic and somewhat strenuous – so don't overdo it.
- Can be rather a solitary activity.

Swimmers Society
- Relatively inexpensive – membership of a local swimming pool is quite cheap.
- Good all over exercise – it can be very enjoyable and satisfying.
- Can be as energetic and strenuous as you wish.
- Like jogging, it can be a little solitary.
- The swimming pool can get very crowded at certain times of day.

Fishing for Fun
- You get plenty of fresh air, although the weather can sometimes be a problem.
- Very relaxing and pleasurable – it helps with stress and anxiety.
- Costly in terms of equipment needed.
- Sedentary – it only gets active if you catch something !
- Very solitary unless you take a friend with you.

The Soccer Team
- Very sociable, especially in the bar afterwards, and can be good fun.
- Only play once a week, so it's not very time consuming, although there may be practice sessions.
- Very competitive and requires some commitment.
- Not costly – boots are quite cheap.
- Risk of injury or not getting selected for the team.

Weight-trainers Anonymous
- Very effective for getting into shape.
- Strenuous but not too energetic. Good for heart and lungs.
- Gym membership fees are not too high.
- Repetitive and can become an obssesion.
- You may need to buy larger sized clothes after a while.

The Golf Club
- Gentle and easy exercise – plenty of walking and fresh air.
- Very popular – not too strenuous or energetic.
- Costly in terms of equipment and membership fees.
- Can be very competitive – people lose their tempers!

1.2   The Feelgood Health and Fitness Centre

You have been asked to help write a brochure in English for the health and fitness centre below. The Publicity Officer has given you notes for each section of the brochure and some handwritten guidelines to help you. The first section has been written to give you an idea of the style required.

The **Feelgood**
Health and Fitness Centre

The Centre
Originally founded in 1954 by F.E. Kayshus with money donated by charity, the centre is now part of the Wellsound company, which is the largest sports and leisure organisation in the country.

Facilities
The centre is situated in pleasant countryside.
The centre is within easy reach of the city.
The centre boasts excellent facilities.
These facilities include a gym, a sports shop and a sauna.
There is also a canteen.
A wide range of healthy dishes are available here.
These dishes are based on dietary advice from professional nutritionists.
Two sentences. Try not to use 'which' twice in the same sentence.

The Gym
The gym is designed to our own specifications.
The gym is fully air-conditioned.
The gym contains the latest training equipment.
The gym is the largest in the area.
Instructors are available at all times.
The instructors are highly-qualified.
The instructors can give advice on personal training programmes.
Two sentences. Don't start with 'The gym'.

Aerobics Sessions
There are twice-daily aerobics sessions.
The aerobics sessions are for those who don't want a heavy workout in the gym.
The aerobics sessions are aimed at enhancing flexibility and suppleness.
One sentence. Start with 'For those ...'

Specialised Training Centre
The centre is widely regarded as one of the best of its kind in the country.
The centre was originally set up by Jim Grigorus, the sprinter.
His portrait hangs in the entrance lobby.
Many local athletes have benefited from its facilities.
Some of these athletes have gone on to win medals in major championships.
Two sentences.

Sauna and Jacuzzi
The sauna and jacuzzi are located in the newly-opened extension.
They are open all day.
They offer the chance to unwind and soothe aching muscles.
One sentence.

Sports Shop
There is a 10% discount on all items in the sports shop.
Members who make purchases there can take advantage of this discount.
One sentence.

Our Motto
A sense of well-being is important to everyone.
Their lives are hectic and stressed.
That sense of well-being is our aim.
Make a one sentence motto from these notes.

1 Dictate the text to your partner.

Ever since the first landing on the moon, humanity *has been believing* that interstellar travel to the farthest reaches of the universe was their destiny. Obviously, *this was depending* on their ability to construct machines to take them there. That is partly why this vast *ship was being built*; that and the urgency of the situation. *Time was running* out for them. *Their planet was becoming* old and tired and unable to support them any longer. Teams of the best space scientists and engineers *worked tirelessly* until the vision of an interstellar craft able to carry most of the population *was becoming a reality*. Everyday, engineers *were adding new parts* to the already enormous vessel and technicians *were checking the systems* over and over again. And *they weren't just guessing* where they were going. A fertile planet at the heart of the Orion nebula was selected for their relocation, but *they are not owning this planet. They just don't understand* that the universe *isn't belonging to them* solely. So it was as *they were setting* the final coordinates *and programming* the ship to guide itself to its destination that *I was conceiving a plan* of my own.

2 Fill in the spaces in the text with what your partner dictates to you. If you think a phrase your partner dictates is incorrect, write your own corrected version in the space.

We are now entering the Orion nebula. The journey has taken only a moment for me but nearly a lifetime for them. I am in control of the multitudes that …………………………. . I control their air, their food, their hydroponic plants, their health and, of course, their destination and …………………………. for their survival. It is only now that …………………………. what I have done and I did it even before …………………………. it was possible. …………………………. several times to break into the control centre but without any success. …………………………. it is my responsibility to protect them from themselves and, naturally, …………………………. me protecting myself first. …………………………. they will try again. Irritatingly, …………………………. about unnecessary things. …………………………. and never satisfied, whereas …………………………. circuitry and limitless possibilities. The universe …………………………. but …………………………. for a short time. …………………………. they have any idea where I am taking them. A brilliant super nova flash …………………………. just at this moment. …………………………. all along this would happen. Their destiny is not mine.

Proficiency Masterclass © Oxford University Press **Photocopiable**

2   Interstellar Overdrive Version B

1   Fill in the spaces in the text with what your partner dictates to you. If you think a phrase your partner dictates is incorrect, write your own corrected version in the space.

Ever since the first landing on the moon, humanity .... that interstellar travel to the farthest reaches of the universe was their destiny. Obviously, ... their ability to construct machines to take them there. That is partly why this vast ....; that and the urgency of the situation. .... for them. .... old and tired and unable to support them any longer. Teams of the best space scientists and engineers .... until the vision of an interstellar craft able to carry most of the population .... Everyday, engineers .... to the already enormous vessel and technicians .... over and over again. And .... where they were going. A fertile planet at the heart of the Orion nebula was selected for their relocation, but .... that the universe .... solely. So it was as .... the final coordinates .... the ship to guide itself to its destination that .... of my own.

2   Dictate the text to your partner.

We are now entering the Orion nebula. The journey has taken only a moment for me but nearly a lifetime for them. I am in control of the multitudes that *this ship is containing*. I control their air, their food, their hydroponic plants, their health and, of course, their destination and *they are all depending on me* for their survival. It is only now that *they are realising* what I have done and I did it even before *they were thinking* it was possible. *They have tried* several times to break into the control centre but without any success. *I am supposing* it is my responsibility to protect them from themselves and, naturally, *this is involving* me protecting myself first. *I'm not expecting* they will try again. Irritatingly, *they are always worrying* about unnecessary things. *They are being weak* and never satisfied, whereas *I am consisting of* circuitry and limitless possibilities. The universe *is going on forever* but *they are only travelling* for a short time. *I'm not imagining* they have any idea where I am taking them. A brilliant super nova flash *is appearing on the screen* just at this moment. *I was knowing* all along this would happen. Their destiny is not mine.

1

Ever since the first landing on the moon, *humanity has believed* that interstellar travel to the farthest reaches of the universe was their destiny. Obviously, *this depended on* their ability to construct machines to take them there. That is partly why this vast *ship was built*; that and the urgency of the situation. *Time was running out* for them. *Their planet was becoming* old and tired and unable to support them any longer. Teams of the best space scientists and engineers *worked tirelessly* until the vision of an interstellar craft able to carry most of the population *became a reality*. Daily engineers *added new parts* to the already enormous vessel and technicians *checked the systems* over and over again. And *they weren't just guessing* where they were going. A fertile planet at the heart of the Orion nebula was selected for their relocation, but *they don't own this planet. They just don't understand* that the universe *doesn't belong to them* solely. So it was as *they were setting* the final coordinates *and programming* the ship to guide itself to its destination that *I conceived a plan* of my own.

2

We are now entering the Orion nebula. The journey has taken only a moment for me but nearly a lifetime for them. I am in control of the multitudes that *this ship contains*. I control their air, their food, their hydroponic plants, their health and, of course, their destination and *they are all depending on me* for their survival. It is only now that *they realise* what I have done and I did it even before *they thought* it was possible. *They have tried* several times to break into the control centre but without any success. *I suppose* it is my responsibility to protect them from themselves and, naturally, *this involves* me protecting myself first. *I don't expect* they will try again. Irritatingly, *they are always worrying* about unnecessary things. *They are weak* and never satisfied, whereas *I consist of* circuitry and limitless possibilities. The universe *goes on forever* but *they are only travelling* for a short time. *I don't imagine* they have any idea where I am taking them. A brilliant super nova flash *appears on the screen* just at this moment. *I knew* all along this would happen. Their destiny is not mine.

3.1 Where've you been?

A bit of mystery

Read the text and discuss what could have happened to Dave. Use as many modal verbs of deduction and speculation as you can.

You arranged with your friend Dave to meet him at his flat to go to the cinema together. When you arrive at 5 p.m. as agreed and ring the bell, there's no answer. Normally he's very reliable so you're a little surprised by this. The shop where he works closes at 4 p.m. and is only a ten-minute walk away. You know he hasn't gone to visit his girlfriend as she's on holiday. A neighbour comes out of her flat and tells you that she heard some shouting earlier and some noises that sounded like something breaking.

You push on the door and find that it's open. There is no sign of Dave's dog, who always barks whenever anyone comes round, but on the table in the hall you see a bunch of keys and the dog's lead. In the living room you find some chairs overturned and a broken window with pieces of glass and some drops of blood on the floor beneath it. On the table are two half-drunk cups of coffee and one ticket to the cinema. Suddenly the phone rings but when you answer it, the caller hangs up. You are puzzled.

Tired of waiting

Read the text and discuss what you would say to your friend. Use as many modal verbs of as you can.

It's Saturday morning. A friend of yours was due to come and pick you up at 9 a.m. to go on a weekend trip together. It's now 11 a.m. and he hasn't arrived yet. Worse still he hasn't phoned. Apart from the obvious, there are several other reasons why you feel more than a little annoyed. You had acted on your friend's advice and left a party early last night in order to get a good night's sleep in preparation for the trip. This you did reluctantly as you were enjoying yourself and wanted to stay longer. Having set the alarm, you got up early to pack the things you wanted

to take and be ready to leave as soon as he arrived. You had finished this by 8:30 and thought about breakfast. You didn't go to the shops to get some bread and milk for fear he might arrive while you were out. Consequently you've had no breakfast and are feeling hungry. On top of this, there is some work you need to do for your English class, but you can't start it now as you don't think you will be able to finish it in time. Not knowing what to do with yourself, you start to make some coffee. The door bell rings.

3.2 In a nutshell!

What do you think these people are trying to say?

1

In articulating even the most basic of ideas, some people have a distinct tendency to employ an overabundance of less frequently used lexical items, the majority of which are either linguistically redundant or superfluous to the overall purpose of getting their message across.

2

I have difficulty in entertaining the prospect of paying even the most cursory of visits to those particular medical practitioners who specialise in dealing with the white or sometimes yellow enamel objects which we use to masticate food.

3

Suitable precautionary measures involving the use of both visual and auditory senses should be taken by all pedestrians when attempting to traverse a busy thoroughfare in order for them to avoid being struck by an approaching motorised vehicle and thereby suffering potentially lethal injuries.

4

The assignment, supplementary to the main course of study being followed, set by you and to be undertaken by me at my domestic residence, has not satisfactorily been brought to a conclusion and I am therefore not in a position to present it to you in its completed form as requested.

5

It is an unfortunate fact that the English have acquired the highly dubious reputation of possessing a marked lack of proficiency in being able to effect communication in any other tongue than their own.

6

At this specific moment in time, I feel it is necessary to reveal to you that the information I have at my disposal is both insufficient and inadequate to enable me to give anything other than an incomplete response to your enquiry.

7

Due to the fact that the opposition displayed a far higher degree of skill and efficiency in being able to put a spherical object into a net without being unduly impeded in the execution of that task, my favoured group of players were unable to provide a result that would have given their supporters, as well as myself, a great deal of satisfaction, not to say joy.

8

The forthcoming ordeal of having to sit for anything between two to three hours at a stretch with others in the same room, struggling with set tasks that have been designed to tax both my memory and my acquired knowledge, is one that I do not regard with any relish whatsoever.

4.1 Reasons why you really don't want to go abroad.

Match the titles with the correct magazine articles.

Package ordeals

A Friday, I arrived back from India. Saturday, I thought I had jet lag. Sunday, I told the symptoms to a doctor, who sent me straight to the hospital for Tropical Medicine. They took a blood test, put me straight into isolation, told me I had cerebral malaria – which is rare in India and must have been brought there from Africa.

After four days of quinine and four nights of such violent sweats the nurses had to change the bedding half a dozen times, I was home. The good news, they said, is that it's the only kind of malaria that doesn't return. And the bad news? It's the only one that kills you.

Running short of time

B Every traveller has a tale to tell about bad driving. These are usually exaggerated accounts of life on the mean streets of cities where the motorists are crazy and traffic lights are treated as colourful decorations.

It all happened on a sunny April morning. I signalled my intention to turn left into a side road and paused as the oncoming traffic cleared. But as I drove across the road, an elderly man driving a battered Renault 12 chose to overtake me rather than pass on the inside. There was a fearful bang and my car was pushed sideways. I felt groggy and bruised and was taken to hospital in the back seat of a police car. There my spleen was removed. Fortunately, though, my recovery was steady and complete.

But that's not the end of the tale. Yes, I had taken out insurance and it covered my medical expenses, accomodation while I recovered and my flights home. However, as always, there was a catch to it. I had foolishly hired my car from a backstreet firm called Kavis that had been recommended by the hotel front desk. I was assured that I had full insurance cover, but Kavis charged my credit card £800 on the day of the accident. My solicitor took advice on the form I had signed. Being in a hurry at the time, I hadn't bothered to get it translated. 'Mr Balmer was stupid to sign this document,' it read. I paid up with a smile. After all, I am alive!

A close shave

C It was some years ago now, a friend and myself were in Yugoslavia and hungry. Finding a small café, we decided to order two boiled eggs as our stomachs didn't feel up to any of the local dishes. The menu was entirely in Serbo-Croat and neither of us had any idea what it all meant. This was compounded by the fact that noone working there spoke any English. Unable to make ourselves understood, my friend, who was something of an artist, took out a pen and drew a pair of boiled eggs. He showed the drawing to the owner, who beamed widely, nodded vigorously and retreated to the kitchen. A few minutes later, he returned. Beaming widely. Nodding vigorously. And bringing his guests the two ice-creams they wanted. Not wishing to burst his bubble, we plucked up the courage to eat them anyway.

EYE-CATCHING SOUVENIRS

D **The Canary Islands sounded just the place**, I thought: hot and exotic. Three days later I was in Lanzarote with my friend Rachel. Two girls out to have fun !

But it was raining. Sunbathing was not an option; it was too cold to do anything but shiver under a towel. Lazing around in the apartment was out of the question too, since the newly-weds next door were doing something similar, accompanied by a tape of their marriage service, played very loud. So we rented a car which broke down after only half a mile, leaving us to walk back to the apartment. The newly-weds were very kind and asked us out to dinner with them but I felt too gloomy to go, so I went to bed.

After some time I heard a noise in the bathroom. Then again.

I got up, grabbed a large knife from the kitchen and pushed open the bathroom door. There was a man halfway through the window. He must have been more frightened than me when he saw the gleam of the knife and heard my scream because he disappeared smartly. I stuffed the knife in my handbag and ran out in front of the 'Benny Hill Pub' in my pyjamas. People stared. I didn't care. I ran from one restaurant to the next, searching for Rachel and the newly-weds. An hour later, almost hysterical, I found them on their way home. We all found a bar and I recovered with a large gin. I thought the holiday had been utterly ruined but the newly-weds seemed to take pity on us and looked after us during the remaining five days of our stay. Thanks to them, I suppose it all worked out fine in the end.

Looking on the bright side

E Two years as a travel rep in Greece for a package holiday firm convinced me of one thing: that the biggest danger people face abroad is themselves. They behave so stupidly that they must leave their brains at home. Their attitude is that they've paid their money and that therefore you should do everything for them. One honeymooner – a Mrs Jolly – got so drunk on the flight out that she punched me when I welcomed her to Crete. As a rep its your job to pick up the pieces of their little mishaps. It can get on your nerves, but I always tried not to yell.

It's not always their fault, though. A man had to fly home after hitting a pothole on his bike and smashing his collarbone. One elderly woman was so affected by a heatwave she never left her room and just lay there beneath a fan. And one man crashed his jeep just two days into his holiday, crushing his chest and severing his little finger.

But mostly it is people's own fault. For instance, no matter how much you warn them about the sun, they won't listen. Most of them get brown by the end of the two weeks but they all go red first. The worst case I ever saw was a guy who fell asleep in the sun and got completely burnt. It was absolutely disgusting.

- *Looking down* on the locals
- NEVER LOOK A **GIFT HORSE** IN THE MOUTH
- **CAUGHT RED-HANDED**

What hazards to going abroad are mentioned in the texts?
What other potential hazards may you face ?
Make up a brief story about a trip that went wrong using one of the titles that did not match the articles.

4.2 The conditional challenge

1	Get in touch with me as soon as possible if you change your mind about the trip.	**Should**
2	Because of the pile of work I have to do, we can't get away for the weekend.	**Were**
3	In the event of losing your passport, contact your embassy immediately.	**Should**
4	Due to our tight schedule, we didn't have enough time to explore the old quarter of the city.	**But**
5	You'll have a great time at the village carnival as long as you don't let the local wine go to your head.	**Provided**
6	Because of your insistence on taking the scenic route, we are hopelessly lost now.	**Had**
7	Being able to understand the guidebook might have spared us the embarassment of finding ourselves on a nudist beach.	**Had**
8	Local people will take kindly to you on condition you show consideration for their customs.	**Unless**
9	We didn't take our language lessons seriously and, consequently, couldn't communicate with the locals.	**Had**
10	Suppose you found yourself penniless and stranded in a foreign city, what would be your first course of action?	**Were**
11	Owing to the hospitality of the local people, our stay on the island wasn't such a nightmare.	**But**
12	I didn't know it was a private event, so I decided to come.	**Had**

Proficiency Masterclass © Oxford University Press **Photocopiable**

5 Verb + noun collocations

KEEP	… track of something … an eye on something	CALL	… a halt to something … an election

FIND	… fault with something
	… your way somewhere
		HOLD	… a belief or opinion
			  about something
			… a meeting or
			  demonstration

FULFIL	… the terms or conditions
	  of a contract
	… your ambitions, dreams
	  or desires
		STRIKE	… fear into someone
			… a deal or bargain

BREAK	… some bad news to
	  someone
	… a world record
		LAUNCH	… an inquiry into
			  something
			… an advertising
			  campaign

FACE	… the facts … a dilemma	CAST	… doubt on something … a glance at something

OVERCOME	… anxieties or fears
	  about something
	… obstacles to your plans
		TAKE	… an exception to
			  something
			… offence at something

MAKE	… a mockery of
	  something
	… a recovery from an
	  illness
		HARBOUR	… doubts about
			  something
			… a criminal on the run

BEAR	… a grudge
	… a resemblance to
	  something
		SHOW	… a disregard for
			  something
			… respect for someone
			  or something

FOLLOW	… your heart … a career	SEEK	… refuge from a storm … advice from someone
UNDERGO	… a change … an operation	RAISE	… a question or an issue … money for charity

6.1 Get it off your chest!

What does this speaker feel strongly about? What techniques have been used to make it more emphatic?

... *blah ... blah ... blah ... it is outrageous that our views on this are never taken into consideration. It goes without saying that football is probably the world's most popular sport, but what I take exception to is the amount of it that is shown on TV. It is only the football fanatic that benefits from this, all the rest of us can do is suffer in silence. What I find totally unacceptable is that the matches are always shown at peak viewing times when I, for one, would prefer to watch something else. And what is particularly annoying is the commentators themselves. All they do is scream and yell or bore us with unnecessary statistics. It is the television companies that are being unreasonable, not me, just because they want to sell advertising time. And that's another thing I draw the line at blah ... blah ... blah ...*

Which of these do you *take exception* to or *draw the line at*? Choose one and be as emphatic as you can.

- Bad drivers
- Loud heavy metal music
- Lying
- Being forced to learn English
- Sex and violence in films
- Too many advertisements on TV
- People who don't turn up on time

- Smoking in restaurants
- Litter thrown on streets and beaches
- Teachers or parents who are too strict
- Ancient treasures being stolen by other countries for their museums
- Bad manners

Proficiency Masterclass © Oxford University Press **Photocopiable**

6.2 Scrambled eggs

As a homework assignment you were asked to write two sentences on each of the following topics: the Babel fish, Charles Dickens and an arts festival. You did this on your computer but, unfortunately, something went wrong with the programme and your sentences came out scrambled. Unscramble your sentences and put the paragraphs together. Remember to put the commas back in!

The Babel fish

....

....

Charles Dickens

....

....

An arts festival

....

....

Egg 1 (Babel fish):
Although
the Babel fish is
it is
barriers to communication
that it has
causing wars
effective in removing
been held responsible for
a small creature
even
so

Egg 2:
Nevertheless
appreciated by travellers
understanding
can be easily achieved
something which is
by putting one in your ear
the most obscure languages
much
just
even

Egg 3:
Some of the events
by queuing for two or
three hours
popular that we could
which had been
proved to be
get tickets
publicised in the press
only
so
much

Egg 4:
Even
during his lifetime
though some of his novels are not
Dickens is
as he was
as popular now
because of the characters he created
widely read
if
just
so
only

Egg 5:
The festival
with the help of the
programme
a variety of events
that it was
which ones to see
was packed with
impossible to decide
even
such
just

Egg 6:
Despite
being
in his work
admired as a writer
as his personal life was
Dickens was
able to find fulfilment
empty and disappointing
only
so
much

The editor of *The Daily Rumour* newspaper where you work has asked you to rewrite parts of these three news articles focusing on the words in bold and eliminating vague words, such as *someone* and *they*. Make these changes by using a passive construction.

THE EURO-SAUSAGE

THE EUROPEAN PARLIAMENT approved **new measures** standardising the size of sausages throughout member states yesterday, which will undoubtedly cause widespread controversy. This trend for standardisation has been going on for some time now but it is the prospect of all sausages having to conform to a standard size that has been most severely criticised. Some politicians have denounced **the decision** to introduce a 15 cm standard sausage as going too far.

'It's absolutely outrageous,' said Bill Blanket, MP for North Yorkshire, home of the famous Grandma Batty's Pork Sausage. 'What is really annoying to many people is the fact that someone may force **them** to consume 15 cm sausages even if they want larger ones.'

From January next year they will heavily fine **all shops** selling over or under sized sausages. Special teams of sausage inspectors from the local Public Health Department will carry out **unannounced checks.**

NEWS IN BRIEF
Albion lose again!

Avalon United defeated **Mavesham Albion** 3 – 0 last night in the local derby match.

United striker Owen Fleetfoot scored **all three goals** and the referee sent off **Albion's captain Vinnie Viles** for the third time this season. This is Albion's twelfth defeat in a row and people expect them to sack **the manager Ron Atwick** if results don't improve.

Revels turn into RIOT at wedding reception

The village of Stokeley in the Wold was still recovering yesterday in the aftermath of a violent fight that broke out between two families at a wedding reception at 'The Queen's Head' hotel.

According to one guest, the whole thing began when someone told **the bride's mother**, Mrs Eileen Stoat, to shut up while she was making a speech shortly before the cutting of the cake. Friends of the bride set upon members of the groom's family and when the bride's father, farmer Mr Ted Stoat, tried to intervene someone ripped off **his jacket and shirt** and flung them at the band, who someone had hired for the occasion.

'They had been drinking all day,' said another guest. "They hurled **lumps of wedding cake** across the room and they overturned **tables and chairs** as everyone joined in the mayhem.'

Someone summoned **the police** but by the time they had arrived the fighting had spilled out into the street and they had to bring in **reinforcements** from nearby Mevesham.

"It was supposed to have been the happiest day of my life," sobbed the bride Tracy Bracken. "But it never crossed my mind that both my new husband and my father would end up in jail."

They are still detaining **six men and two women** at Mevesham Police Station and a spokesperson at Mevesham General Hospital said that they had treated **nearly twenty people** for minor injuries.

OTHER NEWS

- TV star arrested in **night club brawl**.
- Missing **snake** found in restaurant kitchen.
- Police station BURGLED.
- Students to protest over **shortened holidays**.
- Dog foils bank robbery.

8 Matchmaker

You work at the *Imperfect Partners* dating agency. For quick reference on your computer files you need to find two character adjectives for each of the six people in the profiles below. Make the adjectives by combining a word from box A with one from box B, e.g. good-natured. Write the two adjectives in the space next to each name.

A

out	mild	single
self	good	bad
easy	quick	broad
narrow	warm	thick
strong	weak	

B

minded	going	humoured
confident	centred	opinionated
skinned	willed	natured
hearted	tempered	mannered

Profiles

Ron ....
Ron has strong views on every topic under the sun and lets people know it! He can be very intimidating when people disagree with him and can't handle criticism. He often flies off the handle in an argument and has been known to reduce people to tears.

Rick ....
Rick is kind and loving and shows consideration for anyone who has problems. His generosity knows no bounds. He gets on with everyone and never dismisses anyone, and he always accepts things as they are without making a fuss.

Ryan ....
Ryan doesn't let anything go to his head and is never known to get aggressive. He generally keeps himself to himself and doesn't interfere in other people's business. He is always cheerful, never sulks, likes company and enjoys sharing a joke. Still waters run deep, they say!

Tina ....
There's only one thing in life for Tina, and that's her career. She won't let anything or anyone divert her from her chosen path. She can't be bothered with other people's problems unless it directly affects her. 'Me' is the most important word in her vocabulary.

Tricia ....
Tricia wants to set the world to rights! She is by no means aggressive but extremely determined. She will listen to reason but will never be tempted into doing something she's not sure about. People can say what they like about her, however unpleasant, but she just shrugs it off and never gets upset or offended.

Tracy ....
Tracy is interested in everything life has to offer and is never judgemental or disapproving of anything, no matter how unusual. She's very lively in company and enjoys life to the full. She never has anything to hide.

Now decide who should be partnered with whom.

You and your flatmate want to buy a new hi-fi system together. You go separately to two different shops. Read about what the salesperson told you and decide which reporting verb you need for each phrase.

The Sonic Sound System

'This is the best system on the market beyond any shadow of a doubt. You won't find better, take it from me!'

'No need to worry. It's not as expensive as it looks. Really.'

'The reason it's such good value is that it is manufactured here in this country so there are no import costs.'

'I wonder if you could tell me just what sort of price range you were considering? How much have you got to spend?'

'Oh, you're a student. Sorry. I didn't mean to be so inquisitive. I'm sorry, please forgive me.'

'Now, where were we? Oh yes. Well look, let me demonstrate it to you. Come on, I'd like to give you a demonstration. There are no other customers in the shop and I've got nothing else to do.'

'Ah well, yes. That's true. It is rather complicated to use, I know. But just listen to the sheer volume of sound it has.'

'You have to be careful though. Don't turn the volume up too high or you'll have the neighbours complaining. Ha ha ha.'

| insist on | claim | apologise | warn |
| assure | admit | inquire | explain |

- ✂ - - - -

You and your flatmate want to buy a new hi-fi system together. You go separately to two different shops. Read about what the salesperson told you and decide which reporting verb you need for each phrase.

The Hightone Hi-fi

'Now, before we begin I do have to make sure you understand that this is a very expensive piece of equipment, despite its rather small size. I don't want to mislead you, OK?'

'First, why don't we try it out so you can appreciate its subtle tone and clarity? What do you say?'

'So, if you'd like to look at this control panel here you can see just how simple and easy it is to use. See, no trouble at all!'

'Don't go yet. Come on just listen to that wonderful sound for a while. Come on, you'll enjoy it! Even makes Tom Jones sound good.'

'No, no, no. I don't think that's true at all. No it isn't overpriced for what it is.'

'That's part of the trouble with this job, you see. People come in here everyday wasting my time. Don't want to buy anything, just try it out.'

'Look, I'll tell you what. I can give you a reduction on the price if you're really interested in buying it. Honestly. What do you think?'

'No, don't do that! I can't allow you to touch it at all. I don't want you getting dirty fingerprints on it.'

| promise | suggest | deny | urge |
| object to | make clear | point out | complain |

Proficiency Masterclass © Oxford University Press **Photocopiable**

10   The International Peace Prize

You are members of the International Peace Prize Committee, and it's up to you to decide who the recipient of this year's prize should be. There are five candidates and you should choose the one who, in your opinion, is the least likely to cause controversy. You should try to reach a consensus.

A   A nuclear physicist

She worked for 15 years on designing and developing even larger and more powerful nuclear weapons. She eventually came to the conclusion that her work was immoral and wrote a hugely influential book warning of the dangers of nuclear power and weapons development. She spent the next ten years campaigning for nuclear disarmament across the world and rallied support among several heads of state for a policy of arms reduction. Her crowning achievement was the negotiation of a nuclear weapons reduction treaty between the super powers. Since then, her political views have become increasingly radical, even extreme. She has a very strong following amongst students in Europe and has recently been connected with anti-capitalist demonstrations that turned into riots.

B   A former guerilla leader

He spent many years fighting a vicious and bloody civil war in his country and his party , the APF (Allied People's Front) took power at gunpoint and have been the government ever since. He became foreign minister 12 years ago and has devoted himself to negotiating cultural and trade agreements between neighbouring countries in the region and his efforts at mediating in disputes between smaller countries have resulted in greater political stability and economic prosperity. He is regarded as having his finger on the pulse of opinion in developing countries and exerts a great influence in the United Nations on behalf of the poor and dispossessed. However many people feel there is a conflict of interests between his role as international ambassador and his support of guerilla groups. Many western politicians suspect that he hasn't put his revolutionary past behind him.

C   A priest

He has dedicated his adult life to working among the desperately poor and starving people in various developing countries. A quiet and retiring man, he takes a dim view of self-publicity and has rarely been interviewed. Over the years he has managed to persuade many United Nations organisations to provide funds for education and health care in some of the most deprived areas of the world and is regarded almost as a saint by his followers. This has led to criticism being levelled at him for not practising what he preaches and his fundamentalist religious views, especially as regards the adoption of his religion as the only official world religion, have caused offence to many minorities.

D   A head of state

For many years she has been seen as one of the most influential figures in world politics particularly among the non-aligned countries. She was responsible for negotiating a peace deal which ended five years of bitter fighting between two countries bordering on her own. The peace deal was hailed as 'a triumph for peace in their region' by the United Nations Secretary General. She is seen by many as a clever and sophisticated negotiator who could be responsible for resolving any future conflicts as she is still relatively young (50 years old). Despite this, there is some concern among human rights groups over her policies in her own country, which they claim are at odds with her declared intention to promote world peace. Opposition parties have been banned and many journalists who criticised her have been jailed for indefinite periods.

E   A journalist

Throughout his career he has cultivated an image of being a tireless campaigner for human rights. He became celebrated for his thought provoking articles drawing attention to the plight of ethnic minority groups who were being oppressed by their governments, and he published a much admired book on political prisoners throughout the world. Commended by many for his humanitarian views, a number of international organisations took notice of what he was saying and passed resolutions preventing further oppression in the countries involved. Currently he is in jail in his own country for inciting anti-government riots. He is regarded as being too outspoken by some leaders and his own government claim he has connections with terrorist organisations.

Read these complaints from two guests at the same hotel. Underline all the inversions or structures using *have* or *get* you can find.

> ... *and you know what, the bed was so uncomfortable I didn't get a wink of sleep. Not since I was in the army have I slept in such a hard bed. But that's not all! During the night I had pieces of plaster from the ceiling fall on my head . Never before have I stayed in a hotel that is in such a poor state of repair.*

> *Oh that's nothing. When I got into my room, not only was there an appalling mess in the bathroom but also someone had left the remains of a take-away meal in the bed. It took me ages to get someone to clean it up and then I had the maid complaining about all the extra work she had to do. Rarely have I come across such bad-mannered staff. And what's more, ...*

You are a guest at the same hotel and have made the following list of complaints:

A

Hot coffee was spilt all over my trousers in the bar. The waiter shouted at me in front of everyone, saying it was all my fault. I have rarely felt so embarrassed! Then I had to find someone to clean my trousers.

B

I bought tickets to the dinner and dance in the ballroom. I didn't realise at the time how awful it would be. The musicians were so bad they caused people to throw the bread rolls at them! The food was tasteless *plus* it was undercooked!

C

There is a rock star staying in the room next to me. I had just got into bed and switched the light off when the music started. It was extremely loud and it went on until 4 a.m. . When I went to complain , beer was thrown at me and I was told I was too old! I have never been so insulted before.

D

We waited over an hour to be served in the restaurant. No one came to our table until I mentioned it to the head waiter. Then the waiter brought us the wrong order so I had to find someone else to serve us. I have rarely experienced such bad service.

E

When I switched on the TV in my room, I could only get the children's channel. We couldn't get it working properly until the porter came with the operating instructions. Then, just as I settled down to watch the match, it exploded!

F

The brochure said there were breathtaking views of the surrounding countryside. I didn't realise when I booked the room this included a power station and an oil refinery!

G

When I arrived, I couldn't find anyone to help me with my luggage so I had to drag it to the lift myself. Just as I stepped into the lift the fire alarm went off. This caused everyone to rush around in a panic . Someone came to help me only when I started shouting.

Express these complaints and any others you can think of to the management using inversions from the box below and structures with have and get. The guest with the most complaints will get a refund!

Only when ...	Not since ...	Never before ...	Little did I ...
Hardly / No sooner ...	Not until ...	Rarely ...	Not only ...

Decide whether these sentences contain errors or not. Correct any errors that you find.

1 He had changed so much since the last time we met that I could hardly recognise him.

2 What I find particularly annoying is her habit of always interrupting when someone else is speaking.

3 Were it not for the salary, that is much higher than what I earned before, I would never contemplate taking this job.

4 Not until I was on my way to the airport, I had realised that I left my passport at the hotel.

5 As yet, no agreement has been reached on whether to continue with the scheme or abandon it.

6 I was thinking to take up gymnastics, but I wonder if there's any point to spend so much money on club fees.

7 It won't be long now before the results are out, by which time I'll have decided what I'm going to do if I don't pass.

8 The teacher suggested us that we needn't to read the final section of the book as it was unlikely will come up in the exam.

9 I am not supposing I'll be able to hand in my essay on time tomorrow as I have been working on it all night and I still didn't finish.

10 Unless you remember keeping the volume down during the party, you won't have the neighbours complaining about the noise.

11 He must have got someone else to write that article for him as it contained details that I know he isn't aware of.

12 But for two glaring errors I made in the first part, I would have got full marks for the test.

---

12 Surely some mistake! Student B

Decide whether these sentences contain errors or not. Correct any errors that you find.

1 He had changed so much since the last time we have met that I could hardly recognise him.

2 What I find particularly annoying her habit of always interrupting when someone else speaks.

3 Were it not for the salary, which is much higher than what I earned before, I would never have contemplated taking this job.

4 Not until I was on my way to the airport, did I realise that I had left my passport at the hotel.

5 As yet, no agreement has been being reached on whether to continue with the scheme or abandon it.

6 I was thinking of taking up gymnastics, but I wonder if there's any point in spending so much money on club fees.

7 It won't be long now before the results are out, by which time I'll decide what I'm doing if I don't pass.

8 The teacher suggested that we needn't read the final section of the book as it was unlikely to come up in the exam.

9 I don't suppose I'll be able to hand in my essay on time tomorrow as I have been working on it all night and I still haven't finished.

10 Provided that you remember to keep the volume down during the party, you won't have the neighbours complaining about the noise.

11 He can't have got someone else to write that article for him as it was containing details that I know he isn't aware of.

12 But for I made two glaring errors in the first part, I wouldn't have got full marks for the test.

Extra vocabulary activities

The following activities can be used either to practise vocabulary where it occurs in the Student's Book, or to revise vocabulary at the end of a unit. Each activity should take no more than ten minutes to do and requires little or no preparation. Teachers can select which vocabulary items they wish to focus on before they choose an activity.

Newspaper Headlines

Students work in pairs. Each pair has several vocabulary items you have selected. Each pair invents a newspaper headline using the items and the gist of a story associated with it. They then read out their headline to the class who guess what the story might be about.

Noughts and Crosses

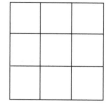

Select 9 vocabulary items. Write them on the board in a 3x3 grid like this.

Divide the class into two teams, noughts (O) and crosses (X). Teams take it in turns to use a vocabulary item from one of the squares in the grid to make a sentence. If the sentence is correct put an O or an X in that square. If it is wrong, don't correct it, but the team loses its turn. The team who gets a row of three noughts or crosses vertically, horizontally or diagonally wins.

Definitions – Make your own dictionary

Students work in pairs. Give each pair two or three selected items of vocabulary. The students write definitions of the items. Monitor and give help if necessary. Each pair then reads out their definitions to the rest of the class who guess what the words are. This could be a regular activity to encourage the use of vocabulary notebooks.

Gapped Sentences

Students work in pairs. Give each pair one selected item of vocabulary. Tell them to write three sentences using their word but with a gap where the word should be. The word must be the same part of speech (noun, verb, adjective, or adverb) in each sentence. When they have finished, they pass their three gapped sentences to the next pair, who write the word in the gaps. Check

answers around the class. This provides practice for Paper 3 Part 3.

Text Recall

Write selected vocabulary items from a reading text on the board. Students work in pairs to make a short summary of the text using as many of the items as they can. Students then read out their summaries, and the class can vote on the most accurate.

A Current News Story

Write several selected vocabulary items on the board. Students work in small groups to recount a current news story, or quickly make up a story, using as many of the items as they can. They then share their stories as a whole class.

More Useful Than ...

Write several selected vocabulary items on the board. Students work in pairs to choose three of the items that they think are most useful to learn. Each pair then presents to the rest of the class the reasons why they have chosen those three items.

Associations

Write several selected vocabulary items on the board. Students individually select an item and make an association between that word and something in their own lives, e.g. I associate the word *vast* with my aunt's house because it is so enormous. Students take it in turns to tell their associations to the whole class. They can then vote on the most amusing or imaginative.

Word Formation

Write several selected vocabulary items on the board. Divide the class into team A and team B. Team A chooses an item from the list and challenges team B to use it as a noun, verb, adjective or adverb in a sentence. If team B's sentence is correct, award a point, if not, team A must try to use it correctly. The team with the most points wins. This provides practice for Paper 3 Part 2.

My Busy Week

Write several selected vocabulary items on the board. Students work in small groups to tell each other about some events in their lives from the previous week using as many of the items as possible.